650.1 W198r
The reputation game :the
art of changing how people
see you /
Waller, David,   NOV 3 0 2017

THE SA

LOGY OF REPUTATION

GAME ★★★ TRUST

D0428982

REPUTATION  WITHDRAWN

BARRIE SAVORY'S HEALING HANDS

FRAUD IN US HISTORY

UTATION NETWORKS

THE POWER OF CLOSED NETWORKS

REPUTATION IN THE EUROVISION

PUSHING FOR CHANGE

HEADHUNTING IN THE DIGITAL AGE

MORE PRAISE FOR
THE REPUTATION GAME

'An insightful and really rather fascinating study of what one might argue is the issue of our age: the creation and management of a reputation. The authors have clearly managed to get great access to a huge number of people and the results make for very compelling reading. It's well-written, too. In fact, it's required reading for anyone who truly wants to understand the modern media age.'

Tom Bradby, Presenter, ITV News at Ten

'You'll learn why reputations are more valuable than money; you'll learn how they're built and tended and enriched; and how, if neglected, they can catastrophically implode. It might have been called, "How to ensure that everybody knows just how good you know you are really".'

Sir Martin Sorrell, CEO, WPP

'The insights in *The Reputation Game* are a masterclass of pattern recognition. This book shows us that no matter who you are, your industry or hustle, reputational capital is at the centre of success or failure. Waller and Younger use as examples the rise and fall of great companies, countries, gangsters, and pop-culture icons to show us the moments and choices that are truly the "art of changing how people see us all".'

Steve Stoute, CEO, Translation LLC

David Waller THE Rupert Younger

REPUTATION

GAME

The Art of Changing How People See You

ONEWORLD

A Oneworld Book

First published in North America, Great Britain, the Republic of
Ireland and Australia by Oneworld Publications, 2017

Copyright © David Waller and Rupert Younger 2017

The moral right of David Waller and Rupert Younger to be
identified as the Authors of this work have been asserted by them in
accordance with the Copyright, Designs, and Patents Act 1988

All rights reserved
Copyright under Berne Convention
A CIP record for this title is available from the British Library

ISBN 978-1-78607-071-5
eISBN 978-1-78607-072-2

Typeset by Hewer Text UK Ltd, Edinburgh
Printed and bound in Great Britain by Clays Ltd, St Ives plc

Oneworld Publications
10 Bloomsbury Street
London WC1B 3SR
England

Stay up to date with the latest books,
special offers, and exclusive content from
Oneworld with our monthly newsletter

Sign up on our website
oneworld-publications.com

FSC
www.fsc.org
MIX
Paper from
responsible sources
FSC® C018072

To our families: Max, Pippa, Munro;
Catherine, Alec, Honor and Lorna

David Waller and Rupert Younger, 2017

NOTE ON THE AUTHORS

David Waller was a journalist with the *Financial Times* for the best part of ten years, working in Frankfurt and on the influential Lex column. More recently, he is a partner in a global consulting firm and has been an adviser to companies and governments on reputational issues. He has also written four books on business and historical subjects.

Rupert Younger is founder director of the University of Oxford's Centre for Corporate Reputation, a leading academic teaching and researching how corporations and institutions create, sustain, destroy and rebuild reputation. He is a member of the senior common rooms at Worcester College, Oxford and St Antony's College, Oxford. Rupert is also co-founder and global managing partner of Finsbury, the strategic communications consultancy headquartered in London.

CONTENTS

The purest treasure mortal times afford
Is spotless reputation.

William Shakespeare, *Richard II*

INTRODUCTION

On the morning of Friday, 27 January 2017, British Prime Minister Theresa May met with President Donald Trump at the White House. It was the first meeting with a head of government in the Trump presidency and was heralded as a diplomatic coup for Theresa May at a time when she was under pressure to show to her detractors that Britain, following the contentious Brexit vote, was still a world power.

There was much to discuss. British newspapers had in the days prior to her visit called on the prime minister to tackle Trump directly on his stated support for torture and his protectionist policy agenda, but May was determined to make this a charm offensive. And that she delivered. The most iconic image from the trip was a picture of the two leaders holding hands while walking through the colonnades surrounding the White House. The picture sent a signal that the 'special relationship' between the UK and the US was alive and well, but it was also perceived as evidence that the abrasive Donald Trump had a softer, perhaps more chivalrous, side to his character.

Yet thirty-six hours later, President Trump was reported to have slammed the phone down on Australian Prime Minister Malcolm Turnbull after only twenty-five minutes, following what was by all accounts a bad-tempered exchange. Trump himself described it as 'the worst call so far' with a world leader. At issue was a deal agreed by the Obama administration to accept around 1,250 refugees, primarily from Iran, held in detention camps in the Pacific islands off the Australian coast.

When pressed to honour this agreement by the Australian prime minister, Trump reacted angrily, according to reports in the *Washington Post*. He alternately berated the deal and bragged about the size of his electoral college victory. A few days later he tweeted 'Do you believe it? The Obama administration agreed to take thousands of illegal immigrants from Australia. Why? I will study this dumb deal!'[1]

So what can we conclude about President Trump from these two very different events? Who is the 'real' Donald Trump? A chivalrous, polite, courtly and respectful leader with a keen eye for diplomacy or a bullying, intemperate and irrational man prone to outbursts of uncontrolled anger?

Contrasting reputations have been at the heart of the various controversies surrounding Trump. For some, he has been perceived as misogynistic, racist, bullying and egotistical – a figure so divisive and unpredictable that he is unfit to hold the most powerful political office in the world. Yet for others he is the campaigning outsider, the successful businessman who is unafraid to 'drain the swamp' of Washington elites and officials who have enriched themselves and left the majority of the electorate marginalized and without a political voice. Trump understood this, and used reputation as his most effective weapon.

This book's central argument is that reputation is more valuable than money. We seek to define reputation, arguing that it is different from marketing, PR, branding, status or image. We set out why such distinctions matter. We show how personal, corporate, institutional and national reputations matter in visceral terms. And we go on to explain the key elements of reputation engagement: how reputations are created, sustained, destroyed and rebuilt; how leaders in business, the military and politics use reputation to achieve their goals; how celebrities and criminals build and exploit their reputations for their own advantage; and how our reputations precede and follow us, online and in other social networks.

What other people say about us dramatically affects our ability to achieve what we want, even if what they say is gossip. Our personal reputations are vital to our self-esteem and can make us feel happy, fulfilled and appreciated. A good reputation helps us to find a soulmate, sell a table on eBay, rent out a room on Airbnb, get invited to parties or secure a new promotion. By monitoring what we say and do online, and what others say and think about us, huge corporations are also able to build up a picture of our shopping habits, sexual preferences and behavioural quirks in ways that are only now becoming apparent.

'When you ask people if they live in a networked age, most people would say yes,' LinkedIn co-founder and Silicon Valley titan Reid Hoffman told us. 'But the vast majority of people have not internalized this at all – and understood that everything becomes a reputational issue. It is a major component to everything – relationships, decision making and so on – but most people don't actually parse this out.'

In the commercial world, reputation is everything. According to a *Harvard Business Review* article by Bob Eccles, Scott Newquist and Roland Schatz, some seventy to eighty per cent of all value on the stock market derives from 'hard to assess intangible assets such as brand equity, intellectual capital, and goodwill'.[2] Companies with top-flight reputations hire and retain the best people, charge more for their products, achieve better profit margins and benefit from higher share ratings, creating a virtuous cycle. Companies with poor reputations, on the other hand, have trouble hiring and keeping people, get treated with suspicion by government and regulators, and are shunned by customers and investors alike.

High-profile crises at organizations such as BP have shown what it looks like to lose a corporate reputation. The banking industry has inflicted enormous reputational damage on itself in many parts of the globe. Reputation is the biggest risk faced by many big companies,[3] and a great opportunity for those who figure out how to build and maintain the right kind of reputation. It provides organizations with their broad licence to operate. Big insurance companies have developed policies to protect corporate clients from the quantifiable consequences of reputational disasters. These include 'disgrace' policies that come into force when, for example, an athlete such as the Russian tennis player Maria Sharapova fails a doping test: most of her sponsors dropped her overnight, severely damaging her $20 million-plus annual income.

Countries have reputations, too. Nineteenth-century Britain built a reputation as the undisputed engineering capital of the world, exporting everything from machine tools to billiard tables, ships and locomotive engines. Charles Babbage, Victorian polymath and inventor of the computer, observed that English-made goods had quite a cachet, enjoying a reputation for reliability and robustness that meant customers would not only pay a premium price, they would bypass all the usual due diligence associated with placing a big contract. There were direct commercial benefits: complete strangers from overseas would place their orders sight unseen and, as a result, the factories of Manchester and Birmingham could ship their goods around the world with the minimum of costly paperwork. Likewise, the reputation of the City of London dominated world finance for centuries, and to this day helps explain why it is a leading centre for finance and professional services, despite the fact that the UK's economic hinterland is much diminished.

Today, 'Made in Germany' signals the highest level of quality and reliability, particularly for engineering products, to the point that the customer is prepared to pay a premium. The emissions scandal at VW, the quintessential German car company, has arguably damaged that reputation. 'Made in China' tells a story of cheap mass production – though given that the iPhone and many of the world's top consumer products are now assembled in China, that reputation is evolving. Say the word 'Switzerland' and we think of chocolate, cuckoo clocks – and tax evasion. Russia, meanwhile, has a reputation (in the West) for bellicose behaviours that reflect deep-seated national pride. These national reputations drive commerce and underlie foreign policy. They influence the price a country has to pay to borrow money from international investors. Luxembourg is currently trying to change its reputation as a tax haven, by telling anyone who will listen that its tax rates are actually *higher* than many others.

It's not just businesses and countries that care about their reputations. The more uncertain our social world, the more we rely on reputation as individuals. 'If I ain't got my reputation,' declares one crime boss in *The Wire*, 'I ain't got nothing.' Dominic West, the British actor who plays Sgt McNulty in *The Wire*, agrees: 'Avon and Stringer's reputations were their weapons. You did not need a gun.' And in real life, non-corporate organizations including the Islamic State of Iraq and Syria (ISIS), Mexican drug cartels and the Mafia continue to use reputation, and a reputation for violence in particular, as a signalling mechanism, as a means of enforcement and as an economic weapon.

We are all playing the reputation game. This book will show you how the game works, laying out the rules and winning strategies. We show how some individuals are able to rebuild shattered reputations, while others never recover; why some organizations achieve the reputations they deserve where others never do; why some industries are pariahs while others benefit from a halo effect; and how to play for strategic advantage.

But first, you have to ask the right questions about the kind of reputation you want, for what, and with whom.

PART I

REPUTATION STRATEGIES

A good reputation is more valuable than money.
Publilius Syrus, Latin writer and scholar, 85–43 BC

1

THE RULES OF THE GAME

There are three 'dice' in the reputation game: behaviours, networks and narratives.

The first is your behaviour. **Your actions send signals about what others can expect from you.** In business, always paying your suppliers within thirty days sends a positive reputational signal. As an individual, you should always do what you say you are going to do. If you start turning up to meetings late, people will adjust their expectations accordingly: they will tell other people you are always late, they will 'aim off' when they have a meeting with you and turn up late themselves, or, if they set special store by punctuality, they might invite someone else along instead.

It would be wonderfully simple if there was a straightforward connection between your behaviour and your reputation. Yet this is not the case: philosophers from at least the time of Plato have pondered the paradox that you can enjoy a great reputation, and yet behave really badly. Many chief executive officers (CEOs) complain that their companies do not enjoy the reputations they deserve – typically with investors – while others enjoy reputations they haven't 'earned'. There has been much hand wringing about our new 'post-fact' or 'post-truth' world, but in terms of reputation it has always been perception that matters. Reputation doesn't exist independently of the way people form their judgements. In short, **your reputation is not what you really are, but what others perceive you to be.**

That is partly because **reputation travels through networks.** Your choice of which networks to invest time in, coupled with how you engage, make a huge difference. We all know intuitively that the company we keep, in person or online, tells the world a great deal about who we are. If you are not part of the right networks, it makes it harder for your actions to be appreciated and your reputation to take the shape it deserves. During the Deepwater Horizon crisis of 2010, BP found itself adrift in the US – a British company lacking connections in the White House, as we will see. Or you can be an unpublished author whose self-published masterpiece is ignored by reviewers, a talented actor who cannot get a casting, or a painter who cannot get a show put on: in the creative industries a gifted individual needs to be taken on by an agent who will introduce him or her into networks of publishers, producers or galleries.

So reputations begin with our actions, and travel through our networks. The third element is the message that is being transmitted. In today's world, we are all our own publicists – whether on Facebook, Instagram or Twitter, or professionally through annual reports, blogs and websites. **How we use narratives is critical to the way we influence our reputations.**

Goldman Sachs, on the face of it, has a real reputation conundrum. As one of the largest and most successful investment banks in the world, it is loved, hated, feared and admired in equal measure by different people all over the world. So what is its reputation? It would seem impossible to state with any certainty. Matt Taibbi, a staff writer at *Rolling Stone* magazine, famously wrote a piece on Goldman Sachs in which he described the bank as 'a great vampire squid wrapped around the face of humanity, relentlessly jamming its blood funnel into anything that smells of money'.[1] The piece went on to accuse the bank of 'manipulating whole economic sectors for years at a time, moving the dice game as this or that market collapses, and all the time gorging itself on the unseen costs that are breaking families everywhere'. Harsh criticism, reflecting US public opinion in the aftermath of the 2008 financial crash. And yet, despite this, Goldman retained its prime position as a recruiter of finance MBAs and the investment bank of choice for mergers and acquisitions.

How can it be possible for Goldman Sachs to be simultaneously so reviled and revered? The answer lies in the simple proposition that **we all have multiple reputations, each of them *for* something *with* someone.** Goldman's commercial success is built on hiring the best people, rewarding them generously, and looking after clients' financial interests more effectively than the competition. The bank will only become concerned about any other criticism if that begins to affect the judgement of politicians and regulators, which might have implications for its business.

A modern, multinational corporation has multiple constituencies: it sells to its customers, it buys from its suppliers, it seeks to influence the regulators that govern its markets; it pays dividends to its shareholders and conveys a story about its future earnings potential to analysts and journalists; it engages with pressure groups who pursue a specific agenda, such as mitigating climate change; it also provides a living (and hopefully also the opportunity for self-fulfilment) to its employees. These multiple reputations can mean the difference between success and failure. For example, a long-standing reputation for quality, reliability and trustworthiness with customers will help you maintain high margins and withstand temporary shocks such as a product recall or even a serious accident. A reputation for reliability and predictability with investors should earn you a higher stock-market value and reduce the cost of raising capital when you need it.

Rolls-Royce, the engineering group, has a near fail-safe reputation for producing aircraft engines of the extraordinary reliability and quality: its Trent family of engines are designed to fly for up to forty thousand hours between each shop visit and have only suffered one 'uncontained failure'. This was on 4 November 2010, when one of the engines on Qantas Flight 32 exploded shortly after take-off from Singapore's Changi Airport. The crew managed to land the damaged plane and there were no casualties, yet it was a close-run thing. The accident was later found to be due to a defective component.

Although Rolls-Royce's share price fell after the incident, it is fair to say that airlines, passengers and investors gave the company the benefit of the doubt. This was perceived to be an exceptional event and Rolls-Royce's reputation for engineering reliability prevailed. The company subsequently issued multiple profits warnings in 2014–15, culminating in a record loss of £4.6 billion for 2016, and it has been investigated for bribery and corruption in Indonesia, China, India, Brazil, Nigeria and the UK. The company has suffered reputational knocks as a result, but surely nothing like as severe as if there had been another mechanical failure.

Being known as a great employer that provides rewarding career opportunities will help recruit the brightest and best graduates, leading to lower recruitment costs and greater productivity down the line. Sometimes, however, the contradictions between your different reputations can cancel themselves out. For many years, Tesco enjoyed a reputation with its shareholders for financial and strategic invincibility. Long headquartered in a dowdy office in the suburbs north of London, Tesco seemed to be able to grow profits and market share faster than its competitors. Under the stewardship of former CEO Terry Leahy, the company sought to export its model to other parts of the world, with huge launches in Asia and continental Europe. Even as it expanded, others loathed the company, arguing that its relentless expansion was draining the life out of town centres and putting small shopkeepers out of business. Following the departure of Sir Terry in 2011, the company suffered a series of disasters, from horsemeat being found in its food products, to an accounting scandal and forced withdrawal from the US market. Its profits collapsed, it lost market share in its core home market, and it had to replace new CEO Philip Clarke with no-nonsense outsider Dave Lewis. Having lost its reputation for unrelenting competence, the company found itself with few friends among those who had formed a poor judgement of its character, rather than its competence as a retailer..

We will explore the interplay between competence and character reputations, but note that a good character reputation does not guarantee to commercial success: Cadbury and Rowntree were both proud, progressive companies with fabulous reputations in the communities where they operated, but ended up losing their independence. A reputation for benevolence will not immunize you against commercial threats.

Countries too have multiple different reputations. When President Obama failed to intervene in the Syrian conflict, President Putin of Russia seems to have concluded that Obama would not respond in any serious manner to a military intervention in Ukraine.

'With the Kremlin, the Obama administration gained a reputation for weakness and indecision,' reflects Fred Kempe, president of the Atlantic Council, a leading US think-tank. 'Obama could only have addressed that reputational issue by changing his behaviour, as Kennedy did in 1962 during the Cuban missile crisis.'

Such perceptions often don't grow out of adopting the wrong policy, but rather from a lack of consistency. The Berlin and Cuban crises, as Kempe has written in his 2011 book *Berlin 1961*, show how a reputation for weakness or indecision can be provocative to a rival, whether or not it is based on fact. The missile crisis was in part a result of a perception of American weakness following the US acquiescence to the building of the Berlin Wall a year earlier.

In summary, we all have multiple reputations. Our actions are formulated as a story and travel through networks. We cannot necessarily control our reputation – after all, reputation is what other people are saying about us – but we can learn how to use these three elements to our advantage. Let's look in more detail at the three dimensions of reputation, starting with the origins of human behaviour in the deep past.

2

BEHAVIOURS

THE BEHAVIOURAL BIOLOGY OF REPUTATION

Reputation is bound up with the most elemental animal and human needs: to survive in a hostile environment, to get enough food to eat and to find a mate. Humans are social animals, banding together to fend off predators and hunt large prey. Do you co-operate with others, and if so, who can you trust?

Chimpanzees, our nearest relatives in evolutionary terms, have complex social systems, based on relationships between individuals that have many endearing parallels with the way we humans behave, as any visitor to the zoo can testify. Researchers believe that chimps and other social animals pursue two basic reputation strategies. The first is social learning: they watch other animals' behaviours, making a choice of where to feed or build a nest, for example, and will follow suit without testing the environment directly for themselves. As science writer John Whitfield observes, this 'has obvious similarities with the way humans choose what to buy, where to vacation', and so on. The second strategy is eavesdropping: adjusting your own behaviour based on watching – or being watched by – others. Whitfield cites the example of the cleaner wrasse, a small coral-reef fish, which 'decides whether to cooperate with its clients by removing parasites and dead tissue or to cheat them by biting mucus and scales (which are more nutritious) partly on the basis of whether potential clients are watching'.[1]

Costa Rican vampire bats leave their cave every night to look for a meal of blood. On average, one-third of younger bats come back without anything to eat, and they are bailed out by well-fed older bats who are happy to regurgitate some of their surplus blood. How the well-fed bats decide to share the surplus depends on patterns of past behaviour; whether, in short, the hungry bat has fed them in the past, and there is a favour to be repaid.

Reputation is not just concerned with our beliefs or actions. Our observed behaviour affects status, trust and reciprocity. As humans, we have developed sophisticated mechanisms to respond to danger or opportunity. We learnt long ago that how others see us affects our future. Cave dwellers knew it when they drew paintings of the hunt on their walls. This is thought to be a signalling mechanism – either that they were expert hunters or that there was abundant food in the area.

BEHAVIOURAL SIGNALS

The Godfather movie of 1972 glamorized the life of the mob and contained the immortal scene of the Mafia affiliate waking up to find a horse's head next to him in bed: behavioural signalling like no other. The Italian Mafia in the US had various rules and customs that had to be obeyed by all Mafiosi. The rituals associated with membership ranged from drawing blood from a pinprick on the finger to swearing an oath over a gun or a picture of the Virgin Mary. Once sworn in, Mafiosi lived by *omertà*, the code of silence that meant you should never speak about the Mafia to the authorities. It was *cosa nostra*, our thing, and no one else's business. If you broke *omertà*, you might end up in landfill in New Jersey or mixed into the concrete foundations of a construction site. The behavioural signals were crystal clear, and the Mafia gained a reputation for consistency by punishing breaches of those rules in unarguable terms.

Take the example of Abe Reles, a hitman for the Mafia from the 1920s to the time of his death in 1941. He was a member of what the media dubbed 'Murder, Inc.', the enforcement arm of the National Crime Syndicate that comprised the five main Mafia families in New York. He was a cold-blooded psychopath, nicknamed 'Kid Twist' because of his ability to strangle his victims with his bare hands, but his speciality was to drive an ice pick through a victim's ear and into their brain. On one occasion he killed a parking attendant in broad daylight for not delivering his car quickly enough, and he took pleasure in burying alive one of his enemies. He was an effective enforcer, and his presence alone sent a strong message to those around him. Reles became feared and even admired (*for* killing, *by* other criminals). The Mafia families connected to him gained valuable reputation currency by association.

In 1941, Reles earned himself a new nickname, 'The Canary', when he 'sang' to the authorities. After being arrested on charges of racketeering and murder, Reles squealed, providing details of some eighty-five murders. Various malefactors were identified, including the infamous Harry 'Happy' Maione and even Reles's old school friend Martin 'Buggsy' Goldstein. Thanks to his testimony, many of them were sent to the electric chair.

In the trial of Cosa Nostra boss Albert Anastasia, Reles was the star (and only) prosecution witness. The trial was set to start on 12 November 1941. With help from the five families, a US $100,000 bounty was placed on Reles's head. A bodyguard was bribed, and Reles duly 'fell' from the window of room 623 of the Half Moon Hotel in Coney Island on the day the trial was due to start. There was an investigation into his death, but no suspects were prosecuted, and instead a federal grand jury concluded, some ten years later, that he had accidentally fallen to his death while trying to escape by climbing down a chain of tied-together sheets. But Reles had not shown any great enthusiasm for trying to escape police custody before the trial, and indeed he had shown every desire to remain under police protection. His end sent a clear signal to anyone else who might be tempted to go down that route: Reles might be able to sing like a canary, but he would not fly like one.

It is regrettable to say that violent behaviour can be an effective evolutionary strategy. Anthropologist Professor Robin Dunbar of the University of Oxford studied the benefits that accrued to the families of those Vikings known as *berserkers*, from which the English word 'berserk' derives. These warriors tanked themselves up before battle with a brew derived from bog myrtle, a Dark Age equivalent of Strongbow cider, and were fearsomely violent. This was handy for raiding parties, but made them unpopular at home, where they disrupted community life and often ended up being banished or bumped off by the neighbours. Although as individuals their life expectancy was short, their families prospered by association. Such was their reputation for violence that fellow Vikings were loath to enter a property dispute with the families of a berserker, and often caved into their demands without a fight. Dunbar's study of the intergenerational violence chronicled in *Njal's Saga* shows that members of a berserker's family were 'half as likely to be murdered . . . as those whose families did not boast a berserker'. Over several generations, this meant that the violent families accumulated significantly more wealth and territory than the peaceful ones, not to mention their added life expectancy.[2]

The interplay between actual violence and the reputation for violence is at the heart of the pioneering analysis of Mafia behaviour carried out by Professor Reuter of the University of Maryland, one of the world's leading authorities on the economics of organized crime.[3] Together with Diego Gambetta, Reuter wrote the definitive study of racket-dominated industries, in particular the garbage collection market in New York and its suburbs over forty years from the 1950s to the early 1990s.[4] During this time, the Mafia ran customer allocation agreements whereby commercial premises were designated the 'property' of Mafia-run garbage collectors. (Residential garbage was a legitimate business, collected by the city.) Working hand in glove with the Teamsters Union and indifferent or incompetent city officials, the Mafia acted as de facto regulator of an industry that consisted of hundreds of small, family-run and poorly capitalized businesses. The Mafia-dominated carters charged the end customers up to five hundred per cent more than they would have been able to get away with in non-Mafia markets. As Reuter delicately puts it, the presence of the mob served to 'inhibit customer complaint'. The Brooklyn Trade Waste Association did, in fact, have a grievance committee, although meetings were all about sharing the spoils of the racket and did not address customer complaints.

'It was the simplest possible arrangement,' Reuter explains in an interview. 'Once you had served a business customer at an address you then owned the right to serve any business at that address. It was territorial. You "owned" specific locations. The customer knew that this was a racketeer-dominated industry, and so was never going to initiate a complaint because of the risk of retribution. If the customer started causing trouble, the union picketed the customer for some assumed violation and the customer was vulnerable because you can't have garbage outside your premises.' If the customer carried on protesting, the next step was violence against person or property. The right to serve a particular business was fully tradeable – the customer not having any say – and contracts changed hands at up to forty times monthly gross revenues, far higher than they would have been worth in a legitimate market. This was a real public policy dilemma: the harder the authorities tried to dismantle the racket, the more notorious it became, and the more reluctant the big, legitimate nationwide firms were to enter the market. The reputation of the Mafia was at its perverse zenith in the 1950s, Reuter believes, when senate committee hearings into mob influence were broadcast on TV. It was a riveting media spectacle, serving only to reinforce how terrible the Mafia were.

The Mafia's reputation for violence forced customers to fall into line, but in fact over time the mob's willingness to carry out the beatings, arson attacks and even murders necessary to maintain their reputation declined, Reuter found. Like any economic asset, reputation needs investment, and the families involved in the garbage racket in New York ended up wealthy and lazy, relying too heavily on their past reputations and not 'investing' for the future. 'Reputation became an asset,' Reuter says. 'And in some weird way the Mafia came to understand that it was an asset that you could run down. My theory was based around a view that the Mafiosi did not want to die with any of their reputational assets intact.' The racket ran for more than forty years, but it eventually collapsed when a legitimate firm entered the market. One of the big national garbage firms sensed the commercial opportunity and took the risk of challenging the gangsters. 'The fact that they were able to do so revealed a lack of credible Mafia enforcement,' comments Reuter. 'The firm said that even if a head of a horse had been put in one garbage truck they would have exited the market.'

The Mafia's reputation for violence successfully maintained the effectiveness of the racket for four decades. It imposed order and structure on a market and a community, kept out competitors and sustained profits – a striking result considering just how fragile the actual enforcement arrangements were. The result did not equate to a conventionally 'good' reputation. The Mafia did not want to be seen as fine, upstanding human beings, although the capo does value his reputation for benevolence in the local community.

Signalling using violence created a clear reputation. This in turn proved an effective if amoral tool, delivering long-term commercial advantage. In that respect, it must be said that the Mafia were skilled players of the reputation game.

THE SAS DETERRENT

The Special Air Service (SAS) is known as one of the most effective fighting forces in the world. The group was founded in 1940, when a soldier named David Stirling sold the idea of a small elite force to General Auchinleck, commander of the Allied forces in North Africa. At the time, Stirling was confined to crutches following a parachute accident, but this didn't deter him. Deciding to practise what he preached, he sneaked into the Middle East HQ in Cairo and found himself in Auchinleck's office without an appointment, where he successfully made the case that a small team of ruthless, highly trained soldiers could be more effective than an entire regiment.

The reason that the general was convinced lay in part in the reputation that preceded Stirling. He was highly capable and was known for delivering on his word. Churchill, too, was a strong supporter of the idea, and admired the embryonic commando force that Stirling had belonged to before founding the SAS. No one had any illusions that Stirling's men would be anything other than dangerous and unpredictable. But they had one central advantage – a reputation for being able to undertake highly effective disruption operations involving a very small group of men.

The SAS went on to become one of the most feared and respected rapid response and strategic fighting units in the world. 'The regiment', as it is called by its members, is subject to extreme entry testing. The unit is split into four squadrons, each consisting of around sixty men, which in turn is divided into four 'troops' of around sixteen men. The four troops have specific specialisms: Boat Troop are experts in maritime activities; Air Troop are experts in freefall parachuting; Mobility Troop are specialists in vehicles and desert warfare; and Mountain Troop are specialists in arctic combat and survival.

The SAS has four main roles: raising, training and leading indigenous forces around the world; counterterrorism; strategic reconnaissance; and high-impact operations. The unit's handling of the Iranian Embassy siege in London in 1980 and high-impact military strikes in Afghanistan and Iraq have cemented its reputation for effective and decisive action.

Jamie Lowther-Pinkerton is today best known as the former Private Secretary to the British royal princes William and Harry – during their teenage years and their twenties. His is a quiet reputation, known only to a few in elite circles. But to those in the know, he is regarded as super-smart, steady and diplomatic. He brought to his royal household role a clear-headed, down-to-earth pragmatism and charisma that reflects his time as a senior officer in the SAS. He was in the regiment for seven years, latterly as commander of G Squadron, 22 SAS, serving operationally in a number of different theatres (though specific details of SAS operations remain highly classified for forty years or more, for security reasons). He is clear about the reputation that underpins the regiment's reputation as a fighting force. 'The British army is not, and has seldom been, a "continental" army amassing hundreds of thousands of troops for grand manoeuvre in the way that the French, Germans, Russians or Americans have been,' says Lowther-Pinkerton. 'On the rare occasions that it has been called upon to conduct continental scales of warfare it has been through dire necessity, such as in the World Wars fought for national survival, and frankly we have not shown any great enthusiasm for it as a style of fighting. What we are, though, are great raiders, whether at the strategic level – as in the Peninsular War – or as small bands of determined men. This propensity for raiding is in our DNA, implanted there by our remote history of armed "migration" and centuries of supporting the Royal Navy, the country's senior service, in its operations around the globe.'

The reputation of the SAS – as the guardian of the national genius for raiding – has real value. It attracts the crème de la crème of the British Army, and it acts as a valuable psychological deterrent for the enemy. Lowther-Pinkerton recalls his time with the regiment combatting terrorism: 'The narrative around our capability had huge value – terrorist and insurgency groups did not do stuff because the SAS were perceived to be in the area. Just being thought to be there was a very effective deterrent – they knew that their chances of detection were higher and that their chances of escape were lower if they continued with their operation.'

One can apply similar analysis to other forms of military reputation. For centuries, the Royal Navy gave the UK a strategic edge in its endless conflicts with European powers. Admiral Lord Nelson's victory at Trafalgar was not enough on its own for the country to prevail against Napoleonic France, but without the

Royal Navy, Great Britain could not have fended off invasion and ensured the transport of men and material to fight land battles on the Continent. The Royal Navy remained the world's most advanced and effective naval force until at least the Second World War, and its dominion over the seas gave security to the British Isles, enforced rule over the empire and acted as guarantor to the country's international trade.

Or take the Germans: for centuries, the Prussians were fabled for their military prowess. They also had a habit of starting wars: the war with Denmark in 1864, with Austria two years later, the Franco-Prussian War in 1870–71, the First World War of 1914–18, then the Second World War. Having been roundly beaten in the last of these conflicts, the Germans put their bellicose past behind them, to the point where their allies in the North Atlantic Treaty Organization (NATO) are sometimes concerned that Germany should be better prepared. Indeed, the former Polish Foreign Minister Radek Sikorski quipped that he was the first Polish statesperson in many centuries to have actively called for Germany to be more warlike (in facing up to the threat from Russia). 'I fear German power less than German inaction,' he said in 2011. Germany's reputation for military capability survives, even though it is more than seventy years since the German army has fought a war in earnest. Likewise, Japan has not fought since the country was annihilated at the end of the Second World War, but its reputation for military competence also endures, and no doubt serves to check the expansionary ambitions of its neighbour and historic rival, China.[5] Centuries of history suggest that there is something fundamental in the organization and values of British, German or Japanese society that predisposes these countries towards war.

Reputations for capability are inherently sticky. Once you have a reputation for a particular talent, it is remarkably resilient. You have to work hard to lose that reputation. This is in marked contrast to character reputations, which are much more volatile.

CAPABILITY AND CHARACTER

For an individual, your *capability reputation* derives from how well you are perceived to be fulfilling a specific task: how likely you are to do your job effectively or cook an exquisite meal or deliver good value when you rent out a room on Airbnb. For a company, it is about how dependable it is in providing goods and services: manufacturing a reliable aircraft engine (Rolls-Royce), propelling rockets into space (Space X) or selling cheap clothing (Primark). On the other hand, *character reputation* reflects moral and social qualities. These include openness, honesty and transparency (or their opposites). You can have an outstanding capability reputation, while suffering an appalling character reputation. Sometimes your character reputation can be so bad it overwhelms your capabilities; at other times, your character flaws are forgiven because you are capable when it matters.

In London, we spoke with Sir Roger Carr, chairman of BAE Systems, one of the UK's largest listed companies, in his office off Pall Mall. Sir Roger is now an eminent industrialist who earlier in his career became chief executive of a group called Williams Holdings, which specialized in buying up smaller engineering companies and making them more efficient. Williams Holdings was exceptionally effective at doing this and it grew from modest origins into a FTSE 100 conglomerate. At the heart of the company's success was a reputation for quick and aggressive restructuring of the businesses it bought.

'Reputation was critical for Williams,' Sir Roger explains. 'First and foremost, we generated a reputation for execution. We used to have a small fleet of black BMWs that were driven by our turnaround and restructuring team and that became a very deliberate signalling mechanism for us. This was a small group of people who were very good at what they did post-transaction and they had a very special place in our organization. And people knew that. You only had to put six black BMWs outside the business and you could see the tempo of change accelerating.'

Whether the carloads of accountants wore dark glasses and stony expressions is not recorded: but there was an element of intimidation about the manner of their arrival. It conveyed just how seriously they took the business of squeezing efficiencies out of the companies they bought. They had a well-defined *capability* reputation. The BMW team were very good at their job, and everyone knew it. This reputation preceded them, and became a major asset for the company. But Carr believes that Williams enjoyed a positive *character* reputation as well.

'I like to think that we built a reputation for loyalty with our advisers. So the people we started with were the same people we ended with. And we only departed from them if we had to as a result of conflicts of interest. Second, we built a reputation for being fair with rewards. We did not nickel and dime people. And third, we were generally regarded as people who did what we said we would do, and could be trusted to do that. This meant that people were prepared to transact with us because they knew that we would act honourably and that, while we would be tough, we would not do that at the expense of fairness.'

In the US, we turned to Les Moonves, chairman and CEO of the CBS Corporation. Like Carr, Moonves was at pains to point out that competence and character both have their value. 'I think competence becomes one of the most telling factors about who we are and what we do. But it does go hand in hand with the ability to bring out the best in people, which is about character. I think my strongest ability is to create an environment where the best people can thrive,' he says.

For Moonves, your character becomes a critical factor in a creative industry where you have to be able to turn people down on one idea but at the same time motivate them to come back to you the next time they have a big idea. 'How do you keep your reputation when you are saying no to people ninety-five per cent of the time? How do you say no to someone when you may want their next project? To me that's very important – I would like them to come back in the door and feel very good about CBS. I want people to think of me as someone who they can trust and count on and who if they do good work it will be appreciated.'

Known by allies and competitors alike as the 'Man with the Platinum Gut', Moonves has a reputation as one of the most competent and competitive men in the industry, with an uncanny ability to spot and back the next big thing. For him, unsurprisingly perhaps, it is character that matters most.

'I think character and competence do go hand in hand, but I think that character is number one,' he reflects. 'Character is destiny. Great people who are greatly talented and who have both these things become the idols of our time. They become the Steven Spielbergs, if you will, who not only is a brilliant filmmaker but a wonderful guy. He is considered to be a man of great character and great dignity. Likewise, Tom Hanks on the acting front. Or Bruce Springsteen. These are brilliant talents who are also great people and are seen as such.'

APPLE'S CAPABILITY

The rise and rise of Apple under CEO Steve Jobs was built on its capability reputation. Every Apple product that launched was iconic, the latest in functionality, a must-have device. The value of the company rose from US $3billion in 1996 to over US $350 billion in 2011 when Steve Jobs handed over the reins to Tim Cook. Yet while Apple's products were magnificent in design terms, they suffered a number of embarrassing technical glitches.

It all started in 2008 with what pundits now refer to as 'Crackgate', where cracks started to appear in the casing of the iPhone 3GS. This was followed by 'Labourgate', which saw Apple criticized for suicides at Foxconn, one of its suppliers in Shenzhen, China; and then 'Antennagate', where users holding the iPhone 4 in a certain way impaired the mobile signal. One year later, in 2011, came 'Batterygate', where users of the iPhone 4S experienced rapid loss of battery power. Then 2012 saw two problems: first 'Scuffgate', where nicks or marks started to appear quickly on the newly launched iPhone 5; then the much more embarrassing 'Mapgate', where Apple's long-awaited mapping app failed to deliver accurate directions. This latter problem prompted a full corporate apology from CEO Tim Cook. And finally, three issues emerged during the course of 2014 – 'Cameragate' (problems with the iSight cameras on the iPhone 6Plus); 'Hackgate' (where celebrity hacks placed a focus on the security of Apple's iCloud service); and also 'U2gate' (where Apple was criticized for allowing the automatic download of U2's new album onto every iTunes account without users' permission).

Despite this series of missteps, this did not impact Apple's capability reputation – on the contrary, the company's reputation protected it from any fallout. Once you have won a reputation for a certain type of competence, in this case producing devices that everyone on the planet wants to own, it is hard to shake off.

To shed some light on how Steve Jobs pulled this off, we spoke to Bill Campbell, a Silicon Valley titan who spent a number of years as chairman of the board at Apple but who sadly died in April 2016, six months after we met with him in his Palo Alto home. During his career he chaired Intuit, a leading software company, and was the longest-serving director on the Apple board, serving seventeen years until stepping down in 2014.

'Steve was always design-led,' said Campbell. 'When he started the Mac factory in Fremont, he cared about every box and wanted them all to have logos on them. These were just boxes, for God's sake! But he was like that.'

Apple's strategy of focusing on the design of the product was in marked contrast to Google's strategy, which Campbell sees as more science-led. 'Google is a science machine, trying to think of algorithms to improve search and things like that. Whereas Apple, they think about design and take things that may not be as break-through – although certainly the iPhone and the Macintosh were breakthrough – and what they do is they make them approachable. You have two companies, number one and two in terms of market valuations in Silicon Valley, with very different reputations.'

Both strategies have had huge payoffs. Both companies have strong capability reputations, but Apple has also managed to develop a specific and valuable set of character reputations. In Apple's case, the design-led strategy has opened up its appeal to a mass worldwide audience and led to rock-concert-style queues at stores on the day of product launches. This has underpinned a richer and more visible corporate character, while Google, by contrast, is relatively faceless.

'The reputation recovery was led by Steve. He put the ads out – the lifestyle ads – and people responded to that, saying "I want to be like that." It was brilliant. Instead of it being so simple, it became that this simplicity made the product so much more powerful. That was all Steve,' Campbell said.

It is a testimony to the stickiness of Apple's capability reputation that it has not only been able to survive a number of capability hits, but that it remains one of the most successful public companies on the planet. Every June, Apple holds its annual Worldwide Developers Conference (WWDC), and the $1,599 tickets sell out in just over a minute.

For Google, its capability focus – on science and breakthroughs – has also delivered huge value. 'What does Google want its reputation to be? Larry Page really cares about being enormously creative and trying to advance the case for technology to make people better. Mark Zuckerberg says to me – "I can't even get over Google. They are the leading edge of everything that we are doing,"' said Campbell.

And he was equally clear that this confers real value. 'I think that the reputation Google has is with its peers. It is enormously valuable – [take] innovation, for example. When you think about all the stuff that they are doing, Google is a magnet for ideas, and it attracts the right kind of partners. That is an important thing to have in this industry. And if you are a kid who wants to go and work at Google, you do so because you can expect to be working on breakthroughs. So the value of Google's reputation in also attracting the right talent is huge.'

CHARACTER REPUTATIONS

Simon Cowell has famously been known for many years as 'Mr Nasty' on the hit shows *Britain's Got Talent* and *The X Factor*. His direct and often waspish comments jar alongside the honeyed remarks of fellow judges, and of course make for fantastic TV. The audience love it, and Cowell himself seems to play up to the image.

In reality, Cowell could not be more different. Slight, quietly spoken and extremely courteous, he met with us in his office in west London late in the evening – evidence of a punishing schedule that sees him work all hours of the day and night. It quickly became clear that character has become one of his principal reputational assets – in person, because it is so at odds with his public persona, and in public because it plays up to a bespoke image that delivers great entertainment.

'You could not do the job that I do if you are not interested in people or like people, or want to like people,' he says. 'You also have to be a great listener. The magic of our show is not even so much what they do [on stage], it's what they do before and afterwards. That little Q&A with Susan Boyle before she sang set it up beautifully – she did not say much, but she said she lived on her own, she had never been kissed, and she's got a cat. It was a sort of magic – it was not over thought out, and she was honest, and you were led to believe that she would be terrible.'

Tactfully, we suggested to him that his reputation with the British public was less than perfect. In fact, we ventured, people tend to think of him as downright . . . nasty.

'I always thought I was being funny, rather than nasty!' he says. 'I know what nasty really means, and I would never ever say or be that person. I never thought I was being nasty telling someone that they cannot sing a note in tune when everyone around them is saying that they can. And when I am saying, when they are eighteen [years old], "You can never make a living out of this, trust me, I am not a magician," I think I am being kind. You cannot hold out false hope to someone at such an important time in their career. It's not fair. And it's not right.' So perhaps a good character reputation is less about being nice than it is about integrity.

TRUST AND REPUTATION

Trust plays a huge part. Who can we trust to look after our money, or to be telling the truth? Who can we trust to fly our loved ones across the Atlantic, defying intuition if not the laws of physics? Without trust, how can we function, survive and flourish? Indeed, the course of evolution is a contest between the opposing forces of co-operation and self-interest. Trust helps us to forge alliances and friendships, so we can better negotiate the uncertainties and insecurities of the world.

Trust and reputation are not synonymous, even though they are mutually enforcing. Character reputation is one of the factors that will influence a person in deciding where to place their trust. It is logical to extrapolate this from a person's past behaviour. As the philosopher Baroness Onora O'Neill has said, 'If we are to place or refuse trust we need *either* unmediated evidence of others' honesty, competence or reliability or mediated evidence that can be checked.'[6] Reputation is an example of mediated evidence: it's not first hand, but it's the next best thing. In a situation where we co-operate with others to our mutual advantage, we have to be able to trust others and we also need to have a reputation for being trustworthy ourselves.

Philosophers have advanced a distinction between weak and strong trust. Strong trust is unquestioning and probably instinctive, such as the trust that a child has in his or her mother. It is not, except perhaps in some elemental, unconscious way, about reciprocity: you don't love your child or spouse because you want something in return.

Ask yourself how many people to whom you would lend a month's wages, without considering why the money was needed or when it would be paid back: the number of people falling into that category will be very small indeed. If you were dying of cancer, to whom would you entrust the upbringing of your young child? This is strong trust.

Hill-farmers in the Lake District have developed a unique culture of trust based on character reputation. James Rebanks, in his best-selling book *The Shepherd's Life* (2015), tells the story of a shepherd who realized he had bought some sheep from a neighbour far too cheaply. 'He felt this was unfair to the seller because he'd trusted him. He didn't want to be greedy, or perhaps as importantly, to be seen to be greedy.' He sent the other farmer a cheque for the difference, but the other farmer refused to accept the repayment. The only way out of the impasse was to go back the next year and deliberately overpay for some more sheep. 'They both valued their good name and their reputation far more highly than making a quick buck.'

Weak trust is more contextual and requires a rational assessment of the circumstances and the interests of other people. The kinds of contacts we forge at work are often examples of weak trust, even if we get to know and co-operate with our colleagues very well. Move jobs, and the basis for what you have in common often evaporates.

Professional relationships require trust where character and competence are both vital. If a pensions expert comes to your house to sort out your family's financial future, it is essential that the adviser brings professional expertise, as in knowledge of pensions and investments. Character is also vitally important: you don't want a brilliant financial adviser who wheedles his or her way into your home and then steals your money.

Joyce Berg, a researcher at the University of Iowa, ran an iconic study in 1994 using students to test the value of reputations in trust games. She devised an experiment where two groups played an investment game. Each group received a basic $10 fee for participating in the game. Group A were told that they could give some of their money to a person in Group B, knowing that this money would be tripled. Participants in Group B then had to decide how much of the tripled money to send back to the person in Group A who had sent over the money in the first place. Her findings led to intriguing insights into character and reputations.

This was initially a one-off game and Group A participants knew nothing about participants in Group B. So, on the face of it, players in Group A had no incentive to risk sending any money at all as there was no guarantee that their generosity in handing over the money would be rewarded. Character did not matter. But in fact thirty out of the thirty-two Group A participants sent money – on average, $5.22.

How can this be explained rationally? It seems that Group A players wanted to show what kind of character they had – to demonstrate they were willing to take the risk of getting nothing back. In showing that they were willing to place unconditional trust, they hoped to be trusted in return. And what of those in Group B who received the money? Well, eleven out of thirty players sent back more money than they received initially, suggesting that the reputational signal was understood and reciprocated, if not by everyone.

Intriguingly, gender seems to make a difference. Extending Berg's work on trust, Dr Rachel Croson and Professor Nancy Buchan have found that men and women were equally likely to send money in the first part of the game, but that women were far more likely to reciprocate than men. In other words, women are no more trusting than men – but more trustworthy.[7]

PLAYING THE GAME

The late author David Foster Wallace penned a celebrated tribute to the talent of the tennis genius Roger Federer, writing that it was a form of religious experience to see the Swiss player at the top of his game. Here he describes the final of the 2005 US Open:

> . . . what Federer now does is somehow instantly reverse thrust and sort of skip backward three or four steps, impossibly fast, to hit a forehand out of his backhand corner, all his weight moving backward, and the forehand is a topspin screamer down the line past Agassi at net, who lunges for it but the ball's past him, and it flies straight down the sideline and lands exactly in the deuce corner of Agassi's side, a winner – Federer's still dancing backward as it lands.[8]

The shot was impossible, Foster Wallace concluded, more like something from the science-fiction movie *The Matrix* than a feat of human brain and sinew. He went on to explain that Federer's skill is all-encompassing, defying the limitations of the human body and demonstrating a transcendent form of beauty.

We have all borne witness to such numinous sporting moments, whether it be Cristiano Ronaldo dancing through his opponents on the football field to score a seemingly impossible goal; Tiger Woods on top form, annihilating his opponents; Usain Bolt clearing 100 metres in 9.5 seconds; or Jonny Wilkinson clinching the 2003 Rugby World Cup for England with a winning kick in the last seconds of the match. These displays of talent are life-affirming, all the more so as we have all in our time kicked around a football or sprinted across the park or hit a golf or tennis ball, and we know just how remote from everyday capability are these moments of perfection. In the case of Roger Federer, character and capability are aligned: here is a man of sweet temperament, of incontestable niceness and integrity on and off the court, but who is a ferociously competitive player who has won a record nineteen major tennis singles titles, including winning Wimbledon eight times. He is the sort of man to whom sponsors and audiences flock, even if at the time of writing he is no longer the top player in the world. His serenity of character is the wellspring of his sporting success.

The case of Tiger Woods is more complex. He was the most successful golfer in the world, the number one player for 545 weeks between 1999 and 2010. He was the outstanding player in a sport that requires physical fitness, skill and grace, but also demands psychological dominance over your opponents. His golfing capability overawed other players. Then, in December 2009, having become the first sporting billionaire, he took time out from the sport to address problems in his marriage after it emerged that he was a serial philanderer.

His reputation for being a great golfer should not have been affected by his extramarital affairs, but when the psychological effects of a dissolute personal life spilled over into his game, that was another story altogether. Woods returned to the sport the following year, eventually going through a painful divorce, but he never recaptured his winning form. This period of self-immolation stripped away the psychological advantage he had enjoyed. No longer flawless and unassailable, he became merely human. He was nothing like as intimidating with a golf club in his hand, just another guy who looked for some action on the side. There were thousands of other golfers around the world with the very same human flaws.

The US swimming champion Ryan Lochte demonstrated a worse error of judgement. While in Rio de Janeiro for the 2016 Olympic Games, he was found to have fabricated a story about how he and two other American swimmers had been robbed at gunpoint by men with a police badge. In fact, it turned out that the twelve-time Olympic medallist and his teammates had been confronted by security guards after vandalizing a petrol-station toilet. His actions and the subsequent attempts at a lie denigrated his host country and shamed his own. All Lochte's major sponsors dropped him. So in sport, it's often not enough to simply play the game. Bad character can put you off, and even if it doesn't, you will almost certainly lose the goodwill of your sponsors.

The most egregious example is that of Lance Armstrong, whose capability as the world's leading cyclist was largely unquestioned between 1999 and 2005 when he won the Tour de France seven times in a row. This is a sport that relies not only on psychological but also physical intimidation, as well as talent and fitness, and Armstrong's reputation as a winner gave him a competitive edge. The Texan cyclist earned $218 million for himself and hundreds of millions more for charity, after he made a spectacular recovery from testicular cancer.[9] His success brought him a messianic following in his native America, his fame and popularity appearing to presage a career in public life. Yet his capability as a cyclist turned out to have been built on lies: he had cheated his way to the top by taking performance-enhancing drugs such as EPO, steroids and corticoids.

French rider Christophe Bassons remembers Armstrong's public intervention in the 1999 Tour de France. Bassons had voiced suspicions that this race, the so-called Tour of Renewal, was far from drug-free. 'Lance Armstrong reached me,' Bassons recalled in an interview with BBC Radio 5. 'He grabbed me by the shoulder, because he knew that everyone would be watching, and he knew that at that moment, he could show everyone that he was the boss. He stopped me, and he said what I was saying wasn't true, what I was saying was bad for cycling, that I mustn't say it, that I had no right to be a professional cyclist, that I should quit cycling, that I should quit the tour, and finished by saying [*beep*] you . . . I was depressed for six months. I was crying all of the time. I was in a really bad way.'[10]

Rumours had swirled for years, always denied categorically by Armstrong. At last, in June 2012, the US Anti-Doping Agency (USADA) filed charges against him, a few months later accusing Armstrong of masterminding 'the most sophisticated, professional-ized and successful doping programme that sport has ever seen'. He finally admitted wrongdoing in January 2013 in an interview with Oprah Winfrey, although by that time the damage had been done and many questioned the sincerity of his apology. Thereafter he was stripped of his Tour de France titles and banned from the sport for life. He was also dropped by sponsors including Anheuser-Busch, Nike and Oakley.

Armstrong now faces multiple lawsuits from his former spon-sors and possible financial ruin. Describing himself as the Voldemort of the cycling world, the man everyone loves to hate, he rebuffs suggestions that he is the sporting world's biggest fraud of all time. He seethes at the accusation that he was somehow uniquely corrupt, suggesting that he won according to the unwritten rules of the sport that prevailed at the time. Everyone was doing it; he simply did it better than everyone else.

David Foster Wallace believed that 'high-level sports are a prime venue for the expression of human beauty.' They are also, it is sad to say, an arena for the darker aspects of human nature.

'Sport is a global phenomenon engaging billions of people and generating annual revenues of more than $145 billion,' writes Gareth Sweeney, author of a Transparency International (TI) Global Corruption Report in February 2016.[11] 'While corruption in sport is not new, the recent pervasiveness of poor governance and corruption scandals threatens to undermine all the joy that sport brings,' Sweeney writes

The most prominent scandal to date involves the Fédération Internationale de Football Association (FIFA), the organizing body for global football, where in May 2015 nine current and former FIFA officials were arrested at the five-star Hotel Baur au Lac in Zurich on charges of racketeering and money laundering. The US Justice Department charged a total of sixteen officials – including six present or former members of FIFA's executive committee – with corruption, and at the same time arrested two of FIFA's vice presidents. They were accused of receiving over £100 million in bribes, while former FIFA vice president Jack Warner was accused of taking £500,000 that had been intended for the victims of the Haiti earthquake in 2010. There have been multiple allegations of corruption surrounding the choice of Russia and Qatar as hosts for the World Cup in 2018 and 2022, respectively, including a hard-hitting *Panorama* documentary by BBC reporter Andrew Jennings, who has spent many years investigating corruption in world football.[12] To demonstrate just how topsy-turvy were the moral values of the world of football, Sepp Blatter, the FIFA president who had presided since 1998, was re-elected two days after the arrests, though he was finally kicked out later in the year, facing his own criminal charges.

Note that none of this was about a reputation for competence. Steve Easterbrook, president and CEO of McDonald's, was one of the senior corporate leaders who had to assess the reputational consequences of an association with FIFA, having been a major sponsor of the game since the mid-1990s. 'We had chosen to be associated with football and the organizing body of football because around the world football resonates with our customers.

29

But when the behaviour of the organizing body falls out of line there is no doubt that there is reputational damage by association. We have had to consider this very seriously,' he says.

'When you think about the reputational ripple effect, you either walk away from the game that our customers and staff love and that we have invested a lot in around the world, or we see if we can use our convening power with the other sponsors to deliver change. I spoke with all the other sponsors and we discussed what we were seeing, but we all liked being associated with football. Our view was that if we could use our association to drive the case for a change in the way that the game governed itself – its reputational character – then we could use our involvement to help make a meaningful contribution to the future governance of the game.'

Easterbrook, together with three other major sponsors – Coca-Cola, Visa and Budweiser – were as good as their word. In a dramatic and very public intervention at the height of the crisis, the four CEOs issued a joint statement demanding that Sepp Blatter, FIFA's president, step down with immediate effect. For Blatter, that moment signalled to the outside world that his tenure was over.

THE CHARACTER OF BANKERS

Ten years on from the start of the 2008 financial crisis, the global economy is still on a fragile footing. Banks are still singled out as being the root cause of the crisis. The UK banking sector, for example, has suffered a 'collapse of trust on an industrial scale', according to the Parliamentary Commission on Banking Standards. The 2015 Edelman survey found that banks and financial services were two of the four 'least trusted' sectors of business (together with chemicals and the media). And in the US, a recent Harris Interactive poll found that forty-two per cent of people agreed either 'somewhat' or 'a lot' with the statement that Wall Street 'harms the country'.

The absolute core competence of the world banking system is to provide finance for governments, companies and individuals, to provide customers with bank accounts and access to our money twenty-four hours a day, and to manage our savings. It is a statement of the obvious that the financial system, and the individual institutions that form the system, should be above all safe, even if risk taking may lead to greater profits. If a bank goes bust through misjudgement or incompetence, the whole of society should not suffer: shareholders should bear the brunt as in any other company. That is what happened with the much-reviled hedge fund sector: many funds collapsed during the crisis but the impact on wider society was minimal since the losses were borne by shareholders.

There has in fact been a dramatic but largely unacknowledged increase in the competence of banks, largely because of regulations enacted after the 2008 crisis. Wholesale banks have up to ten times more capital than they did ten years ago. Their ability to place outrageous bets by 'leveraging up' (that is, borrowing against their assets) has been dramatically curtailed. The rules that allowed bankers to be paid millions, even as they placed bets that made the system riskier, have been tightened considerably. There is more liquidity in the system. And there is legislation to make sure that no European bank is too big to fail, and that failing banks can be wound up ('resolved') without recourse to the taxpayer (as happens dozens of times a year in the US, without great fanfare). In the UK, further measures are in place to ensure that risky investment banking activities are split off from taxpayer-insured high-street banking.

In short, banks in the developed Western economies of the US and Europe are safer, stronger and more liquid than they were before the crisis. The risk of going bust has been reduced, and the consequences of bank failure should not be as dire as when Lehman crashed (though no one wants to be the first to put this to the test).

But the reputation of bankers has not improved – because the underlying culture remains. 'The pattern of bad behaviour did not end with the financial crisis,' claimed William Dudley, the president and CEO of the Federal Reserve Bank of New York (the Fed), 'but continued despite the considerable public-sector intervention that was necessary to stabilize the financial system. As a consequence, the financial industry has largely lost the public trust.'[13] And by mid-2015, big banks had paid a staggering US $235 billion in fines since 2008, more than the annual gross domestic product (GDP) of Portugal.[14]

These fines have been imposed because of deficiencies in culture, incentives, ethics and oversight. Just two rogue traders – Jérôme Kerviel at Société Générale in France, and Kweku Adoboli at UBS in Switzerland – caused total damages of nearly US $10 billion between them. In 2012, the UK-based HSBC was fined $1.9 billion for money-laundering violations. In July 2014, the French BNP Paribas was fined a record $8.9 billion for violating sanctions against Iran, Sudan and Cuba. Then there was the LIBOR affair, when many banks were found to have colluded in rigging this key interest rate, and hundreds of millions were paid out for violations in the global foreign exchange market. The list goes on and on – in early 2016, for example, Goldman Sachs agreed to a record $5 billion settlement for its role in marketing and selling faulty mortgage securities in the run-up to the 2008 financial crash, and later in the year Deutsche Bank agreed a $7.2 billion penalty. Bernie Madoff, an informed insider (if you'll forgive the joke), told us:

> Anyone who had been in the industry for any period of time knew how corrupt these investment banks were. Don't forget I served more than twelve years on the SIA federal regulation committee, and five years as NASD compliance committee chairman . . . You had to be *blind* or stupid to not realize what was going on and [see] the difficulty of getting the regulators to have the courage to take on the powers that be and thereby losing their chance to get hired by the industry in the future at double the salary. No, the fines throughout the banking industry were simply a slap on the wrist. Prosecution was never a fear, to this day.

Are we talking about a few bad apples, or is the barrel itself rotten? William Dudley of the Fed puts the onus squarely on the leadership of the banking sector, arguing that it is their responsibility to ensure that the culture is right. 'Culture reflects the prevailing attitudes and behaviours within a firm. It is how people react not only to black and white, but to all the shades of grey. Like a gentle breeze, culture may be hard to see but you can feel it. Culture relates to what I *should* do, not what I *can* do.'

The Group of Thirty (G30), in its Culture in Banking Report dated July 2015, agrees. 'Events that precipitated the global financial crisis and the subsequent issues that have emerged have revealed a multitude of cultural failures,' the report states. 'Problematic cultural norms, and subcultures within large banks, have caused widespread reputational damage and loss of public trust. These events have been economically costly to firms in terms of fines, litigation and regulatory action. The cultural failures also came at a cost to the public, directly in some cases, and in terms of lost bank-lending capacity.'

Davide Taliente, a partner at the global management consultancy firm Oliver Wyman, led the research team behind the report. 'We interviewed about fifty banks across most big jurisdictions – a pretty comprehensive selection. Culture cannot be solved by regulation – not least by the fact that rules are slow and pedantic,' he says. 'What we were trying to do is to recommend substantial strengthening of organizational checks and balances that deliver the "right" behaviours, over and above respecting laws. The real irony here is that most written banks' codes of conduct are reasonable, there is nothing wrong with them. But they are not enforced and are not embedded in the way staff are managed. They become just a piece of paper.'

What is it about bankers that makes them behave so badly? A study published in *Nature* by Alain Cohn, Ernst Fehr and Michel André Maréchal, three economists from the University of Zurich, offers an intriguing answer: bankers behave as honestly as any other profession when on their own, but together they behave worse than others.[15] Using the economic theory of identity – which proposes that we all have multiple social identities based on gender, ethnicity, profession and so on – they ran an experiment increasing the weighting given to the professional identity of a group of 128 bankers from a large international bank. They split the group in two and gave each group a questionnaire to fill out. One group was subjected to a questionnaire that focused more on their professional identity as bankers, including such questions as 'At which bank are you presently employed?' and 'What is your function at the bank?' The other group was presented with a questionnaire filled with more general questions such as 'How many hours of television do you watch per week?' After filling in the questions, those with the predominantly banking-related questionnaire were primed to see themselves more as bankers, while those who had completed the more general questionnaire saw themselves in a more neutral light.

In the experiment, each person was asked, privately, to toss a coin and input the result into a computer. If they flipped heads, they would get US $20, but flipping a tail would earn them nothing. And in order to mimic the competitive nature of banking, participants were told that they would only be paid out if they flipped more heads than a randomly drawn person from a pilot study. The average would suggest, of course, that a person would in general flip fifty per cent heads and fifty per cent tails. But the results showed that while the control group reported heads in 51.6% of cases, the group primed to behave as bankers reported 58.2% heads. In other words, bankers clearly cheated.

Given all this, is it possible for banks and bankers to have good character reputations? In one respect, history would suggest not. Banking has for millennia been a pariah profession. Traditionally seen in Christianity as immoral, and with the practice of charging interest banned by the Muslim faith to this day, bankers have been persecuted in literature and political discourse throughout history. But more recently, as technology and automation since the 1970s have led to a dramatic expansion of lending, banks and bankers have found themselves in the position of being the new masters of the universe, perceived as highly skilled enablers of commerce and progress when they are not selfish or cavalier.

For a very long time, reputation mattered in banking. John Whitehead, who spent thirty-eight years as chairman of Goldman Sachs before retiring in 1984, was responsible for the creation of the bank's twelve original business principles. The second of these states: 'Our assets are our people, capital, and reputation. If ever any of these is diminished, the last is the most difficult to restore.'[16] Alan Greenspan, former chairman of the Federal Reserve Bank, spoke about this in a speech in 2008, saying: 'In a market system based on trust, reputation has significant economic value. I am therefore distressed at how far we have let concerns for reputation slip in recent years.'

One reason for this is the rise in the trading activities of investment banks and the decline in relative importance of the advisory activities. Trading, as an execution function, relies less on the character aspects of reputation that traditionally held banks to account. In a world where one's word was one's bond, bankers were held in check by the possibility of being blackballed within the close personal networks of the City. The threat of this was enough to secure good behaviour. Trading activities, by contrast, are done at arm's length and are often completely automated. This automation has diminished reputation as an effective regulatory mechanism.[17]

Fortunately, there are specific changes we can make to change the behaviour and reputation of banks, not least a cultural revolution at the world's major financial institutions. Banks have been poor players of the reputation game because they thought they could ignore it while they got rich. But poor reputations have led to increased regulatory oversight and political intrusion, which in turn have resulted in huge fines and problems attracting and retaining clients and staff. And for individual bankers, poor reputations have left them social pariahs.

Both banks and their employees need to change, if they are to be respected and trusted again. 'The leadership required comes not only from the top but all the way through the system,' says Lord Green, former CEO of HSBC. 'After all, even the person with no one reporting to them on any organization chart has the opportunity to influence others – colleagues, clients – for good or ill.'[18] This, Lord Green says, is like the cleaner at NASA who, when asked what his job was, replied that he was helping to put someone on the moon.

'WE'RE NOT ACCUSING YOU OF BEING ILLEGAL . . .'

Monday, 12 November 2012 saw the start of an uncomfortable week for three companies – Starbucks, Amazon and Google. A four-month investigation by Reuters had identified these companies as paying a bare minimum in corporation tax – in some instances, that meant zero – despite running large businesses in the UK. It would prompt very different reactions in each company, and highlight the different ways in which reputations for capability and character develop.

Journalists juxtaposed a number of seemingly incongruous facts. Starbucks, the international coffee giant, had paid zero corporation tax on sales of just under £400 million in the UK in the 2011 financial year, even though the headline rate for corporations was twenty-four per cent. Google was found to have paid just £6 million on £2.6 billion of UK sales in 2011, while Amazon had paid zero on £3.3 billion of sales in 2010. The result of these disclosures was an outcry of indignation from newspapers, and also from the UK Parliamentary Accounts Committee, headed at the time by the formidable Margaret Hodge MP.

One of this book's authors asked successive years of his Oxford MBA class to evaluate these figures. It was made clear to all students that the payments were not illegal in any sense. Around one-third of each class each year focused on the *capability* underpinning these tax payments, commenting that these companies are demonstrably highly expert and capable at minimizing their tax liabilities – thereby helping to maximize returns for shareholders. The class felt that if the purpose of business was to deliver returns for the owners, these companies have been tremendously successful – and they were highly financially literate and expert at navigating complex international accounting laws.

The other two-thirds of the class immediately focused on a *character* assessment. Taking a broader view of the purpose of business in society, they felt it signified a poor corporate culture that paid little regard to the societies in which they operated. To this group, the companies were villains.

The Public Accounts Committee (PAC) seemed to agree with the latter interpretation. 'We're not accusing you of being illegal, we're accusing you of being immoral,' Ms Hodge told the nonplussed head of Google's operations in northern Europe, who was under the impression that his job was to make money for shareholders, delight customers and stay within the law. The PAC report following the hearings, released over the first weekend of December 2012, accused the companies of immoral behaviour, prompting one of the three companies to reconsider its position. Starbucks announced that it would review its UK tax policies. Kris Engskov, the former White House aide who was now the company's European boss, said just three days later that the company would 'voluntarily' pay £10 million in corporation tax in each of the following two years, 'regardless of whether our company is profitable during these years'. This unprecedented announcement was not required by law, and was a reaction to a widespread sense of public outrage at the tax revelations of the previous week. In Engskov's words: 'These decisions are the right things for us to do. We've heard that loud and clear from our customers.'[19]

In February 2016, Google reached a settlement with the UK's Inland Revenue after a seven-year investigation into its tax affairs. Google agreed to pay US $185 million (£130 million) in back taxes. At first, Chancellor George Osborne was tempted to celebrate the deal as a triumph for the government. The Treasury called it 'the first important victory in the campaign the government has led to ensure companies pay their fair share of tax on profits made in the UK and a success for our new tax laws'. But considering Google's UK revenues were £5.6 billion in 2013 (and tax paid a measly £20.5 million), the settlement soon looked decidedly underwhelming. Matt Brittin, the company's European chief, was hauled in front of PAC for the usual public grilling. 'We have long been in favour of simpler, clearer rules, because it is important not only to pay the right amount of tax, but to be seen to be paying the right amount,' Brittin explained afterwards. 'But changes to the tax system are not Google's call. Reform must come from governments, not from the companies who are subject to their rules.'[20]

Brittin is right: governments around the world need to fix clearer rules and eliminate the opportunity for arbitrage between different tax regimes. International tax is in truth a highly complex issue, and multinational companies have always taken advantage of ambiguities in the system to minimize the tax they pay, particularly in their overseas operations. But Google did not help its moral case when, a few weeks later, it awarded Brittin's boss, global CEO Sundar Pichai, a share package worth US $199 million, dwarfing the tax settlement. Its obligation to the country where it operates a near $6 billion business should surely be greater than to the one talented individual who heads the company.

Google's behaviour was, in reputation terms, entirely rational. Users of the search engine generally do not care about Google's 'character' – they care about the ability to find what they want with the greatest accuracy in the shortest time – or in other words, Google's 'competence'. Its decision to negotiate over seven years with the UK tax authorities, and then settle, relates to its reputation with an audience of regulators and politicians. Google ultimately decided that it was worth reaching an agreement in order to neutralize any further political attacks, given the government's ability to create new and additional regulatory costs for the group in the future. In doing so, the settlement reached needed to be seen as reasonable by the group's shareholders. Google would have wanted to make sure that its reputation for financial competence remained intact, and settling on such a minimal amount of tax after such a lengthy negotiation would certainly have achieved this.

It is worth drawing a final key lesson from these cases: behaviour that is legal is not always going to protect your reputation. On the contrary, your reputation, especially your character, can take a hit, even if you are following the letter of the law. For Starbucks, this reputational hit also became a competitive whipping stick. Costa Coffee, one of its major competitors, used the publicity surrounding the Public Accounts Committee to trumpet the fact that it had paid its tax in full.[21]

REPUTATION GAME THEORY

Reputation has a powerful effect where there is any form of uncertainty about the person or organization we are dealing with, which is most of the time.

Nowhere is this more evident than in negotiations – where not only are you uncertain about the capability and character reputation of the other person, but also there is a great deal of uncertainty about the eventual outcome. Take Britain and its Brexit negotiations. The stakes could hardly be higher – for the UK and for the European Union (EU) – and there has been a huge amount of uncertainty about the process, the people and the final outcome. In this febrile environment, everyone has focused on the reputation of each protagonist in this grand and unfolding political drama.

It has a colourful cast list. In one corner, we have the Europeans, led by Jean-Claude Juncker, the EU president, whose heavy drinking is alleged to make him a political liability after lunch.[22] Alongside him, and leading the EU negotiating team, is the former Polish prime minister and now president of the EU Council, Donald Tusk, reputed to be a warm, smooth political operator.[23] Completing the EU troika is Michel Barnier, the pugnacious and tough lead negotiator for Brexit, who was once described by a British newspaper as 'the most dangerous man in Europe'.[24]

In the opposite corner, the British team is led by UK Prime Minister Theresa May, the 'vicar's daughter in kitten heels' who has sought to build a reputation as a safe pair of hands, driven by an old-fashioned sense of public service.[25] She adopted a tough but pragmatic approach to the initial negotiations, stating that 'Brexit Means Brexit', while indicating that the talks should focus on securing a good deal for both the EU and the UK. Alongside her are UK Foreign Secretary Boris Johnson, a demagogue seen as a political maverick with a reputation for 'professional chaos';[26] and David Davis, the minister of state in the newly formed Department for Exiting the EU, whose Eurosceptic views are legendary and who delighted in the moniker 'Monsieur Non' that was given to him when he was Europe Minister in David Cameron's government. As if that wasn't enough, the UK team also had to deal with the 'feisty' Nicola Sturgeon,[27] Scotland's first minister, who called for a second Scottish independence referendum on the basis that the Scots electorate voted to remain in the EU.

Whatever the truth of these reputations, there can be no denying the fact that they created significant early fault lines in the negotiations. Britain was perceived as being ill-prepared, unrealistic or irresponsible, while the EU was perceived as being bellicose, divided and insular.

As with all reputations, perceptions of capability and character are the dominant frames of reference. Theresa May, as home secretary in the Cameron government that preceded her own, took the UK out of the Justice and Home Affairs Chapter of the Lisbon Treaty, subsequently opting back in to specific initiatives where she felt it was in the UK's interests to co-operate. EU watchers cite this as evidence not only of her competence, but also of her ability to focus on achieving sensible outcomes – a character reputation that will undoubtedly play a large role in the forthcoming negotiations.

Tim Cullen, a former World Bank executive who directs the Oxford Programme on Negotiation at the University of Oxford's Saïd Business School, cites two distinct elements to any negotiation. He believes that it is important to separate out the specifics of the matter under discussion from perceptions about the people you are negotiating with. He believes that it is critical to ensure that engagement with one does not destroy the relationship with the other.

Like many who have researched negotiation, he believes that reputation plays a critical series of roles in negotiations. First, the reputation of each party colours our initial perceptions, and informs initial strategies. If you have a reputation as a tough negotiator, the other party's strategy for engagement will reflect that. Second, a reputation for competence in a specific area will be seen as a major asset in any negotiation. Take, for example, the UK's reputation for intelligence-gathering. This is regarded around the world as first rate, so it can be used as a critical chess piece in any settlement between Britain and the EU.

Cullen also makes the case that reputation is dynamic in negotiation. While it may be advantageous to be seen as hard, inflexible and determined at early stages in a negotiation, it may become useful to be seen to be open to persuasion and discussion at later stages. But as with our broader analysis, people have different reputations *for* something *with* someone – and, in negotiation, being seen as flexible within the negotiating team may also come across as being weak or unprincipled by the wider public.

THE PRICE OF LEMONS

The economist George Akerlof won a Nobel Prize for showing how reputation works in uncertain markets. His most famous work, 'The Market for "Lemons": Quality Uncertainty and the Market

Mechanism',[28] published in 1970, focuses on the role of reputation in the second-hand car market, which he used because it was one where there was considerable uncertainty about the reputation – and motives – of the buyer and seller.

At the time, he struggled to get the study published, as fellow academics wrote off the subject of dodgy second-hand cars, what he called 'lemons', as essentially frivolous. But, in fact, that is how the world works, with people having to make decisions based on uncertain information that is subject to rumour and gossip.

Akerlof showed how buyers would always suspect the motives of sellers. If you are selling a second-hand car, you know more about it than the buyer. The buyer is almost certainly going to think, 'If he really wants to sell me that car, do I really want to buy it?' As a buyer, the price you will be prepared to pay will reflect your caution and lack of knowledge. So even if the car is only a week old, you will expect a heavy discount on the price of a nearly new car, on the assumption that there must be a good reason it is being sold. If you are the seller, and you know the car is still as good as new, you are simply not going to sell it for the same price under such conditions, which simply reaffirms the market suspicion that any second-hand car that is for sale must be a lemon.

The analysis works whether you are selling illegal drugs, second-hand cars, horses, stocks, shares or bonds. The cycle of suspicion and mistrust means that this kind of market will seize up, with no business being done. But if there is a middleman who has developed a reputation for selling second-hand cars at a fair price, it allows the market to function, allowing for a reasonable degree of certainty that the car being sold is not a lemon.

Akerlof's paper was an early example of a serious economist applying proper analytics to the slippery concept of reputation. A decade later, David Kreps and Robert Wilson of Stanford University used the evolving science of game theory to analyse the problem of 'Reputation and Imperfect Information'.[29] Their research looked at chain stores and asked a deceptively simple question: suppose you dominate one regional market, indeed enjoy the benefits of being a monopolist – how should you behave if a new department store opens up on your patch?[30] Should you co-operate by meekly accepting the arrival of a new competitor, or should you behave aggressively, reducing prices in an attempt to make life as uncomfortable as possible for new entrants? Both courses of action are costly: if you roll over, you concede ground to your competitor, while if you fight, you lose profits in the short term. Your expectations of how they will respond matter, too.

With even a tincture of uncertainty about what the other player would do, the reputation effect becomes crucial, especially if the player suspects that the new entrant is seeking to build their reputation. In essence, the research suggests that it is always better for the incumbent to respond to the new entrant with aggressive pricing.

There are many real-world examples, from contract and labour relations to international diplomacy, where it is highly worthwhile to acquire and maintain the kind of reputation that enhances your bargaining position. President Obama reflected on this theme in his long, valedictory interview with the *Atlantic* magazine, asking aloud about the value of military deterrence in international relations. Traditionally, he muses, countries have gone to war to demonstrate the credibility of their threat to go to war. One consequence of this logic was the Vietnam War, which he describes as a humanitarian tragedy that killed millions and held back the development of Asia for decades. In Syria, Obama famously did not intervene militarily when President Assad crossed the US 'red line' of using chemical weapons against his own people. In stepped Vladimir Putin to broker a decommissioning of such weapons. Whether this was a good outcome is a tortuous ethical and policy question: Obama enraged those who feared that US credibility had been undermined. He himself believes that US interests were best served by keeping out of the conflict. But has this damaged the reputation of the US for sticking to its word?[31]

In 1983, US economists Alvin Roth and Francoise Schoumaker devised a simple game where players were divided into two groups (plus a control group) and given the chance to bargain for a set of lottery tickets.[32] They had to reach agreement, or else neither group was allocated any lottery tickets at all. Everyone was then told there was a catch: a winning ticket was worth $40 to one group and only $10 to the other. In simple economic terms, then, the rational split for the lottery tickets would be eighty per cent of the tickets for the $10 outcome players and twenty per cent of the tickets for the $40 outcome players – so that they would have an equal chance at capturing equal value.

In the experiment, players were told that there would be twenty-five rounds. In rounds one to fifteen, both sets of players played against a computer, without realizing that they were doing so.[33] But when game sixteen started, players received full information about the offers and eventual choices made by the others in their group over the last five games.

This new information created new reputation capital for the players in the game. Up to that point, they had acted without fear that their prior strategies would become public. In the remaining rounds of the game, players suddenly became highly sensitized to the reputations that they had inadvertently built up through their past behaviours, and also became highly attuned to the other players' reputations as seen through the lens of their chosen strategies. As a result, in the last few rounds, players sought to pursue winning strategies based on a new set of expectations, showing just how such expectation frames contribute to character reputations. Unsurprisingly, perhaps, the outcomes were sharply different in the closing rounds.

THE LARGEST FINANCIAL FRAUD IN US HISTORY

There is no gilding the lily: Bernie Madoff perpetrated the largest financial fraud in US history. He founded his own securities firm in 1960 with a US $50,000 loan from his father-in-law and $5,000 of his own savings from working as a lifeguard and installer of sprinkler systems. He started to produce attractive returns to investors, and was seemingly able to weather the economic cycle, delivering consistent returns irrespective of global economic conditions. It turned out that Madoff was robbing Peter to pay Paul, paying out these returns by borrowing forward against the new investment funds flowing into his firm from investors. Over the course of his career, it is estimated that around US $36 billion was invested in what has become the world's most infamous Ponzi scheme.

Madoff currently resides in a cell at the Federal Correctional Institution in Butner, North Carolina. His release date is 29 June 2159, around his 221st birthday. Madoff agreed to correspond with us over several months at the end of 2015 and into early 2016. Communication with a federal prisoner is made by post and via the Federal Correctional email service, CorrLinks. The system works like this: you write a letter to the prisoner to ask if they would be prepared to correspond with you. If they are happy to do so, you get an email informing you that an unnamed federal prisoner wants to correspond with you, asking that you download the CorrLinks communications app. Once downloaded, you then receive the email sent by the prisoner and are able to start corresponding.

Our first email from Bernie Madoff stated that he had received our letter, and that he would indeed be happy to correspond with us. However, he asked (and he was 'embarrassed' to have to be doing this) if we could send US $200 to cover the costs of correspondence. To us, that seemed like a lot of Internet time, or indeed, postage stamps, but we wanted to talk to him. We asked how the funds should be sent, and were told by Madoff to send funds via Western Union or MoneyGram. Not having used either of these before, we checked with our banks and they told us that these services were untraceable, and as such could be used by those seeking to hide the transfer of funds from authorities and others.

We persevered, and sent the money to the PO Box specified by Madoff – an address in Des Moines, Iowa. A small alarm bell did ring in our minds. Why would a federal prisoner, located in Butner, North Carolina, want money to be sent to a PO Box in Des Moines, Iowa? And if it reached there, how was he going to be able to collect it, given that he is unable to leave the prison?

After sending the cash, we waited but heard nothing. So we sent Madoff an email asking if he had received the funds. He replied that he had not received anything. Bemused, we set about explaining again what we had done and he then apologized and said that he had got the address wrong. This time, we were to send money to him at a new address – a generic one using his federal correctional name. This we duly did, sending another $200 as per his new instructions. Again we waited for a response from Madoff, and received none. We chased him; he replied again: 'I am at a complete loss. Your wire has not come yet and the people here claim they have no ability to clear this problem up.' By this time, we started to feel that we might be onto a bigger story, but far be it from us to impugn his motives.

So we tried again, this time through an American friend who would be able to navigate the online payment system using a US registered credit card. This time, now $600 down, we succeeded. Madoff confirmed he had received the funds and was good to go. (We never found out what happened to the US $400 that we had already sent.)

When did the Ponzi scheme start? The prosecutors, and other detractors, have said that Madoff was congenitally predisposed to fraud, and that he systematically started to defraud investors in increasingly large amounts from the early 1970s onwards. But he was able to maintain a positive reputation against internal market grumblings due to the fact that he was seen as what we could today call a 'disrupter' – his original business was based on innovations not offered by the major banks.

In a letter, he explained his version of events:

Everything went along fine for years and then we ran into the 1987 market crash. My US clients, particularly three families, started to panic and were concerned that the significant unrealized long-term gains [they had made] would disappear in the chaotic market environment that seemed destined to continue. In spite of my objections they ignored their commitments to wait until [the investments] were ready to unwind, and they forced me to sell their positions. I complained that the premature unwinding was a violation of the agreement and would put me in a terrible position with my foreign clients, particularly in the current market environment.

There followed a complex negotiation between Madoff and his clients, in which he took on certain client liabilities, while he also liquidated some of their assets so he could give them back the money they wanted. His account casts himself as the wronged party.[34] The way he explains it, his clients had to pursue riskier investment strategies, because of financial pledges they made to him. To some extent, the details are irrelevant: what seems incontrovertible is that by the early 1990s, Madoff was under pressure to deliver higher returns to his old clients. He also enjoyed such a good reputation in the industry that new clients were knocking on the door, demanding that he take their money and try out a new investment strategy. In his mind, he had thirty-five years of generating legitimate profits for his clients, and some sixteen of fraudulent ones.

His attorney Ike Sorkin confirms: 'Bernie never solicited anyone. He never asked for money. People were turned away. I had a friend who I played golf with who asked me if I could put in a word for him with Bernie because Bernie would not return his calls. I chose not to for any of these requests. But Bernie used to sit at the Palm Beach Country Club and people would offer him money for investment.'

'My plan was to utilize an option arbitrage strategy I had been using with great success for a couple of years with a number of individual clients and limited partnerships,' Madoff explains. 'Because of my earlier success with this model . . . I was approached by a number of European hedge funds to take them on as clients. I was concerned with the reputation that European hedge funds had as "Hot Money" investors, [that is] they would flee at the first sign of poor performance. I was assured that if I would commit to a long-term commitment to keep their money, they would bring in the desired type of investors. Although my success to date with the . . . strategy was good, the amount[s] of money I was investing was limited. I decided to forge ahead and things went well. More monies started to flow in as word got out that Bernie had a new strategy for hedge funds and high net worth clients.

'Then the market stalled due to the onset of the recession and the Gulf War. I started to find it difficult to employ the strategy and had to sit with the money in US Treasuries waiting for the market to become receptive. This led to the funds pressing me to get into the market to trade as well as the high net worth clients also growing impatient.'

As the market went against him, he tried out what he thought would be a short-term strategy to get the money back. Of course, that did not work either.[35] 'The rest is my tragic history of never being able to recover,' he muses from his prison cell.

Sorkin naturally agrees with Madoff's version of the timeline. One of the most respected names in the legal profession in New York, Sorkin has, for many years, served on the other side of the fence as a prosecutor for the federal government – first as a trial attorney with the Securities and Exchange Commission (SEC), then as an assistant US attorney, and then as deputy chief of the criminal division of the US Attorney's Office for the Southern District of New York in the 1970s. From 1984 to 1986 he worked as the director of the SEC's New York office. Sorkin's words carry weight.

'Bernie says that the beginning was after the recession of 1990. You will recall that President Clinton was elected on the basis of the mantra "it's the economy, stupid". Bernie says that investors asked him if he could still get the returns that he was getting before the recession, and to his shame he said yes. He started his firm in the 1960s with a loan from his father-in-law and he would cover the shortfalls in his trading by loaning the shortfall. So it was pride and his reputation that brought him down. He did not want to let people down,' says Sorkin.

Madoff has never disputed the fact that he enacted the fraud, and he has dedicated his activities since being imprisoned to helping the authorities – including the Madoff Recovery Initiative led by Trustee Irving H. Picard – to recover as much of the lost client funds as possible. 'After my arrest I assured my attorneys that I believed that with my assistance [they] would be able to receive enough assets from those parties that contributed to my problem. Rather than using my information to negotiate a lesser sentence I chose to use this information as leverage over those above parties to return the money they withdrew from the advisory side of my firm over the years. Money that was composed of both legitimate profits I earned for them in the first thirty-five years as well as those false profits generated in the last sixteen years.'

Madoff becomes animated in our correspondence when discussing the work being done to recover funds. He regards the effort that he has put into this area as one of the most important things he can do to atone for the fraud perpetrated for so many years before his incarceration. He is irritated by comments made by Irving Picard, the trustee appointed by the Securities Investor Protection Corporation (SIPC), that he has been unhelpful in seeking the return of money to investors. Madoff is also clear that major players and counterparties in the investment banks all manipulated the markets for their own gain, consistently, and that this is an endemic problem within the culture of financial markets today. It may seem like the pot calling the kettle black, but his words resonate in the light of the 2008 financial crisis.

In corresponding with Madoff, it is hard not to feel personal sympathy for him. Since going to prison in 2009, both of his sons have died – his elder son, Mark, committed suicide exactly two years after his father's arrest, and his younger son, Andrew, died of lymphoma on 3 September 2014. His name is now synonymous with fraud. It is fair to say that both his character and capability reputations have been comprehensively destroyed. After many years of success, he has lost the reputation game.

3

NETWORKS

BARRIE SAVORY'S HEALING HANDS

One of the authors has an intermittent back problem: about once a year, his lower back seizes up and he finds himself in unremitting pain. As he has found, there is only one thing to do: call Barrie Savory in Harley Street, speak very politely to his receptionist, plead for an appointment, and turn up for a half-hour session ready to be fixed.

Savory has been practising as an osteopath for more than half a century. Born in London in 1939, the son of a chiropractor, he is a slight, good-humoured man with wise, intelligent eyes. He has the strength to lift you off the floor if the need arises, and the delicacy to realign the way your skull sits on top of your neck, without you noticing. He shakes your hand and makes small talk for a moment or two while appraising you expertly as you stagger towards the examination couch. He glances at your notes, asks a few pertinent questions and then lays on his hands. He presses and prods for half a minute, and invariably delivers a quick and simple diagnosis: your lower back is out of shape; one leg is longer than the other; you're seized up here; you have a nerve trapped there; have you been spending too much time at your desk writing another book?

Barrie is possibly London's leading osteopath, and has been for decades. Film stars, members of the royal family and prime ministers have all beaten a path to his door. He is fabulously discreet about his customers, but since Sean Connery wrote an endorsement for his book *The Good Back Guide*, as did HRH the Duke of York, one can reliably assume they are among his satisfied patients.

Analysing Barrie's reputations, they are clearly based on skill – in our model, competence and capability. He delivers results, fixing bad backs and eliminating pain. But there is more to it than that. He is at the heart of a network – of doctors, orthopaedic surgeons and patients – where every successful treatment reinforces Barrie's reputation. This leads to a virtuous circle of further referrals and more gratified patients. This has been going on for more than fifty years, and Barrie has long been as busy as he wants to be. In his late seventies, he can pick and choose when he works and for whom, and interleaves his professional work with lecturing to impart his skills to new generations of osteopaths. He does charity work and spends as much time as he pleases with his granddaughter or on the golf course (though he still makes himself available to patients at short notice).[1] This is the kind of professional nirvana to which many of us, in many different fields, might aspire, but which is very difficult to attain.

We asked Barrie how he had made his name. 'Ah,' said Barrie, 'I can date it to one letter back in 1976.' It was early in his career and he was already a skilled osteopath, but it was a bit of a struggle building up a practice. The breakthrough moment came when a leading orthopaedic surgeon referred a patient to him. Barrie laid on his hands, did a good job and then wrote a letter to the surgeon, copying in the patient's GP, explaining the treatment and the outcome. It was a short, straightforward letter without a hint of self-promotion, an unpremeditated master move in Barrie's personal reputation game. It prompted the GP to get in touch with Barrie, and say that he would be sending patients directly to him in future.

As it turned out, the GP was a partner in a discreet and still flourishing practice in the heart of Knightsbridge. The doctor's patient list included peers of the realm, members of the royal family, cabinet ministers and so forth: an unparalleled network of well-heeled, middle-aged, influential people, many of whom suffered back pain from time to time. Barrie did a good job for one influential patient, then another, then scores and hundreds more. 'Looking back on my patient records I can quite literally date the development of my practice to that one letter, and the access it gave me to the GP's patient list,' says Barrie.

So Barrie Savory's reputation was made when skill was connected to a network of influential people who were predisposed to have back pain and who would tell all their influential friends about Barrie's magical hands. 'I had the skill,' Barrie reflected, 'but I needed the stage on which to display the skill. It needed to be a high-end stage. It's no good playing rep in Bromley.'

THE SCIENCE OF REPUTATION NETWORKS

We all belong to social networks of one form or another – whether through social media, alumni networks, work groups or simply our family. Unless we are professional headhunters, or competing for business in a world where contacts and connectivity really matter, we probably don't give them much thought. Yet the networks that humans form have been the subject of intense study, by online businesses such as Facebook which are looking to exploit them for commercial gain, but also by social scientists fascinated by 'organic' networks of human beings. These unplanned networks have a 'structure, complexity, function, spontaneity, and sheer beauty not found in organized networks, and their existence provokes questions about how they arise, what rules they obey, and what purpose they serve', write social scientists Nicholas Christakis and James Fowler.[2]

Networks are fundamental to what makes us human. The typical size of a group of sophisticated primates like chimps or baboons is around fifty, and they all know each other personally. Chimp brains cannot sustain social relations with any more than fifty or so fellow creatures as it is just too mentally strenuous. Humans have much bigger brains than their nearest relatives and many scientists believe that human intelligence evolved not to cope with basic survival, but in order to handle interactions within larger and more complex social groups. Robin Dunbar of the University of Oxford has done pioneering work on the relationship between brain size and social interaction, and even has a number named after him. The Dunbar Number is 150: the number of individuals we can know well – well enough to remember their name and be able to sustain a conversation if we met them in the street. His research shows that this is the average number of friends we interact with on Facebook, the typical size of a fighting unit in most modern armies and the ideal number of people to work in an entrepreneurial business. This is not the same as the number of people we count as close friends or family we could turn to in an emergency: research suggests that the average person has between two and four really close friends (while sadly, many have none). We have the brain capacity to recognize around five hundred people, but in the age of mega-cities and online networks numbering billions this is no constraint to the size of our communities.

The most basic network consists of just two people, sometimes called a dyad. Put three people together and you have a triangle of connections, a triad. A more complex example given by Christakis and Fowler is a line of sixty people passing a bucket along a line from a river to a burning house: this involves a lot more people but in a simple relationship with one another. The network is the vehicle for the transmission of water. 'But it also could be germs, money, violence, fashions, kidneys, happiness, or obesity,' they write. 'Each of these flows might behave according to its own rules. For example, fire cannot be transported in buckets toward the river; germs cannot affect someone who is immune.' Reputation flows through networks, with its own dynamics.

If you mapped Barrie Savory's professional network, it would have him at the centre, connected to thousands of individuals ('nodes'). But Barrie is also connected to a much smaller number of medical professionals who are responsible for making referrals. These are the crucial players: the so-called 'network brokers' who make or break reputations and bridge the gap between two different networks.

Your position in a network depends on a few key variables: the sheer number of people you know; the density of the network (do they all know each other?); your centrality to the network; lastly, do you know others really well (a strong tie) or less so (a weak tie)?

You might think we would always want to group together with people we have something in common with, yet there are real benefits to having lots of weaker connections, too. A well-known experiment carried out by Stanley Milgram in the 1960s showed that we are all connected to everyone else in the world by a maximum of six degrees of separation.[3] At the time of writing, the experiment was repeated by networking supremo Julia Hobsbawm on BBC Radio 4. The world's first professor of networking, at the Cass Business School, part of the University of London, managed to reach a complete stranger on the small Scottish island of Coll in six phone calls. Intriguing though this is, our brains are not set up to deal with six degrees of separation. Back in the primordial past, human brains evolved to cope with three degrees of separation at most, in other words to be influenced by friends of friends of friends. Our moods, behaviours, weight, health, happiness and, of course, reputation are all affected, typically unconsciously, by our connections at three levels of separation.

If your behaviour is the message, your network is the method of travel. Put bluntly, if no one knows you, you don't have a reputation.

SOCIAL CAPITAL

In *Bowling Alone*, Robert Putnam's celebrated book about the atomization of US society, there is a chapter given over to the many different manifestations of social capital. It may not be physical capital (like machinery) but it is incredibly valuable nonetheless. Putnam cites a forgotten educational administrator from early twentieth-century rural West Virginia, who defined the term as 'good will, fellowship, sympathy, and social intercourse among the individuals and families that make up a social unit'. The community will benefit 'by the cooperation of all its parts, while the individual will find in his associations the advantages of the help, the sympathy, and the fellowship of his neighbours'. Or, as Yogi Berra defined the benefits of reciprocity: 'If you don't go to somebody's funeral, they won't come to yours.'

Ron Burt is the Hobart W. Williams Professor of Sociology and Strategy at the University of Chicago's Booth School of Business, and he has spent his academic career studying the ways that social networks create competitive advantage. The first, most obvious conclusion is that successful people are simply more able, more intelligent, better with words, more skilled or charming.

But there is another aspect to success in any field: social capital. Burt's research shows that people who are better connected just do better. They have the benefit of exchanging ideas, information, goods or services. By dint of their connectedness, they are able to secure better prices, find the right partners for their professional or personal life, and open up opportunities that others are unable to secure. Understanding these networks is the key to understanding the alchemy of success.[4]

Joel Podolny, now head of Apple University, is a leading sociologist in this field, and he uses status to explain the way in which networks create advantage. Social capital has real power and meaning where there is imperfect – or obscured – information relating to quality. That could be the quality of the advice you are getting from an adviser, or it could be the lack of consensus on the quality of a particular wine.

In a much-cited 1993 paper, Podolny described how investors who are not able to get an accurate read on the quality of an investment bank look instead to the bank's standing in the social network of other investment banks. This became a proxy for bank quality, and his findings showed that higher-status banks were, as a result, able to borrow funds at a lower cost. It wasn't what the banks were doing that conferred this advantage – it was simply where they were in the network.

THE POWER OF CLOSED NETWORKS

A network is 'closed' when all the people or entities are connected to each other. Everyone has some form of connection or tie with at least two others in the network. Open networks, by contrast, are ones where two people or organizations are tied, but their networks of contacts are not connected to each other.

Figure 1, taken from Burt's work, shows this well. In this example, Robert and Jessica are the two people connected to each other. In the closed network shown on the right, Robert knows Jessica well and Jessica knows Robert well, and Robert's friends also know Jessica's friends. Conversely, in the open network on the left, Robert and Jessica know each other a bit, but their networks of friends are completely separate.

Figure 1 Open and closed networks

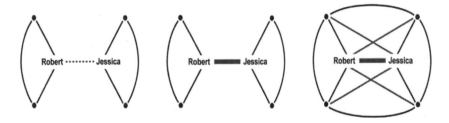

Source: Courtesy of Professor Ron Burt, Hobart W. Williams Professor of Sociology and Strategy at the University of Chicago Booth School of Business

In a closed network, relationship ties are personal and, typically, very strong. A perfect example is the family. Each and every family member knows everyone else, and each member of the family is connected to everyone else. By contrast, an open network is one where you have a weak tie to someone else, and that other person's network is separate from your own. In other words, you know one person – perhaps a colleague from work – reasonably well, but your friends have never met each other.

Information moves fastest in closed networks. The speed of connectivity enables people in the network to take rapid action, and information moves with greater certainty. This is because closed networks facilitate high levels of trust. People know each other well, and all the other people in the network know each other well too. It becomes much harder to behave badly in closed networks. Bad behaviour will be immediately visible not only to the person directly affected, but also to everyone else in the network too. This creates a huge reputation risk when it comes to transgression – every action is amplified by dint of the connectivity of the network.

For centuries, financial markets relied on reputational networks. From the earliest minting of clay coins by Phoenician traders, through to the promissory notes issued by insurers in the London markets, and more recently the development of sophisticated credit scores, reputation has been a critical mechanism underpinning the functioning of financial transactions.

Don Robert, chairman of Experian, one of the largest financial information companies in the world, agrees: 'The roots of credit and credit scoring were informal. Local information was shared about the credit worthiness of this or that individual, and these local information networks actually persisted right up to the early 1970s. Today, the networked information that we use in credit scores comes from a combination of sophisticated mechanisms but they all rely at their core on information shared through closed networks.'

The British Army knows the value of network closure. Its platoons of men and women work in extreme situations where high levels of trust allow for rapid decision making and can save lives in the heat of battle. Major General Jonathan Shaw commanded the 2nd Battalion of the UK's Parachute Regiment, 12 Mech Brigade, in Kosovo and commanded coalition forces in Basra in 2007. He was also Director of Special Forces before being appointed Assistant Chief of Defence Staff (Global Issues) in January 2011. This role saw him responsible for chemical, biological and nuclear policy; arms control and counter proliferation; and cyber security for the UK's Ministry of Defence. Shaw believes that trust – and the reputation of individuals with their immediate colleagues – lies at the heart of any unit's effectiveness when it comes to warfare:

> Trust gets stronger between people the more danger you face. Hence regimental spirit is cultivated most strongly in the infantry. They fight for their mates more than for queen and country, and far more than for the cause set by the politicians ... who get the least loyalty, being the least trusted. The result of this bonding inside a unit is that they trust each other with their lives. That is what they fight for. Soldiers care deeply what others think of them but it is secondary as a motivation; their primary motivation is their internal reputation, their mutual respect. They don't want to be seen to let the regiment down or fail to live up to their own code of selfless behaviour, which in turn forms part of their self-regard.

Another interesting example of the trust that exists in a closed network is the New York diamond industry. Nearly half of the world's US $70 billion annual diamond jewellery sales are in the United States,[5] and the diamond area of New York centred around 47th Street in Manhattan handles over ninety-five per cent of the diamonds imported into the US. Supporting this trade is the Diamond Dealers Club (DDC). Located just by St Patrick's Cathedral at 47th Street and 5th Avenue, the DDC calls itself 'the largest and oldest organization active in the US diamond trade, and the most important diamond exchange in the United States'. It operates a strict series of rules around the exchange of diamonds between dealers, and it forbids dealers to challenge decisions through the courts made by the DDC. The whole network operates completely on reputational capital and sanction – amazingly, deals are not even written down.

Glenn Spiro is a bespoke jeweller based in London. While his clients today are some of the richest and most glamorous people in the world, he started in the industry as a junior benchworker in

London's Hatton Garden. Reputation underpinned everything in this market, from the stones to the clients and even the way you dressed:

> I used to go to Hatton Garden, where there was the diamond bourse. All the dealers would sit with their goods. Everyone had a desk, and it was their little empire. I was working as a bench-worker, I was a craftsman. I wore torn jeans, plimsolls, T-shirt and so on. And my grandfather, who had nothing, came with me occasionally when I was asked to run errands. For three months, I delivered a package from Cartier's workshops to this man in the bourse called Monty. I would occasionally pass him in the street and would say 'Hi Monty' and he would never acknowledge me. My grandfather said to me, I think you should wear a pair of trousers, a shirt and a jacket. So I did that, and I was too early for the bourse so I went next door and got a cup of coffee and who, lo and behold, came up and said 'Good Morning'? It was Monty. And not only did he say 'Good Morning', he said, 'Would you like a cup of tea?' He had no clue who I was, but he knew he had met me before. But because I had the trousers and jacket on, because I looked the part, he gave me the time of day. If a man is smartly dressed, if he looks the part, looks great, it makes a difference. You get taken seriously. Our perceptions of people are very much ruled by image.

Spiro knows the diamond market inside out. And reputation, he says, is central to the way it functions. He says, 'In our business it is the same as it is with life in general – you are only as good as your word. The nature of our business is the same as it has been for hundreds of years, with no legal paper contract. We all sell and acquire millions of dollars of gems amongst each other on basically a verbal agreement or handshake. If you are ever to break this unwritten law you are very much on the way to being considered outside the "circle". That is the way it is done in this industry – it's done on reputation, and my word is my bond.'

The DDC provides a trading floor, where information about other traders, market conditions and general gossip is shared. The wall of the trading floor is a public repository of all relevant background information on the reputation of members. There are pictures of and background references for any visitor to the club, each of whom has to be sponsored by one of the club's members. There are also nominations for potential new members, where existing members are invited to comment on the reputation of anyone proposed. But also, and perhaps most importantly, on the wall are published any judgements made through the DDC's internal arbitration process along with 'wanted'-style pictures of anyone with an outstanding debt. Diamond traders hope never to appear on the wall.

The majority of traders come from similar Jewish backgrounds, and often multiple generations of family members enter the trade – and so enforcement mechanisms for misbehaviour extend into the community itself. 'If a particular family or merchant has behaved badly, members of the community may choose to walk by on the street and not help if they have a problem, or may refuse to help in the case of a medical emergency. The networks are that tight,' says Lisa Bernstein, a law professor at the University of Chicago, who has studied the workings of trust in the diamond industry.

Modern industrial companies increasingly organize production teams into small, specialized units to benefit from the advantages of closed networks. Paolo Scaroni, chief executive of British glassmaker Pilkington from 1996 to 2002, understood this well when he implemented a key change to the float glass process, a quarter-mile-long production line created by Pilkington for the production of sheet glass for cars and buildings.[6]

In the late 1990s, Scaroni tells us, 'the potential for disruption in the production line was huge. In a process lasting over a quarter of a mile, there are many parts that can wear out or break, and when that happened the entire line would have to close, sometimes for up to three days at a time.' Scaroni asked each team to name the parts that needed replacing most often, and made sure they were always available. 'This meant that we could restart a broken line within hours, not days. As a result, we dramatically improved our productivity. And there was competition and pride among each team – no one wanted to be part of the team that let the side down when it came to an extended stoppage of the line. It became a mark of professional pride, a reputation badge of excellence.'

German Mittelstand companies operate in closed networks, so far as the communities in which they operate are concerned. These are the family-owned businesses that form the backbone of Europe's largest economy. Michael Diekmann, a former CEO of the Allianz insurance group, comes from a classic Mittelstand background: his father was proprietor of a family-owned company that made bridges. It was a leading employer in the small north German town where he grew up. 'Everyone knew what car my Dad was driving, the kids at school were the children of people who worked for the company, you played football with them, were part of the same theatre group or the fire brigade,' he told us. 'In the long winter when people didn't have work they would never have understood if my Dad drove an enormous Mercedes and spent long vacations in Hawaii. You are not anonymous: there is a direct connectivity between your actions as a capitalist and the social environment. You have to ask yourself are you part of something or just exploiting the community.'

As CEO of a large, publicly listed company like Allianz (with more than 147,000 employees and a market capitalization of €66 billion), Diekmann says it is easier to hide. 'You have a virtual world rather than the direct world of the Mittelstand,' he reflects. But he is among many CEOs of big German companies who have a social conscience and have sought to impart the Mittelstand ethos to a much bigger organization.

Back in the old days, when the City of London was a closed network, the only way to become a partner in Cazenove, the ultimate insider's stockbroking firm, was to be a public-school-educated landowner. We once met the son of the first partner in Cazenove to have been to grammar school rather than a posh public school. On attaining partnership, his new partners insisted that he sell his suburban house (which, to their horror, had a *number*) and buy a farm. His sons were taken out of grammar school and sent off to boarding school. It proved a very expensive promotion, as this was in the mid-1970s and the markets were in a long-term slump.[7]

In this context, the top public schools still represent a closed network at the top of public life in the UK: certainly that is true of former prime minister David Cameron's inner circle (just over half of his May 2014 Cabinet were educated at private school, compared to seven per cent of the population). Similarly, in France, almost all top civil servants, politicians and industrialists graduated from the top few elite universities, for example the École Normale Supérieure. The graduates of these schools, the so-called *énarques*,[8] are notoriously a closed network of super-bright intellectuals, including president Emmanuel Macron and his predecessor Francois Hollande. Yet for all the hope invested in Macron, they are having trouble steering France a path to prosperity and relevance in the modern world – a lack of innovation being one of the downsides of a closed network.

Chairpersons, CEOs and non-executive directors of the UK's big listed companies form another closed network: they come from a small pool of talent and they all know each other's strengths, weakness and foibles, to the extent that they obsess about their reputations with each other. 'I really worry that top executives care more about their reputations than the reality, in some cases,' reflects a top UK headhunter. 'The better their reputation, the higher salaries and bonuses they can command. It becomes absolutely everything to them, to the point where if you lose your reputation you are losing not just your self-esteem but your earning power, your very identity.' In this particular closed network, reputation becomes so precious that it must not be put in jeopardy, even if it becomes detached from reality.

When everyone knows everyone well, there is a danger that you create an echo chamber where everyone repeats the same information over and over. New thinking and new people are not encouraged. People play safe, out of fear of offending the majority, or because it is not worth risking a reputation for competence or reliability or trustworthiness. 'They really don't want to be seen to be the person associated with failure, or to be in the hot seat when things start to deteriorate,' comments one City insider, describing the closed world of big company boardrooms.

The case of the ex-Sir Fred Goodwin, the former CEO of the Royal Bank of Scotland, illustrates this well. In his early career, he was a rare example of a man penetrating a closed network – in this case the upper echelons of Scottish finance – through raw talent. His father was an electrician and he was the first of his family to go to university. He graduated as a lawyer from the University of Glasgow before retraining as an accountant, joining Touche Ross as a management consultant, and becoming a partner in 1988, aged thirty. He moved to RBS in 1998, subsequently driving through the £21 billion takeover of NatWest, the largest ever UK banking merger. In 2001, he was promoted to Group CEO. His initial impact was transformational: through twenty-six acquisitions, he turned RBS from a regional player to the fifth largest bank in the world, with a market capitalization of £80 billion and more than one million employees. Naturally, Goodwin had the ear of Prime Minister Blair and Chancellor Gordon Brown. He received a knighthood for services to banking.

As his success grew, his network started to close around those people who either agreed with him or were useful to him. The first sign of grander ambitions came in 2005 with the move of the bank's corporate offices from its old headquarters in the historic centre of Edinburgh to a new £350 million mini village set in a hundred acres of woodland at Gogarburn, adjacent to the city's airport. As part of that move, he selected for himself an office the size of a football field. He also relocated the directors' kitchen to make sure that the scallops that he loved eating wouldn't get too cold on the way to the dining table. According to Alex Brummer, *Daily Mail* City editor, Goodwin personally ordered the bank's twelve chauffeur-driven Mercedes S-class cars be spray-painted the same specific shade — Pantone 281 — so they precisely matched the RBS corporate blue, also ordering that the interiors be furnished in a beige that exactly matched the colour of the carpets in the management offices back at Gogarburn.[9] He initiated an affair with a female colleague, despite being married since 1990. He began micromanaging the company. For example, he disliked the use of adhesive tape in public areas so much that he banned it across the bank. He ordered thousands of filing cabinets with rounded tops at the bank's HQ in order to stop papers being placed on top of them. He personally commandeered the design of the bank's Christmas card.

No one on the close-knit board sought to challenge his behaviour. In the autumn of 2007, the bank went a deal too far with the £49 billion consortium bid for the Dutch bank ABN Amro. Along came the crash – the whole financial edifice was revealed to be risky in the extreme, and in 2009 RBS announced the biggest loss in financial history. The bank was eventually rescued by taxpayers at a cost of £45 billion. At the time of writing, the UK taxpayer still owns seventy-two per cent of the bank, its shares worth three per cent of what they were at their peak in 2007, and half what the taxpayer paid for them. Only one of the former eighteen board directors of RBS has been censured (former head of the investment bank Johnny Cameron was banned from the City).

Fred was stripped of his knighthood. His own capability reputation (for cost-cutting) had been made as an outsider in a closed network, and was lost when his board failed to impose any checks on his behaviour. In his early career, he was a deft player of the reputation game. Following the worst financial collapse in the UK's history, he lost the reputation game on a grand and irrecoverable scale.

THE VIRTUE OF WEAK TIES

In open networks, the links between individuals are looser. There are more people in an open network than in a closed one, because it is less strenuous to maintain casual connections (think of

LinkedIn or Facebook). What you lose in terms of trust, coherence and efficiency is counterbalanced by increased creativity. Innovation and ideas fly around open networks, precisely because of the serendipitous impact of acquaintances or strangers. When you are connected to multiple people, each of whom has their own diffuse networks, it is more likely that you will encounter new ideas. These ideas will have more time to take root, rather than being immediately quashed in a closed network. John Stuart Mill, the nineteenth-century English philosopher and political economist, put it perfectly: 'It is hardly possible to overrate the value . . . of placing human beings in contact with persons dissimilar to themselves, and with modes of thought and action unlike those with which they are familiar . . . Such communication has always been, and is peculiarly in the present age, one of the primary sources of progress.'

In 1973, the sociologist Mark Granovetter wrote a seminal article on the strength of weak ties, which investigated the basis of Mill's intuition.[10] Because information flows into the network from its extremities, the system benefits overall, Granovetter demonstrated. In closed networks, he wrote, 'New ideas will spread slowly, scientific endeavours will be handicapped, and subgroups that are separated by race, ethnicity [or] geography . . . will have difficulty.'[11] He gave the example of the working-class communities of Boston's West End, who were unable to fight off developers who wanted to rebuild and gentrify the area. Granovetter's analysis suggested that the residents were closely tied by class, friendship and ethnicity, forming subgroups that had little connection between one another. He suggested that these groups were lacking the weak ties that might have helped them present a united front. Bartenders and shopkeepers served all members of the community, providing a bridge between the different subgroups – but not enough for a fight against the bulldozers.

At the most extreme, this is the difference between a closed society such as North Korea, and open ones like the US, Germany or the UK, which are able to absorb ideas and innovation from all around the world. Historically speaking, a maritime nation like the Netherlands or the UK was more open to innovation and influence from overseas than a closed political culture like Russia. Under Peter the Great, Russia opened up to the world, seeing great advances in prosperity as a result. At other times, it was closed off, as under Stalin. The Industrial Revolution originated in the UK rather than elsewhere, in part because British entrepreneurs were especially open to the flow of new technology and knowledge. The French came up with many epochal discoveries in pure science, but were less good at finding practical applications for them (and, at a crucial time, French society was convulsed by revolution). Economic historian Joel Mokyr has argued that it was the UK's ability to absorb Enlightenment ideas that helped the country to gain the edge over its continental competitors.

Technology has been a massive contributor to economic growth and jobs in the developed world, and continues to change the way we live. Intuitively, we know that it is an industry characterized by open rather than closed networks. Open-source research and development touches all kinds of technology. In this model, intellectual property is not developed in secret, it is shared, allowing complete strangers to appropriate, improve and disseminate innovations. Obvious examples include Android, the open-source mobile operating system, or Wikipedia, which has displaced encyclopaedias as a repository of the world's knowledge. The information is supplied by an army of volunteers from around the world. This philosophy underlines many cutting-edge technologies, from software to the Internet of things to big data and MOOCs (Massive Online Open Courses), which are designed to make top-class education (for example, lectures from Harvard professors) available to a potentially unlimited audience via the Web.

In open networks, new ideas have the time and the ability to travel around different groups of people, growing and changing until they become fully formed and valuable. Reputation in open networks becomes a mechanism through which new ideas propagate and evolve, whereas reputation in closed networks primarily drives efficiency.

In reality, the networks we inhabit are neither fully closed nor fully open. While our family unit may be mainly closed, each family member will have other connections that create more open structures, and so on. Mapping the architecture of real-life networks requires considerable mathematical skill and familiarity with sociological jargon. But there is one very simple, useful concept for players of the reputation game to grapple with: 'structural holes'. These are the curious voids that arise between different parts of the same network. Those who bridge the gaps are the ultimate reputation brokers.[12]

THE IMPORTANCE OF BEING A NETWORK BROKER

Network brokers enjoy a number of advantages. First, a broker receives a higher volume of information than someone sitting in a closed network. Second, this is high-quality information, because the broker is getting it from multiple different sources. Third, the broker will, by dint of his or her network position, be able to spot new opportunities faster than someone in a closed network. And finally, the broker also has a 'control advantage': the ability to make – before anyone else – the connections that he or she wants.

'These structural holes create a competitive advantage for an individual whose relationships span the holes,' explains Professor Burt of the University of Chicago. 'The structural hole between two groups does not mean that people in the groups are unaware of one another. It only means that the people are focused on their own activities such that they do not attend to the activities of people in the other group. Holes are buffers, like an insulator in an electric circuit. People on either side of a structural hole circulate in different flows of information. Structural holes are thus an opportunity to broker the flow of information between people, and control the projects that bring together people from opposite sides of the hole.'

One example of network broking in action is the development of the drug Viagra as a treatment for erectile dysfunction. It was first trialled on humans in 1991 as a possible cure for angina, but it proved worthless for heart disease. Burt explains that the test drugs were recalled in the normal way, but an unusually high proportion of the samples were not returned. Some curious individual had the gumption to ask the question: why were fellow researchers not returning the trial drugs? The answer was that they had an interesting and unexpected side effect, which was leading to unofficial experimentation among the research scientists, presumably outside office hours. This led to further trials and in 1998 Viagra was launched, the first treatment for erectile dysfunction and still a blockbuster today. Scientists at Pfizer were able to see that failure in one part of the organization could be an exceptionally good idea somewhere else.

The engineer Eugene Stoner was the inventor of the M16 rifle and a man deemed by experts to be a genius among small-arms manufacturers. Before he joined the Fairchild Engine and Airplane Company, he worked as an ordnance technician in the Marines. He was familiar with the use of ultra-light plastics and aluminium in the aircraft industry, and when he was tasked with developing a lightweight rifle for Fairchild it was obvious to him that these materials should be used in the design of the new weapon. The result was the AR-10, ultimately supplanted by the M16, which is now used throughout the US armed services. His innovation was seen as revolutionary in the small-arms world. 'But it was nothing particularly new to what I'd been doing all along in the aircraft equipment, in the fibreglass and all that.'[13] Stoner was seen as a genius simply because he was able to bridge the two worlds of aerospace and armaments.

In various studies, Burt has shown that senior managers who bridge structural holes are more likely to get promoted early, to get higher bonuses and win the respect of colleagues. In a celebrated analysis of the networks of 345 bankers in a leading global invest-ment bank, Burt found two intriguing results. First, reputation trumped rank: in other words, how your peers thought about you (as reflected in 360-degree evaluations) was more important than where you were in the bank hierarchy. So, while senior people tended to have good reputations – that was one of the reasons why they got promoted in the first place – it was possible for more junior people to get bigger bonuses than their superiors if they enjoyed a better reputation. The second finding was that the rate of decay in networks – by which Burt meant the rate at which one connection in one year has become redundant by the next year's evaluation – is extremely high. In fact, nine out of ten disappear from one year to the next. But he also found that the true brokers retained their network ties. In other words, they were the one out of ten. They were the ones who understood the value of social ties.

Professional intermediaries such as PR executives are classic network brokers. Tim Allen, a former spokesman for Tony Blair who set up Portland, his own very successful PR firm, explains that the function of top players in PR is to be a 'junction box between the worlds of politics, media, industry and the City'. People like Allen sit at the interstices of these different worlds, ensuring that a CEO develops his or her network in Whitehall, or that a City editor develops personal connections with industrialists, or that a top banker gets to know those who are shaping regulation and policy. This is helpful to all parties, but especially to the companies who pay the bills: they cannot operate in isolation from media and polit-ical scrutiny, and these choreographed connections smooth the way to successful outcomes in takeover battles, planning applications and the like.

And as the power of reputation networks has grown, so too has the remit and influence of these powerful network brokers, particularly in times of crisis. There is a lively battleground for ideas among advisers to companies, and the prize is to have the trusting 'ear' of the chairperson or the CEO. 'There is sometimes a tension between the lawyers, who focus on the court of law, and our role, which is the court of public opinion,' says Roland Rudd, one of the founders of global communications company Finsbury.[14]

These network brokers exist in all major financial capitals of the world. Allen and Rudd's peers in London include Sir Alan Parker, founder of the Brunswick Group. Christoph Walther of CNC and Alex Geiser of Hering Schuppener play similar roles in Germany, as do Anne Méaux of Image 7 in France or Joele Frank in the US. Quite apart from canny intelligence and unrelenting charm, such PR entrepreneurs typically display an unstinting appetite for bringing people together. Night after night, their homes are open to editors, ministers, ambassadors, EU commissioners and CEOs, many of whom are themselves brokers in their chosen field, who are invited with the promise of fine wines and electrifying conversation. Guests might include top journalists on the *Financial Times* and key officials from Downing Street. When these PR titans go on holiday, they go to their yachts or *fincas* with bankers and politicians.

Recently, one highly successful PR entrepreneur gave a sixtieth birthday party. Some two hundred favoured guests sat down for dinner in a basement specially constructed to house his collection of classic cars. 'I seem to have a gift for turning friends into clients, and clients into friends,' he told his guests: an apposite motto for this class of indefatigable and effective networkers. Guests might not be aware of it, but they are in the process of bridging structural holes – and, in the process, positioning their host at their centre.

Other examples of network brokers include the Knightsbridge GP who made Barrie Savory's career: the doctor acts as a bridge between his patients and the specialist osteopath who can make them well. Or the literary agent who connects writers with publishers: in this day and age, publishers want their relationships with authors to be mediated by a third party who can vouch for the quality of the writing. The movie producer is another example of someone who straddles different worlds, linking bankers and financiers with talent, and bringing the whole project to market. Ditto the dealer in second-hand cars identified by the economist Akerlof:

71

he bridges the gap between buyers and sellers in a world of imperfect knowledge and limited trust – someone to turn to when all you see is lemons.

Ron Burt explains the benefits accruing to network brokers as a form of social capital, which has broader relevance than the amount of money you get paid. For successful network brokers, their reputation precedes them, opening up connections and opportunities that enable them to become more productive in future. The more connections you have, the more you are talked about and the more connections you can make – making this kind of reputational capital very sticky.

LET'S STICK TOGETHER: REPUTATION IN THE EUROVISION

Over two hundred million people worldwide watch the Eurovision Song Contest. It is the longest-running international TV music competition in the world, established in 1956 and held annually since then.[15]

Each participating country performs a song, and this song is then awarded points by other countries. Great emphasis is placed on the process by which winners are chosen. But unlike the judging in competitive sports (such as diving), the winning song has no universally agreed traits: no single harmony is universally regarded as better than another; no one orchestration is regarded as the way things are done. Songs reflect national tastes, rhythms and cultures, as well as the musical influences of the performers themselves. How, in this environment, can judging be objective?

Despite its image as a showcase of national cultural and artistic prowess, the organizers take impartiality and the process by which winners are selected very seriously indeed. First, the order of the performances is selected by lottery. Second, each nation selects sixteen people to be its national judging panel. This group must be comprised equally of men and women, music industry experts and the general public, and equally above and below twenty-one years of age. The organizers believe that this uniformity across nations produces the most representative and unbiased view of the entries.

Once selected, each panel member is given a booklet containing tear-out slips, each marked one to five. They meet just one hour prior to the contest, and they are asked to rank their top ten songs. The method by which this is done is simply by the panel member tearing off their mark – one to five – immediately after hearing each song. They are not allowed to vote for their own national entry. An administrator immediately collects the slips, and a notary public adds up the points and signs the final mark sheet. The use of a notary is meant to stamp out any possibility of fraud. There is also a second process consisting of the public vote.

Every effort is made to ensure that there is impartiality in the voting decisions. The voting power of each nation is equal irrespective of geographical size, population or economic power; the panel decision is made public before phone lines open in order to make sure it is not influenced by the popular vote; the random order of the performances means that there is no bias given to early or late entries.

This process should produce a meritocratic procedure that reflects the quality of the songs performed. There is, in other words, a veil of ignorance around the judging process, which is designed to protect against bias. If this were true, one would expect the results to reflect a reasonably random distribution among nations. Yet this is not what the results show. The results show a consistent bias reflecting the underlying cultural and political networks in modern-day Europe.

Gad Yair and Daniel Maman, two sociologists from the Hebrew University of Jerusalem, made a study of Eurovision, finding that European nations coalesce into five meaningful cliques: the first consisting of tax havens Ireland, Malta and Luxembourg; the second centred around the Balkans, spanning Turkey and the former Yugoslavia; the third consisting of Mediterraneans Italy,

Spain, Monaco and Greece; the fourth of independent-minded Britain, Switzerland, the Netherlands, Israel and France; and the fifth of social democratic states Germany and Sweden, together with Norway, Denmark and Belgium. Three other nations – Austria, Finland and Portugal – have no consistent reciprocity with other European nations; in network terms, they are relatively isolated. Taking this as a starting point, Yair and Maman find that European nations are connected by a number of weak ties, held together by a small number of tight networks or cliques.

This model shows which nation directly votes for which other nation but does not take into account all the wider voting relationships that exist. Taking this into account, a more consist-ent pattern emerges of three voting blocs with votes reflecting wider cultural and political network ties. Their analysis shows three meaningful blocs. First, a Western bloc, consisting of Britain, Ireland, France, Switzerland, Luxembourg, Belgium and the Netherlands. Second, a Northern bloc consisting of Sweden, Denmark, Norway and Germany. And third, a Mediterranean bloc composed of Cyprus, Greece, Slovenia, Macedonia, Turkey, Italy and Spain.

Nations in the Western bloc consistently receive more votes than members of the other blocs. Everyone favours them over others when it comes to the allocation of votes. Why should this be the case? The answer lies in network ties, underpinned by political and cultural factors that accrue from reputational dynamics – how nation states perceive each other within the network. So, contrary to some of the conspiracy theories of the late Terry Wogan, coun-tries in the Western bloc actually have a better chance than the others of winning the Eurovision Song Contest.

THE NAZI ANTI-SMOKING CAMPAIGN

Gary Alan Fine is a professor of sociology at Northwestern University. He has written or co-written over twenty books about networks. His office, in a small building housing the sociology faculty just outside the main gates of the university, carries all the hallmarks of a highly productive scholar. Books cover every spare surface and papers are spread in a seemingly random distribution over his desk. The only space seems to be a low armchair in one corner, where the professor sits when meeting with his students.

Fine introduces us to the critical notion of reputational entrepreneurs.

'The argument is that there are three models of thinking about how reputations are developed,' he says. 'The most obvious one – the most intuitive one – is that people deserve their reputations. Warren Harding gained a reputation for being one of the worst [US] presidents based on his record, on his lack of competence. But who is to judge this? Irrespective of that, this is what I would call the *objective* argument.

'Then there is the *functional* argument. Society has slots, and so it needs people to fill these. Heroes, villains, incompetents, and so on. This argument centres on the view that reputation formation occurs within society's functional requirements.

'And then there is the *constructed* view, where meaning is up for grabs and so it depends on who has the interests and resources to use material available for creating and constructing reputation. This is where I see the argument for the existence of reputational entrepreneurs, people who have the motivation to engage in creating or destroying reputations. In US politics, for example, we have this two-party division that we have had for 150 years now, and it means that Democrats are always going to be looking to discredit Republicans and vice versa. We are all potential reputational entrepreneurs, but some of us don't have the incentives to do anything about it.'

This is a valuable way of looking at reputation: networks are not just passive distributors of behaviour. They can play an active role in selecting or shaping information to suit prior objectives. Different people in the network will pursue their own agenda, and so reputations are not simply units of information passing along a line like buckets of water. Each time they reach someone new, reputations are contested.

The most extreme examples of contested reputations are those where negative evaluations or perceptions predominate. Take, for instance, the advancement of medical science under the Nazi Party in Germany.

Robert N. Proctor, a professor of the history of science at Stanford University, has studied this in detail. He is one of the world's leading authorities on medical science, and coined the term 'agnotology', the study of culturally induced ignorance or doubt – especially the publication of misleading or inaccurate scientific data. He is certainly no apologist for anybody, being fiercely independent-minded. In fact, he was the first historian to testify against the tobacco industry. But his work on the Nazi Party offers an interesting example of how negative reputations can become solidified and universal.

During the course of his research on Nazi medical horrors – including the Holocaust and the tortures inflicted on people in the name of medical research – Proctor discovered documents showing that the Nazis conducted the most aggressive anti-smoking campaign in history. Digging deeper, he found that Hitler's government also passed a wide range of public-health measures, including restrictions on asbestos, radiation, pesticides and food dyes. Nazi health officials introduced strict occupational health-and-safety standards, and promoted such foods as wholegrain bread and soybeans. Taken on their own, we might recognize these as the forward-looking policies of a government from the early twenty-first century.

What Proctor found was that Nazi Germany was decades ahead of other countries in promoting health reforms that we today regard as progressive and socially responsible. Most startling, perhaps, was that Nazi scientists were the first to definitively link lung cancer and cigarette smoking. Yet despite all of this evidence, it would take a very brave person indeed to argue that the Nazi regime was responsible for anything this positive – to be seen to contest their reputation would place the person arguing this case in a very weak position.

As Fine puts it, 'It would take a lot of legitimacy on behalf of the claimant to make any positive argument about Hitler or his party's health policies. While it is a very plausible argument, historically it is not one that has legs. In other words, the negative reputation of the Nazi Party in one specific sphere – medical science – has become solidified, irrespective of some specific evidence to the contrary.'

The Nazi Party is of course an extreme example – almost everyone is motivated to view and talk about the Nazis in a negative way. But motivations matter, and certain reputations are apt to be contested.

PUSHING FOR CHANGE

Change.org has grown into one of the most important campaigning websites in existence. Describing itself as 'the world's platform for change', it was launched in 2007 by Ben Rattray with support from friends Mark Dimas, Darren Haas, Rajiv Gupta and Adam Cheyer, who was also the co-founder of Apple's Siri.

The site, at the time of writing, has over a hundred million users in nearly two hundred countries. Campaigns launched may be intensely local – a mother campaigning against bullying in her daughter's school – or they may be global, such as the successful campaign to save Mariam Yahia Ibrahim Ishag, a mother, doctor and Christian living in Sudan, from being sentenced to flogging and death unless she recanted her Christian faith. The range of campaigns is breathtaking, but they all share one common feature – getting enough signatures in a campaign creates reputational pressure for change.

'You have had the democratization of an increasing number of industries,' says Rattray in his crowded and buzzy office in San Francisco's SoMo (South of Market) district. 'First, content – now anyone can be a publisher. Then you have it in commerce – consider eBay, where anyone can be a seller. Then you have it with Airbnb where everyone can be a hotelier. And you have it for transportation with Uber and others. So you have the democratization of massive industries but you have not yet had the democratization of democracy. This is what we aim to change.'

Change.org brings people together on shared interests. It creates groups who are motivated to act on a view, a belief, or simply to right a perceived injustice, creating closure in networks, connecting previously disparate people and bringing them together in groups that are able to communicate quickly. It creates cohesive units, just as in an army platoon, which are highly effective at achieving clearly defined outcomes.

'If you are able to present people with an opportunity for real-time action directly relevant to the content they are consuming . . . that is a very potent political force,' explains Rattray. 'One of the most exciting opportunities is collapsing the spread between awareness and action and we see this in two areas: first, in real-time local opportunities where people are notified about things happening in their location, affording them the chance to engage and be involved to make a change that matters to them where they are. And the second is the media, which is a huge and untapped mechanism for social change. Billions of people read a topic and there is no clear outlet to capture the feeling you have and translate that into action – and if you don't capture these people in real time you have effectively lost them.'

Closure also creates a reputation cost for poor behaviour and 'double speak', where companies say one thing but do another. When it comes to campaigns, this is a highly effective and powerful tool. 'We live in a world where CEOs realize two things. First, that everyone will know the consequences of the decisions they make. Second is that they know that they will have to justify these decisions to their sons and daughters,' says Rattray.

Intriguingly, in this context, closure also enables bigger, slower-moving companies to change. Hasbro is one of the largest toy manufacturers in the world. Since the early 1990s, Hasbro has been producing the 'Easy-Bake Oven', a successful toy oven product that came with the company's acquisition of the original makers, Kenner Inc. The oven was marketed at girls, and was bright pink. In 2012,

McKenna Pope, a thirteen-year-old girl from New Jersey, started a Change.org petition asking the toy maker to offer the product in gender-neutral packaging. Her brother, a four-year-old who wanted to be a chef, felt embarrassed to be looking at products in the pink sections that retailers reserve for girls' toys. In response, McKenna made a video petitioning Hasbro to make a gender-neutral oven and launched her Change.org petition. This public challenge raised the stakes for Hasbro, who quickly realized that how they responded would shape perceptions of their character. The company responded quickly, meeting Pope and agreeing to make a version of the Easy-Bake Oven in black and silver. The prototype Easy-Bake Oven was also made available in blue, and the redesigned products were unveiled at the 2013 New York Toy Fair. It had all the makings of a PR coup – a success story involving a thirteen-year-old girl, gender stereotyping and a climbdown by a major retailer. The media lapped it up, and the company's visibility rocketed.

One of the most effective recent campaigns on the Change.org website was the petition to reverse the long-standing ban on homosexuality within the leadership and youth membership of the Boy Scouts of America (BSA). The BSA is one of the largest youth groups in the world. Until January 2014, the organization prohibited 'all known or avowed homosexuals' from membership of its scouting programme.

The BSA's ban on homosexuals first became known as early as 1980 with membership being denied to openly homosexual individuals applying for adult leadership positions. In 1991 the BSA made its unofficial position explicit, stating: 'We believe that homosexual conduct is inconsistent with the requirement in the Scout Oath that a Scout be morally straight and in the Scout Law that a Scout be clean in word and deed, and that homosexuals do not provide a desirable role model for Scouts.'

Clearly under pressure to make sure that there was no inconsistency, the BSA further clarified its policy in 1993 to include a ban on homosexuality among its youth members. 'Boy Scouts of America believes that homosexual conduct is inconsistent with the obligations in the Scout Oath and Scout Law to be morally straight and clean in thought, word, and deed. The conduct of youth members must be in compliance with the Scout Oath and Law, and membership in Boy Scouts of America is contingent upon the willingness to accept Scouting's values and beliefs. Most boys join Scouting when they are ten or eleven years old. As they continue in the program, all Scouts are expected to take leadership positions. In the unlikely event that an older boy were to hold himself out as homosexual, he would not be able to continue in a youth leadership position.'

While the BSA has not been allowed to ask explicitly about sexual orientation in its application forms, it did enforce this ban where it found evidence that it was being breached. For example, in 2005, a high-level employee of BSA was fired after the BSA received a copy of his bill from a gay resort where he had been on holiday, presumably posted by a disgruntled and conservative parent.

By 2010, the BSA was under pressure to review its position on homosexuality. In response, the BSA announced that it would conduct a two-year review of the policy, which was then discussed and debated by a specially convened committee of the BSA National Executive Board. In July 2012, this committee reached a 'unanimous consensus': they would retain the BSA's current policy.

It was at this point that the reputation network effect kicked into action. On the BSA National Executive Board were James Turley, CEO of Ernst & Young, and Randall Stephenson, CEO of AT&T. Each of these firms had explicit non-discrimination policies in place at their own firms covering all forms of discrimination, including sexual orientation. This left them with a problem. How could they square their membership of a board that had banned homosexuality while also sitting on a board that banned such discrimination?

This inconsistency was a subject tailor-made for a Change.org campaign. 'The Boy Scouts of America banning gay members case was a very effective use of the platform,' says Rattray. 'Pressure was put on the [BSA] board members who were also leading board members of companies who were known to be gay friendly. What the campaign did was to highlight dissonance – doublespeak – which forced these directors to justify their dissonant positions to their family or friends, people they care about. As soon as they were forced to justify this they either had to accept that they were not the people they thought they were or they had to change their behaviour.'

THE GLOBAL VILLAGE

Hundreds of years ago, the French philosopher Blaise Pascal posed the following question: 'We do not worry about being respected in towns through which we pass. But if we are going to remain in one for a certain time, we do worry. How long does this time have to be?'

His question touches on the relationship between reputation, time and space. He is acknowledging that we care about our reputation only if we are part of a community. To belong to a community, you need to stay in one place long enough to build up the reciprocal ties that bind you into a network. If you are only passing through, these questions are irrelevant, but if you are staying for a while, you want to fit in.

For most of history, reputations were tied to small communities. In 1910, for instance, more than seventy per cent of Americans lived in small towns or rural areas. When they moved on, their reputations disappeared. Of course, this is no longer the case. The Internet has made a network of the entire world, and our communities span continents. Geography simply isn't that relevant if, for instance, you are a Justin Bieber fan, as the sociologist Dave Troy discovered when he set about mapping out the network.[16]

Recovering alcoholic Amy Liptrot, in her moving book *The Outrun* (2015), describes how she returned home to the Orkney Islands to dry out after the excesses of her life in London. Stuck on an island in the storm-tossed Atlantic, she is hundreds of miles from her friends in the metropolis (essential for her recuperation). But she considers herself far from isolated. 'I've moved around a lot, but the Internet is my home . . .'

The Internet today is used by staggering numbers of people. DOMO, a data analytics company, stated in its 2014 report, 'Data Never Sleeps', that the global Internet population grew by 14.3% from 2011 to 2013 and that in 2014 it amounted to 2.4 billion users. The company found that – every minute – Facebook users shared nearly 2.5 million pieces of content, Twitter users tweeted nearly 300,000 times, Instagram users posted nearly 220,000 new photos, YouTube users uploaded 72 hours of new video content, Apple users downloaded nearly 50,000 apps, email users sent over 200 million messages, and Amazon generated over US $80,000 in online sales.

'Technology is dramatically increasing the relevance and power of [online] reputation,' says Mike Fertik, founder of Reputation. com and an expert on reputation in the digital world. For example, British actress Ruth Wilson, who has built a successful career on both sides of the Atlantic, including the prime-time blockbuster series *The Affair*, spoke to us about the impact of social media on the TV industry. 'There is something interesting at the moment about social media. Now people are getting cast based on how many Twitter followers they have. It's crazy. It can't be sensible, yet it's what's happening.'

For many millions of people today, the Internet is the fixed point of community. Certainly, that is true emotionally for many like Liptrot, who describes herself spilling 'her heart over the Internet like red wine' and thinks of her own life as a kind of home page, numerous different tabs open and waiting for attention. Assiduously monitoring her scores on various social media plat-forms, she considers herself 'carrying out semi-scientific studies into myself, performing bathymetry of the soul'. With the wind howling outside the door of her croft, she jostles for 'retweets and edgerank . . . I am in an ever-changing process of defining myself, fascinated by counting and plotting and marking my daily activities and movements, collecting bottomless data.'

If the Internet has in effect dissolved space, it has also collapsed time. Any mistake or lapse in judgement that might once have faded with time now lives on for eternity. A prominent example of this is the reputational crisis surrounding Dr. Dre when biopic *Straight Outta Compton* was released in the summer of 2015.[17] In itself, it is a great and gritty movie, but the launch, while commercially successful, was marred by complaints that the film glossed over the rapper's history of physically abusing women. The complaints came from Michel'le, an R&B singer and Dr. Dre's former partner; Tairrie B, another musician; and the hip hop journalist Dee Barnes. The women told the world about being beaten, punched and otherwise abused by the rapper back in the late 1980s and early 1990s, long before the hip hop artist became a billionaire and attained respectability.

The women had been telling their stories independently, but they never gained traction until they found each other online. Tairrie B connected with Barnes via Facebook: 'I said, "Hey girl, I think we have something in common, and we've never talked about it."' Various online accounts of the abuse suffered by the women attracted hundreds of thousands of views, and Dr. Dre was forced into an abject apology. He explained that he was no longer the heavy-drinking wild man of his youth. 'I apologize to the women I've hurt. I deeply regret what I did and know that it has forever impacted all our lives.'

In the pre-Internet era, stories like these would have been ignored or forgotten. Indeed, as individuals making allegations about a rich and powerful person, they were comprehensively ignored until they built a community and a following online. The lesson for others is that misdemeanours perpetrated in your youth can come back to haunt you. For most of us, it is less the risk that a community will be formed to chastize you, than that you post something online that seemed fine at the time, but looks increasingly daft as time goes by. Perhaps there is a picture of you larking around drunk or in a state of undress, which pops up in a potential recruiter's due diligence when you are applying for a job many years later.

The social media scholar and blogger danah boyd has pointed out another example of the Internet's infallible memory. A young man from South Central, the rough area of Los Angeles celebrated in Dr. Dre's movie, applied for a place at an Ivy League university.[18] The college admissions officer googled the candidate and found that his MySpace page was covered with gang insignia. 'Why has he lied to us?' was the lament of the college: the kid had promised that he no longer had any connection to gang life (though it couldn't have been avoided when he was growing up). Unlike the example of a drunken photo, this wasn't a lapse of judgement on the young man's part. 'This was the response of the high-status powerful East Coast elite to what the kid had to do to survive back home,' boyd told us. 'It was an unconscious racial bias showing a complete lack of understanding of how the kid had to perform gang affiliations in order to survive.'[19]

We can't choose our past, but we can take time to curate how it is presented online. And those in authority must be more understanding of the fact that people change over time.

This sort of reputational collision is increasingly prevalent, and has been called 'context collapse'.[20] 'Social media technologies collapse multiple audiences into single contexts, making it difficult for people to use the same techniques online that they do to handle multiplicity in face-to-face conversation,' boyd has written.[21] Context collapse describes not merely online reputational dissonance, but also what happens in the case of companies who are pitching a message at one group ('cutting jobs is good for profits') and then find it blows up when other communities get to hear about it ('what do you mean you are cutting jobs when you are making so much money?').

In everyday offline interactions between people, we make innumerable small adjustments to our speech and behaviour that are calibrated to the context. The online world does not easily transmit such nuances. But teenagers do try . . .

INFLUENCERS

Both authors have teenage children who have expressed amazement about aspects of the research required for this book. For example, we recently returned from an Oxford seminar that featured a twenty-four-year-old online celebrity called Blair Fowler, who beamed in via Skype from Tennessee to explain how to become an 'influencer'. We took a look at her YouTube channel, juicystar07, which has over 1.7 million subscribers. To the amusement of our kids, this contains videos about the 'top ten beauty products for under $10', 'how to do your hair on a school day', 'what's in my handbag this morning', 'my favourite room in the house', 'top ten skincare tips' and so forth. Nothing, it seems, about how to eliminate that middle-age paunch or replace the bald patch on the top of one's head.

Despite the less-than-immediate relevance for our own beauty needs, Blair Fowler's channel is something of a revelation. She posts a short video (five to fifteen minutes) more or less every day of the week. Most are watched at least 200,000 times, while the most popular have been viewed by more than four million people. The most liked video of all was about what happened when her boyfriend did her make-up, but she took that down after they split up. She told the seminar that the channel got started after her elder sister Elle went away to college, and the girls started posting videos to each other to keep in touch. Blair was just fifteen at the time, and the videos were made in her bedroom. By 2010, their videos had been viewed 75 million times. Blair told us how her father had been very sceptical when a man from YouTube had called their home, asking where to send a cheque. She had attracted enough viewers to be paid royalties. Now, in her early twenties, she is reported to earn a significant income from fees paid both by the channel and the manufacturers of the beauty products she endorses online.

There are scores of other influencers in the world of beauty products and lifestyle, including the UK's own Zoe Sugg, aka Zoella, whose YouTube channel has more than eleven million subscribers. The content is hardly forged by Francis Ford Coppola, but its popularity speaks to the trend we identified earlier: young people trust each other more than they trust authority figures or advertisers, even when that person is being paid by the likes of Procter & Gamble or Unilever. Such corporations are extremely keen to be associated with influencers, as traditional billboard and TV advertising is increasingly ineffectual. So long as this is disclosed, it seems to be fine with the audience and, in any case, one is struck by the absolute sincerity of the influencer herself: Fowler says she is bombarded with offers to try out different products, and she only wears what she feels passionate about. It is that passion and authenticity that her viewers respond to.

The phenomenon of YouTube influencers illustrates a special kind of online reputation: a kind of micro-celebrity that is tethered to one very specific subject, giving them a large, narrow network that could only exist online. There are communities dedicated to every subject under the sun, from people with 'autonomous sensory meridian response' (ASMR), whose heads tingle when others whisper, to 'bronies' – adult male fans of the 1980s My Little Pony toy franchise. The Internet is one gigantic engine for generating reputations, as networks form, grow, shrink, mutate, die away, and revive or otherwise evolve, based on age, place, shared interests and so forth. In an effort to make sense of this, danah boyd has studied the trajectory of online reputation from youth to middle age. 'For young people what is absolutely central is the peer group,' boyd told us. 'It's all about figuring out how to be cool within that community. There are these weird pivots as kids say to themselves I want to be cool in this group, or I want to be cool in that group.'

This explains the power of image-based social media such as Snapchat or Instagram. Says boyd: 'Kids are figuring out how to put together an image that makes sense that is funny to their friends and is stylistically cool, so that how you are portrayed makes you look like you are part of the inner crowd. Language is incredibly important but it's not writing, it's about expressing yourself through textual means, using emojis as a playful way of expressing yourself, performing what is normally on the body [clothing, gestures and facial expressions].' Online activity on platforms such as Reddit is also highly performative, all about self-discovery, setting limits, establishing credibility and cool – in other words, going through rites of passage that in a pre-Internet era would have taken place in a physical rather than a virtual community.

Boyd notes a crucial inflection point when people reach their late twenties. For professionals in particular, this is a time when a move away from home has become permanent and career becomes paramount. 'For so many white-collar jobs you have to start performing to your LinkedIn profile,' she says. 'You start seeing a cleavage between the kind of reputation you might sustain in order to stay cool with your friends, and the online reputation you increasingly need for your professional career. People put an enormous amount of effort into keeping the two separate. Facebook is especially awkward in this respect as it forces collision between the professional and personal world.'

She sees parallels between the way kids perform a certain identity to become cool with their peers, and the way middle-aged, middle-class professionals perform to their LinkedIn profiles. Anyone on LinkedIn is probably familiar with the slightly peculiar experience of receiving requests to link with complete strangers, or getting bizarre endorsements (for writing deathless press releases, for example, or for online reputation management skills) from people we barely know. There is an unspoken rule that you should endorse those who endorse you, which leaves us both feeling guilty for our lack of reciprocity. At the time of writing, there are more than 400 million people signed up to LinkedIn. For all its limitations, it feels fairly indispensable for anyone with half an eye on the next promotion.

HEADHUNTING IN THE DIGITAL AGE

Has technology reduced the power of reputation? The argument runs that with the Internet we know more about each other and, therefore, what we hear from others – their reputation – becomes less important. Direct knowledge overrides hearsay.

This argument fails in a number of important respects. First, it assumes an even distribution of knowledge among highly connected people. As we have seen throughout this section, it all depends on networks, which share information in different ways. Second, it assumes that information equals fact, which is plainly not the case. And third, it ignores the fact that technology has dramatically increased the demand for information.

We now research people and organizations far more than was ever possible even twenty years ago. And in the digital age, our extended connectivity makes reputation far more valuable and important than it has ever been. Author Michael Fertik puts it more bluntly: 'Reputation will be the currency of the future.' This is the essence of the second school of thought. Technology is dramatically increasing the relevance and power of reputation.

We spoke to Reid Hoffman, the Silicon Valley entrepreneur who was a co-founder of both PayPal and LinkedIn, which started out in his living room in 2002 and went live the following May. In 2005, he also had the foresight to invest in a start-up networking site called Facebook when it had a valuation of just US $5 million. His $37,500 investment turned a profit of some $100 million. LinkedIn went public in 2011 and Hoffman is now worth around $3.7 billion following the sale of LinkedIn to Microsoft in June 2016. Large, jovial, and very bright indeed, with a degree in philosophy from Oxford as well as one in cognitive science and social systems from Stanford, he has given a great deal of thought to the future of technology and of online networking in particular.

'Most people will assert that they know that they are living in a networked age and are operating intelligently in one,' he says. 'But most people are wrong. We are just at the cusp of what it means to operate in the networked age.' He explains how reputation plays out on the site today:

There is foreground and background reputation. Foreground is essentially what I put forward, my best me. Your LinkedIn profile is meant to be your best self, your shiniest suit. And that's what it's meant to be. Only looking at foreground is still very valuable in reputation terms – for example just seeing how many endorsements someone has, or connections they have, and who those people are. This is valuable. Background information, by contrast, is what people never see in print. What people will never put in print. Background information is got by messaging someone and getting the back story – and that too has some clear reputational shortcuts that can be interpreted. If you ask for a view on someone and the person you contact simply says 'call me', that really only means one of two things – at best it's that it's complicated and the person doesn't have time to write it down, and at worst it's 'don't touch that person'. So your range when it comes to the reputation of that person has just narrowed from complicated to bad.

Even though users may connect with each other quite casually, the evidence suggests that we take very seriously what we write about ourselves on the LinkedIn site. Accordingly, the reputation that it distils and conveys to potential recruiters is very accurate. Hoffman explains:

> You can of course lie in your profile, but a number of independent studies show that when you have ten connections or more the accuracy of your LinkedIn profile is substantially higher than your CV. The reason is that most people realize that they are fully 'public' in whatever they say about themselves when they are connected on LinkedIn. So the usual stuff – role inflation, stretching the scope of what you are responsible for and so on – does not happen because the other members of your team, those people who really know the truth, are going to see it and may call you out.

Hoffman acknowledges the drawbacks of the endorsement system, but defends its efficacy as a way of calibrating reputation. 'The charge that some people make is that these are useless because it's just all friends of friends saying nice things about each other,' he says. 'But when people give endorsements on the back of books these are the very same thing, just in the offline world. Every time you say something in public you are putting your name behind it in front of their friends and other people. Doing so online, on LinkedIn, is no different, except for the fact that it is probably seen and read by many more people, and especially by people who matter to you and your career.'

Looking forward, he believes that we all need to be much more intelligent and proactive in harnessing the power of our online reputation. Most people's engagement with their online professional profile is too reactive, he urges. We tend to use sites such as LinkedIn to build links with people we want to meet or stay connected to, and perhaps also use it to search for jobs that we might like to have. Hoffman believes that LinkedIn should be a much more proactive tool.

'Most people do not have a "be found" strategy. Everyone is active – searching – but really what companies should also be doing is sending up a flare and then seeing who responds and picking the best from that group. And smart people looking for a job should be able to use our tools to find companies populated by people that look like them. We are working now on that,' says Hoffman.

He imagines a world where companies will identify from within their existing workforce the attributes of the most successful people in their organization. This service will be based on a computer algorithm that searches the profiles of the most successful people in the company and pulls together an 'ideal' candidate CV – based on a number of factors, perhaps including educational background, length of time in roles, number of endorsements, connections on different social media and so on. Once an organization has this 'ideal' CV, it can then ask LinkedIn to search for suitable candidates – setting search parameters such as proximity to its head office or even a ranking of the best-suited candidates.

Candidates for the post may not even know that the post is up for grabs, nor that they are being considered. It means that to stand a chance of being considered for your next role in future, you will have to engage with your online profile to make sure that it is engineered to be captured by algorithmic searches. This will, of course, partly rest on what you have to say about yourself.

To some, the idea of companies searching only for 'people that look like them' may sound dystopian. Certainly, this sort of algorithmic activity can end up creating more closure in networks, and more of an echo chamber when it comes to new hires. But irrespective of its potential drawbacks, this sort of innovation is here to stay.

Michael Fertik agrees. 'You have to care about what people say about you,' he says. 'You have to be in the game. You have to be aware that decisions are increasingly being made by machine. You can't "ostrich" and pretend that's not true. Today, employers are increasingly caring very deeply about what machines are telling them about the "hireability" of candidates. It is too soon to call the end of the resumé. But the first cut of resumés is increasingly being done by machines that parse out the data that they need. And you may never even know what that process produces.

'Fast forward to tomorrow. Headhunters or machines that are serving headhunters will automatically analyse the profile of someone who succeeds in your business. Every HR or manager believes that they know who succeeds, but we now know that computers are better at predicting who will succeed. So if a manager gets this, they will ask the computer to analyse the five hundred employees who are in the firm and who are the top talent, and they will ask the computer to go and find three or four people like that. So the computer will review sixty thousand humans who live within fifteen miles of the office and will surface six names who the manager will call. The other 59,994 people never knew that they were in the game.'

VISIBILITY VERSUS CELEBRITY

We tend to think of celebrity as a by-product of our own mass media age, but it has been around for millennia. There were celebrity gladiators and charioteers in Roman times, celebrity courtesans in eighteenth-century England, celebrity music-hall artistes in the Victorian era and celebrity outlaws in frontier America.

Newspaper editors found early on that readers like stories about the private lives of prominent people. In the past, celebrity status was earned through some dimension of competence or capability that justified the interest in the first place: Eugen Sandow, for example, was widely thought to have the most perfect male body in the world circa 1890, and that is why people the length and breadth of the British Empire paid good money to see him flex his muscles on the stage, to buy pictures of him wearing nothing but a fig leaf, and to read fabricated gossip about his love life. Since the emergence of modern consumer culture from the 1930s onwards, personality and lifestyle have supplanted capability. Celebrities now embody the lifestyles that we aspire to, and it is possible to be famous for being famous – leading to the disconcerting phenomenon where some celebrities are best known for having appeared on a 'celebrity' reality show.

Celebrity involves some form of emotional content that builds a bridge between the famous person and his or her public. With the rise of new media, the size of the public with which a celebrity can have a reputation has increased exponentially. On the upside, the financial and social returns from celebrity are enormous. Sponsorship deals and endorsements create significant wealth, as when the rapper Dr. Dre co-founded Beats headphones and subsequently sold to Apple for US $3 billion. In this way, celebrity is a virtuous cycle. Celebrities secure tables at the best restaurants, are invited to the best parties, and become the face of new products and ventures.

But there is a downside, of course. Celebrities are big fish for the media to get their teeth into when things go wrong. They are common property, never more so than when they are on the way down. The sad decline of Amy Winehouse, the staggeringly talented British singer who died in 2011 at the age of twenty-seven, was chronicled in lingering, salivating detail.

In the world of business, the role and importance of celebrity is a function of culture. American society, for example, values success in business exceptionally highly, and celebrity is a respectable by-product of success. The late Steve Jobs founded Apple and reinvented three industries: music (through iTunes and the iPod), film (through Pixar) and of course personal computing. Mark Zuckerberg gave the world Facebook. Jeff Bezos is disrupting retailing, the book industry, cloud computing and many other areas with Amazon. Sergey Brin and Larry Page founded Google, a company that delights billions of Internet users every day. Warren Buffett is the 'sage of Omaha', with a reputation for being the shrewdest investor who has ever lived.

In the US, however, it is possible to be a celebrity business leader without being an entrepreneur. Lee Iacocca, the former CEO of Chrysler, or Jack Welch, the former head of General Electric (GE), were both revered figures who enjoyed many of the trappings of celebrity, including huge earnings and enormous media interest, without setting up companies of their own: they were highly successful employees.

This contrasts with continental Europe, where celebrity CEOs are frowned upon. Jean-Marie Messier, former CEO of the Vivendi media conglomerate, was almost American in his love of the limelight. When he was forced from his position as CEO in July 2002 after the company reported a non-cash loss of €13.6 billion for the prior year, his fall from grace was that much harder as a result. CEOs of big German and French companies may have egos as big as their US counterparts, but they tend to want to keep their heads down. A good example is Michael Diekmann, CEO of the colossal Allianz insurance group from 2003 to 2015, who always shunned personal publicity. His successor, Oliver Bäte, chooses not to live in Munich, where the company is headquartered, but in Cologne, because there in his home town he can live a completely normal life at the weekends. Bosses of insurance companies are perhaps retiring types, but even Dieter Zetsche, head of Daimler since 2006, keeps a relatively low profile, despite his distinctive personal appearance. (He is very tall and has a magnificent moustache.)

In Britain, successful entrepreneurs such as Sir Richard Branson or the inventor Sir James Dyson are admired, but it is a rare CEO who will step forth from the business pages of the press expressed a view on broader social and political issues. When CEOs ventured an opinion on whether Britain should stay in the EU, most huddled together as mass signatories of letters to *The Times* or the *Telegraph*. This in part reflects the more diffident culture of the Brits, but the structure of UK boards is also different from the US. The board of a UK public company is a unitary body that is obliged by law to act with collective responsibility, and the power of the CEO is circumscribed as a result: he or she cannot get things done without bringing the board along with them. In the US, where the chairperson and CEO is often the same person, the boss has much more power.

Celebrity CEOs in the US get paid more than the shy and retiring kinds, research has shown – but if they perform badly, their pay drops below those who are out of the limelight.[22] Violina Rindova and Tim Pollock, together with Matthew Hayward from the University of Colorado at Boulder, have also shown that 'the ability to attract large-scale public attention and to stimulate positive emotional responses provides celebrity firms with access to critical resources (e.g. human capital, capital markets, and sources of raw material or product inputs) and strategic opportunities (e.g. alliances and partnerships, M&A opportunities) that it might have only limited access or no access to otherwise.'[23] Donald Trump's unlikely triumph in the 2016 US election had a lot to do with his status as a celebrity CEO – despite questions around his effectiveness and even his ethics as a businessperson, he was best known to tens of millions of Americans for his TV appearances on *The Apprentice*.

You may think the lessons of celebrity don't apply to your own life, but celebrity is really an extreme form of visibility. When you are starting out in your career, visibility is an asset as it distinguishes you from your peers. Napoleon first came to prominence as a twenty-four-year-old artillery commander when he successfully laid siege to the city of Toulon. He demonstrated courage and competence, and in revolutionary France that earned him the opportunity to prove himself on a bigger stage. After further ruthless acts of valour, he was given command of the entire French Army in Italy at the age of just twenty-six. His ability to deliver military success at times when the stakes were high was the crucial ingredient in building an early, formidable reputation.

In a less bellicose example, Robert Parker, the doyen of wine critics, came to prominence because of his big, bold call that 1982 was a superlative year for claret. The visibility that this gave him launched his career, giving him the courage to quit his day job as a lawyer. William Hague gave a precocious speech at the 1977 Tory Party Conference when he was just sixteen years old, launching a distinguished political career. The fund manager Helena Morrissey came to prominence as a young woman when she made a big bet on the outcome of the 1997 UK election, buying gilts (UK government securities) as she thought rightly that they were oversold.

The British actor Dominic West took on a highly controversial role playing mass murderer Fred West in the TV miniseries and film *Appropriate Adult*, raising the stakes for his career at a time when he could have opted to play it safe. 'I am still a bit naive about reputation when it comes to my career. Fred West was a difficult role to play and I did it despite the fact that it could have done significant damage to my reputation if the script was not as good as it was. And of course I do have a passing resemblance to Fred West so it could have been very difficult for me to do lighter roles if that became the defining role that I was known for. But the reason I did it was that it was a well-written script – the reputation part I deliberately ignored.'

Early visibility linked with indisputable competence is the perfect way to build an enduring reputation. But sometimes visibility comes late in a career: the top defence barrister George Carman was not quite fifty and working mainly in Manchester when in 1979 he successfully defended Jeremy Thorpe against a murder charge. This was deemed a remarkable outcome and Carman shot to national prominence overnight. After years of critical acclaim but little commercial success, novelist Hilary Mantel finally attained global recognition in her late fifties. Before this, she had published a succession of highly regarded novels, but had not enjoyed commercial success. Mantel's literary competence was the kindling of her reputation, but the spark came when she won the Man Booker prize for the first time in 2009 for the novel *Wolf Hall*. It turned into a veritable blaze in 2012 when she won it again for *Bring up the Bodies*.

This multiplier effect of visibility works both ways. Where you are already a winner in the reputation game, expectations are higher, and there is further to tumble if you fall short. One slip, one signal of bad behaviour, and visibility becomes a liability. In business, Enron deliberately and effectively created a very visible presence in order to help it grow and advance in the good times. Repeatedly lauded as one of the world's most respected companies, Enron's apparent business success was built on fraudulent accounting. The company's high visibility accelerated its fall from grace as the evidence of systematic fraud emerged. And in politics, a study of the 2009 MPs' expenses scandal in the UK found clear evidence that those MPs who were more visible faced increased pressure to resign.[24] This is sometimes called 'tall poppy syndrome', where those who are most visible are first to be singled out for retribution.

Being aware of the significance of visibility does not mean more is always better. 'Be hidden, be happy', was the advice given to one of the authors by a Hampshire farmer who wanted nothing more than to live a life of exemplary obscurity, where he was respected by the local community.

Or take the example of Glenn Spiro, the London jeweller. He works to exacting professional standards, and his clientele are some of the most famous and wealthy people on the planet. Yet he has virtually no visibility. He operates out of a discreet townhouse in Mayfair, which has no sign outside it. He never advertises. He has a tremendous reputation for producing beautiful bespoke pieces created from carefully sourced gems – a process that can take months.

'When I look at the way we conduct ourselves in our business model, I suppose it is that of a sniper in the war more than a fully loaded artilleryman firing bullets blindly in the hope of hitting something. This relates to whether we are buying something, creating something or indeed selling something. It all needs careful concentration and execution,' says Spiro. 'We had the option to become very visible. However, we took the view that if we started on that course of action we could easily become what we were not. To this end, we are very comfortable acting with discretion and limited visibility. This allows us to remain true to what we do and who we are.'

THE ELUSIVE FIFTH STAR

A site like eBay succeeds because it operates as a clearing house for reputations – not merely because it is an online marketplace. As Lucy Kellaway of the *Financial Times* explains, 'Trust is vital . . . especially when you are expected to buy things from perfect strangers with user names such as mickey_boy69. It is built through feedback, something which other businesses deploy as a clumsy afterthought . . . [the site] shows there are three conditions for feedback to make a difference: it must be (a) respected (b) universal and (c) instant. On the site, there is no role for politics, PR advisors or social media campaigns in shaping reputation: it is all done by feedback alone. Buyers with 100 per cent scores know they can sell for higher prices – which means there is an overwhelming incentive to behave well every single time.'[25]

Likewise, Google, Amazon and TripAdvisor rankings have a massive impact. One of the authors has an uncle who owned and ran a guest house in Sydney, Australia: during this phase of his life,

Uncle Bobbick lived and breathed the rankings bestowed to the Admiral Collingwood hotel by TripAdvisor. The Internet was alive with celebrations when the Collingwood made it into the list of the top ten per cent of hotels *in the world*, and then went on to be judged the third best hotel in Sydney overall (up from ninety-second). Then social media reverberated to the sound of lamentations after the site unaccountably decided that the hotel was no longer located in Sydney proper, but in Drummoyne, a mere suburb.

For some six months, trade dropped right off as Bobbick lobbied in vain for reinstatement to Sydney. Then he hit on the bright idea of dropping a note to Steve Kaufer, founder and CEO of TripAdvisor, whose email address he found through LinkedIn. 'I wrote to Steve pointing out that the HQ of TripAdvisor is in Newton, Massachusetts, a suburb of Boston, and that Drummoyne was similarly a suburb of Sydney.' He suggested that the TripAdvisor CEO was a poor loser, discriminating against the Admiral Collingwood hotel for historical reasons. 'Back in 1775, as he would recall, when the British beat the American rebels in Boston at the Battle of Bunker Hill, Admiral Collingwood, then a young lieutenant, led a British naval brigade into the battle. In those days, Bunker Hill was freely acknowledged as an integral part of Boston, but I understood that TripAdvisor was now transferring it to outside Boston.' Two weeks after this missive, the Collingwood was reinstated to Sydney. Its rankings on Agoda.com, HotelsCombined.com, Trivago.com and other sites went sky high.

Everyone who stays at the hotel is asked to post an online review. These ratings determine whether the hotel is full or half empty. As the writer John Henry Clippinger puts it, sites such as these 'routinely issue summary judgements, much like a Roman Emperor in the Colosseum who renders thumbs up or thumbs down verdicts upon hapless people, movies, software, hotels and content. Such ratings can have real economic clout. A poor Amazon rating can be a death sentence for a poorly rated product.' A 2012 Nielsen report, which surveyed 28,000 Internet users in fifty-six countries, found that online consumer reviews are the second most-trusted source of brand information after recommendations from friends and family. According to this survey, more than two-thirds of global customers say they trust messages on these platforms. But is this trust misplaced?

There are two ways in which it may be. The first is that the production of fake reviews has become big business. Just as someone with a miserable twenty-five Twitter followers can go online and pay someone to bump up his or her numbers into the thousands, a business that wants positive reviews can pay to get them. In a recent special report in the *Daily Mail*, the journalist Tom Rawstorne posted a request on an otherwise harmless services website called Fiverr, asking for help in securing good reviews for a holiday cottage in Scotland that he was (fictitiously) seeking to market. His request received more than twenty replies, the cheapest offering to write a fake review for £3.50. He was told that he could write the review himself, and that it would be posted by them independently using an 'aged' TripAdvisor account – meaning an account that looked genuine but was inactive. You can find similarly fake reviews on Amazon, for example, and no doubt also on Airbnb, Uber or indeed any sites where the cumulative impact of online ratings creates valuable reputational real estate.

The second distortion is less intuitive: it is the very human tendency to follow the herd. Sinan Aral is both entrepreneur and academic – he is the David Austin Professor of Management at the MIT Sloan School of Management. His academic research focuses on social contagion in networks, in particular the impact of online ratings on sites such as TripAdvisor and Yelp. He describes how he let himself be influenced by someone else's restaurant review. 'A few months ago, I stopped in for a quick bite to eat at Dojo, a restaurant in New York City's Greenwich Village,' he wrote. 'I had an idea of what I thought of the place. Of course I did – I ate there and experienced it for myself. The food was okay. The service was okay. On average, it was average. So I went to rate the restaurant on Yelp with a strong idea of the star rating I would give it. I logged in, navigated to the page and clicked the button to write the review. I saw that, immediately to the right of where I would "click to rate", a Yelp user named Shar H. was waxing poetic about Dojo's "fresh and amazing, sweet and tart ginger dressing" – right under her bright red five-star rating. I couldn't help but be moved. I had thought the place deserved a three, but Shar had a point: As she put it, "the prices here are amazing!" Her review moved me. And I gave the place a four.'[26]

We are all influenced by what we read and by other people's views: it is much easier to declare that you like the challenging quartet of Neapolitan novels by Elena Ferrante when everyone else is saying the same. But this is even more the case when we operate online. 'The heart of the problem lies with our herd instincts – natural human impulses characterized by a lack of individual decision making – that cause us to think and act in the same way as other people around us,' says Aral.

Aral and two colleagues – Lev Muchnik at the Hebrew University of Jerusalem's School of Business Administration, and Sean Taylor at New York University's Stern School of Business – designed an experiment to establish the extent to which we are influenced by positive or negative reviews online. The setting for the experiment was an online news site similar to Reddit. User comments on the site were subject to either a positive vote ('thumbs up'), a negative vote ('thumbs down') or a neutral vote ('level thumb') from other readers. Positive votes were 4.6 times more common than negative votes, with 5.13% of all comments receiving a positive vote by their first viewer and only 0.82% receiving a negative vote. Aral and his colleagues went further and analysed the replies to the original comments over a five-month period. During this time, 101,281 comments were viewed more than ten million times and rated 308,515 times.[27] They set up a test where they added fictitious endorsements to see how users would respond. Views expressed followed the herd, and there were positive ratings bubbles as a result. 'We found that people were willing to go along with the positive opinions of others online, but be sceptical of the negative opinions of others. This creates some dramatic effects,' says Aral. 'You have this potential for herding or snowballing of reputations, which creates winner-take-all or superstar markets.'

So there is a counterintuitive conclusion to be drawn. The online economy relies heavily on consumer ratings, the cumulative impact of which creates valuable reputational capital. That reputation-making power belongs, on the face of it, with ordinary citizens and consumers. Yet in making what we believe are unmediated judgements about our online experiences, we may be succumbing to unconscious bias or fake reviews. And we can be manipulated by big corporations who deploy staggering amounts of computer power to track and anticipate our every move. We are no longer surprised when the ads that pop up on Facebook seem eerily relevant to our needs, but advertising personalization is going to seem like a stone-age tool as the technology evolves.

HOW TO FIND A POLITE DRUG DEALER

Back in 1992, when the Internet was in its infancy, a Californian computer scientist by the name of Tim May wrote a short and highly prescient open letter entitled 'The Crypto Anarchist Manifesto'. He predicted the development of the Dark Web, on which computers today can talk to one another anonymously, and he foresaw a burgeoning online market for any commodity, object or service under the sun, which would promote a social and economic revolution.

'Reputations will be of central importance, far more important in dealings than even the credit ratings of today,' he wrote. 'These developments will alter completely the nature of government regulation, the ability to tax and control economic interactions, and will even alter the nature of trust and reputation.'

Much of what May envisaged has come about. Let's take an extreme example: the market for illegal drugs. More than twenty years after the manifesto, writer Jamie Bartlett conducted some intrepid research into the murky recesses of the Internet while researching his book *The Dark Net* (2014). Exploring the frontiers of investigative journalism, he witnessed an online strip show and more on the apparently highly popular site Chaturbate, observed how Internet entrepreneurs have found a way to commission assassinations, and ordered a small bag of cannabis from the online drugs market known as Silk Road 2.0 (for research purposes only, of course). Silk Road 2.0 was only accessible via the anonymized TOR network, exactly the kind of Internet that May was anticipating. Unlike our interactions in what Bartlett calls the surface Web, where we transact under our own names with legitimate corporations, here all parties are cloaked by TOR ('The Onion Router'), which bounces each connection around its network so that neither party knows where the other has come from, and your IP address cannot be traced. You can pay using Bitcoin, the anonymous online currency that you hold through a digital wallet, and the drug dealer also has a strong incentive to remain anonymous if he or she doesn't want to go to jail.

So how does this market function? The answer is that it works very well indeed. 'Encryption and the crypto-currency Bitcoin have created the technical conditions that allow Silk Road to exist,' Bartlett discovered, 'but it's the user reviews that make it work. Every drugs site has review options, usually a score out of five plus written feedback, and reviewing your purchase accurately and carefully is an obligation for all buyers.' Just as for legitimate sites, there are user forums where customers explain what the really salient features of that feedback should be: delivery times, product quality and quantity. Users also come together to expose scams, just as they do on the surface Web, and there are site administrators who step in to ban unacceptable (though not illegal) behaviours.

Bartlett made a careful study of his options and even asked some of the vendors some questions. It was, he declares, an extremely pleasant consumer experience, as the vendors were bending over backwards to provide service. They take trouble over their brand and self-presentation, just like regular companies. They were keen as mustard to keep him happy. 'Drug dealers on these markets are very polite and attentive – desperate for a positive review because anything else would damage business.' Needless to say, when the product arrived at Bartlett's home, it looked entirely satisfactory. His research did not extend to smoking the consignment.

Crypto-anarchists have used reputation to create not just a well-functioning market, but also public benefits: the merchandise provided through Silk Road 2.0 was of a higher quality by far than the illegal drugs you can buy on the street, and therefore less adulterated and arguably less dangerous as a result. A typical street dealer is not desperately interested in his or her reputation for product quality, but the anonymous online purveyors of cocaine or weed want their customers to tell the world about their experience. 'People who use Silk Road 2.0 are very happy punters,' says Bartlett. 'The average score out of five left by drug users on the site was an impressive 4.85.'

4

NARRATIVES

In the end, we will remember not the words of our enemies, but the silence of our friends.

Martin Luther King, Jr

'TELL SUGE THAT I'M A GENIUS'

How you speak about yourself, and particularly how you persuade others to speak about you on your behalf, is a vital element of the reputation game.

Doug Morris, the charismatic and clubbable chairman of Sony Entertainment, recalls a meeting he had in the 1990s with two other leading figures in the music business: Jimmy Iovine, the founder of Interscope records, and Suge Knight, a former gang member who had become one of the most successful record executives on the emerging rap scene. They were discussing an important distribution deal for Interscope with Suge Knight's Death Row Records, one of the hottest labels around.

Jimmy Iovine, who had already worked with John Lennon, Patti Smith, Dire Straits and many other platinum-selling artists, enlisted Morris's help. 'One day,' says Morris, 'Jimmy, who almost has an ability to see round corners, called me up and said "this stuff is going mainstream, we really have to get into it . . . I've met this guy, I want you to come out and meet him with me. His name is Suge Knight."

'At first I was taken aback by the lyrics and the misogyny of rap music, then I saw all of these little independent record companies buying and selling it. Being a big advocate of the first amendment, I started signing rap artists. The first one I signed was 2 Live Crew, which I got in a lot of trouble for – they actually got arrested in Miami for selling their music. This made me mad, and so we convinced Bruce Springsteen to let 2 Live Crew turn "Born in the USA" into "Banned in the USA".

'We met Suge Knight in a fancy restaurant in California, The Ivy, for lunch. He was a former gangbanger out of Compton, a member of the Bloods. When I met him, I thought: "This guy has the biggest chest I've ever seen!" But after everything else is said and done, Knight was a brilliant, brilliant record executive. He had this label, Death Row Records – I wasn't crazy about the name – and the symbol was a guy being strapped into an electric chair.

'Jimmy weighs about 120lbs, Suge weighs about 280lbs. They were sitting next to each other and I found it very funny seeing the two of them together. It was incongruous. Jimmy had said to me: "Listen, when I wink at you, it means I'm going to the bathroom. And I want you to tell Suge that I'm a genius."

'So I asked, "And because of that, what's going to happen?" Jimmy replied, "We're going to sign Death Row Records." So Jimmy goes off to the bathroom and I'm sitting over the way from Suge. I say: "You know, you're very fortunate." "Why?" he replies. "Because you're going to have the chance to work with a genius," I say.

'Finally, Jimmy comes back and, believe it or not, he made that deal. Interscope picked up the distribution for Death Row Records – including Dr. Dre, Snoop Dogg and a myriad of iconic rap artists.'[1]

Iovine viscerally understood that what others say about you carries more weight than what you say about yourself. What you say about yourself is effectively branding, which people instinctively understand to be partisan and self-interested. What others say about you is never completely within your control, and that means people take it seriously.

THE EVOLUTION OF GOSSIP

Language is thought to have evolved some 100,000 years ago, following a rapid increase in the size of human brains and also the beginnings of organized hunting. Bigger brains allowed humans to talk, enabling our ancestors to co-operate more effectively to track down bigger animals such as giant gelada and mammoths. It was a virtuous evolutionary circle, leading ultimately to the great series of migrations that fanned out from Africa 70,000 to 100,000 years ago. For tens of thousands of years, early humans formed family units that stuck together in roaming bands, loosely affiliated with other groups to form tribes of fifteen hundred or so people. Using language to exchange information about the environment, to speculate, to invoke the supernatural, to sing or chant or to grieve, to identify those making a contribution to the common good or those taking more than their fair share, would have been essential for community cohesion and survival.

By 3,100 BC the pharaohs ruled over hundreds of thousands of subjects. Two thousand years later, the great empires of Assyria, Babylon and Persia ruled over millions. Israeli anthropologist Yuval Noah Harari suggests that it was the human capacity to build epic unifying narratives such as religion, myth and money that undergirded bigger and more sophisticated forms of human organization. 'When the Agricultural Revolution opened opportunities for the creation of crowded cities and mighty empires, people invented stories about great gods, motherlands and joint stock companies to provide the needed links,' writes Harari. 'While human evolution was crawling at its usual snail's pace, the human imagination was building astounding networks of mass cooperation, unlike any other seen on earth.'[2]

Modern studies suggest that, in two-thirds of our conversations, we are not considering lofty themes at all, but basically gossiping about other people. 'If being human is all about talking, it is the tittle tattle of life that makes the world go round,' observes anthropologist Robin Dunbar, 'not the pearls of wisdom that fall from the lips of the Aristotles and the Einsteins.' Much interaction on the Internet falls into this category, with social media often derided as shallow and meaningless. Likewise, office gossip is sometimes seen as being unproductive and unhelpful. But in fact the exchange of gossip online or in the office is fulfilling an ancient human need. Through gossip we are constantly monitoring the way others are likely to behave towards us and using it to calibrate our own behaviour. We build, monitor and challenge our own and other people's reputations, teasing out the complex interplay between words and actions. The process of forging reputations through gossip serves a purpose: to build social cohesion and trust.

In any system relying on reciprocal good deeds, there are opportunities for people to exploit the goodwill of others by being lazy or incompetent, or by cheating. If this kind of behaviour goes unchecked, it threatens the viability of the entire community – whether it is a band of hunter-gatherers or a modern business. Gossip helps flush out the boss who is lazy, the head teacher who is a bully or the colleague who is untrustworthy. The whole system benefits immediately if free riders are eliminated – and in future, changes the way individuals might behave.

THE QUEST FOR LEGITIMACY

In today's world, the opportunity to curate your own narrative has never been greater. The tools at your disposal are extremely sophisticated and available at virtually no cost.

Organizations create narratives around capability, principally in order to highlight the distinctive aspects of their products and services. Capability narratives also serve other purposes when it comes to reputation signalling – they attract the 'right' sort of person to apply for a job at the organization; they signal to investors the competitive strengths that underpin the share price; and they also ward off the regulators.

But it is in the area of character narratives that there has been the most innovation. While one or two companies in the mid-twentieth century did focus on some character attributes

– most notably cigarette companies such as Philip Morris's 'Marlboro Man' in the US, and Quaker companies such as Cadbury in the UK – the majority of companies focused on the utility of their products. Today, corporate narrative is emotional – it highlights not only what the organization does but how they go about it.

Two marketing scholars, Leyland Pitt and Lisa Papania at Simon Fraser University's Beedie School of Business in Canada, have studied the ways in which organizations communicate personality through the narratives that they develop on their websites.

'Whether they mean to or not, organisations create images of their personalities and core characteristics through the words they communicate online,' they write in a 2007 paper in the *Journal of General Management*. 'Frequently, these words are selected purposefully to build certain impressions in the eyes of specific stakeholders. However, sometimes the images formed are unintended; a consequence of combinations and associations between words. This is of crucial importance, since organisations' reputations in the eyes of their stakeholders are shaped by the images organisations convey.'

Take Jack Daniel's. Visitors to its website are in for a folksy southern charm experience. The words 'JACK LIVES HERE' sit above 'A warm Tennessee welcome to all our friends. You've entered The Jack Store, home of smooth sippin' whiskey and all things Jack Daniel's.' The site oozes heritage, and is specifically designed to curate and establish its legitimacy. Dig deeper into the links, and you find videos celebrating the town of Lynchburg, where Jack Daniel established his distillery in 1875. And in a clever twist, the marketing people there are reinforcing its legitimacy and heritage in a contemporary way through links with today's vibrant and highly successful Tennessee music scene. The company has put a lot of effort into creating its origin story, which they call 'our story of independence' and which is told through a timeline that you can scroll through to see the key moments in the company's history. The reputation they are seeking to create is one that is authentic, built on the legitimacy of the original distillery and its iconic founder, but also contemporary and relevant to the young, cool, urban drinkers of today.

The corporate reality is somewhat different. Jack Daniel's is an operating subsidiary of the Brown-Forman Corporation, a New York Stock Exchange listed company with revenues of US $3 billion in 2016 and 4,600 employees. It is a professionally run modern corporation, highly successful and modern in its methods. Its story is not unique. Take Innocent Drinks, which we discuss later (Chapter 6, 'What's in a brand?'), and Ben & Jerry's Ice Cream. Both brands celebrate their heritage as a core part of their identity, and use this to build and maintain their legitimacy in competitive markets.

Capability and character narratives are the two mechanisms through which legitimacy is built. Legitimacy, according to Mark C. Suchman, a professor of sociology at Brown University, is 'a general perception or assumption that the actions of an entity are appropriate within some socially constructed system of norms, values, beliefs, and definitions'. An organization does not need to be seen as legitimate in all areas of society, just within the areas that it chooses to promote or narrate.

Legitimacy is a critical asset in the reputation game. If you are perceived as being legitimate – professionally or personally – opportunities become available to you that would not be otherwise. Legitimacy rests on context: it may be legitimate to behave badly with a group of friends on a stag night, but you cannot behave in the same way on a night out with colleagues.

One of the best ways to project legitimacy in business is through transparency. In recent years there has been consistent pressure on business to increase its transparency, and that pressure is only increasing. There has been an explosion recently in the number of non-government organizations (NGOs), pressure groups and lobbying bodies around the world, putting pressure on the media and politicians globally to ask more questions and to demand more answers. And with this increase in the volume of inquiry comes an increased demand for greater speed when it comes to the release of such information.

In tandem with this, we have seen an explosion of data on the Internet combined with innovations in search technologies – led of course by Google. Transparency, or the lack of it, has as a result become one of the main heuristics used to evaluate the legitimacy of an organization. In the absence of insider knowledge, the perceived openness and transparency of an organization is taken as a proxy for its character, a signal of the way it conducts its business internally and also its willingness to be exposed to interrogation.

In addition to the general signal that being open sends, the specific narratives that organizations use, and the information that they choose to disclose, are now judged immediately against their actions. If there is little or no gap between what we say and what we do, we receive the stamp of authenticity.

THE POWER OF AUTHENTICITY

Authenticity is important in today's complex and uncertain world. Business has long been distrusted by wider society, but the onset of digital communications has accelerated the speed at which any minor hypocrisy will be exposed.

In the days of imperialism, Western powers could murder, rape and pillage in faraway lands, without those stories ever surfacing at home. King Leopold of Belgium owned the resource-rich Congo Free State as his personal possession from 1865 until his death in 1909. Under his rule, it is thought that up to ten million Congolese died. The king's words were pious: at home in Europe, he pretended he was on a civilizing mission, even as the profits from rubber and ivory flowed to the Brussels bourgeoisie. Adventurers such as Henry Morton Stanley were hired to give a gloss of idealism to the country's rapacious behaviours. Rumours of barbarism and atrocity reached Europe, but they were not systematically documented and verified until Roger Casement, the Anglo-Irish human rights activist, published a thorough report in 1903. Joseph Conrad's novella of 1899 had intimated that the kingdom was a veritable *Heart of Darkness*, but it took Casement's work to shine a light on the obscenity of Leopold's rule.

Today, the heightened connectivity of business and society is driving expectations of greater responsibility. 'In an era of unremitting transparency, the world requires much more from the private sector,' write John Browne, Robin Nuttall and Tommy Stadlen in *Connect*. 'The consequences of repeating the mistakes of the past are greater today than they have ever been.' For a number of years, the German engineering conglomerate Siemens paid bribes to win contracts in the developing world. Competitors such as GE looked on aghast as Siemens made profits and delivered a share price performance that seemed impossible to beat. Eventually, Siemens came unstuck and had to pay massive fines after acknowledging institutional corruption.

Organizations are being held to higher and higher standards of behaviour, wherever they operate. It is easier than ever to identify gold standards of behaviour and use them to judge others. This is driving organizations to increase their transparency and communications activity. But there is no sense in being more transparent if you are not also behaving authentically. The risks of actively communicating one story, while behaving in a totally different way, are too great.

Just look at the extraordinary impact of the Panama Papers revelations, published in early 2016 by the International Consortium of Investigative Journalists. At a time when journalists are supposed to be under-resourced and chasing trivia, the publication of stories from 11.5 million files leaked from Panamanian law firm Mossack Fonseca was a triumph of old-fashioned investigative journalism. Quite apart from the revelations about how the rich and powerful shuffle their money around the world, these revelations remind us that there is no longer anywhere to hide, even when communications appear to be confidential.

As Groucho Marx might have said, the secret of success is authenticity: once you can fake that, you've got it made. It is really worth striving for authenticity even if you are not quite there yet.

HOW DID THE STORY PLAY?

'Story is misleading and oversimplistic,' argues Charles Tilly, a leading sociologist. 'But that is what people want to hear.' It manages to punch through and register with people even in a world of infinite distractions. 'The modern world is tumbling us about, shrieking and howling, and we're caught up in the giddy excitement of being part of the whirl,' writes journalist Jenni Russell.[3] Who can make sense of kitten pictures, Donald Trump, Brexit and doping in sport – all at once – to draw on a random sample of today's news?

People reject complexity and embrace simplification: is there anything today that cannot be conveyed in the 140 characters of a tweet? Those schooled in nuance and complexity are destined to be highly frustrated in the modern era. Those who are punctilious about facts will be downright exasperated. Facts tend to be used to justify existing opinions, and there are some who would argue that we are now living in a fact-free world. Many people would prefer to watch a quick clip rather than read an informative, factual article. Certainly, Donald Trump's disregard for factual accuracy did not get in the way of his campaign to become the forty-fifth president of the US.

The writer Farhad Manjoo, in his book *True Enough* (2008), makes some powerful arguments as to why our brains choose to favour certain 'facts' over others when processing information. He cites a 1951 study involving an American football game between two Ivy League institutions – Dartmouth College and Princeton University – which revealed that fans of each team blamed the other side for playing dirty and benefitting from biased refereeing. What the study found was that 'the fans were not choosing to see actions in the game – or deliberately overlooking things – in a way that corresponded with their feelings. Rather, it was a matter of visual perception: their eyes were taking in the same game, but their brains seemed to be processing the events in two distinct ways.'

Manjoo's hypothesis is that modern communications technology allows us to create and choose the evidence that we want. He cites Photoshop as a factor, pointing out that we all now distrust what we see in an image, especially if it is a dramatic one. This also goes for the role that technology has had in creating 'experts' more quickly and easily than in the past. Being able to secure media coverage for a set of views and opinions has its own momentum – others search you out and you can become, almost overnight, an 'expert' commentator, irrespective of your qualifications. 'Today, experts come at us from all directions, in every medium, through every niche . . . We consult experts specifically to learn something about which we are ignorant. The transaction is inherently treacherous because ignorance puts us at a disadvantage, too. How can we know whether the "experts" who dominate the public discourse really are expert?' says Manjoo.

Traditional newspapers are in long-term decline as readership and advertising revenues have migrated online. As Alan Rusbridger, the former editor of the *Guardian*, puts it – the industry finds itself 'in the teeth of a force twelve digital hurricane'. Back in the 1970s, if you wanted to influence your reputation in the City of London through the media, there were two journalists who you absolutely had to speak to: they were Richard Lambert and Barry Riley who wrote the hyper-influential Lex column in the *Financial Times* (FT). This appeared on the back page of the pink newspaper and contained three or four short, unsigned articles. This was an early concession to the notion that less is more. A lot of work went into the articles, and if there was a piece about GEC, for example, City insiders knew that Richard and Barry had spoken to Lord Weinstock, its boss, and to the company's two or three top shareholders. The opinions expressed would be trenchant and superbly well informed. In the days when there were still stockbrokers who had time to read a physical newspaper on their commute from Surrey, they would turn to this column first, and their own views would be shaped by what they read. That way, City reputations were made, affirmed and sometimes challenged or destroyed. To have a chance at influencing the influencers, you had to speak to Richard and Barry.

There is still a Lex column, and it is still on the back of the paper, but it is now one voice among many. And it is likely that most people don't read their FT as a physical newspaper any more, but online, where the old hierarchy of importance is no longer so obvious.

'How was the press this morning?' is a question often asked by CEOs of their media people. 'How did the story play?' It used to be the case that if the story appeared 'above the fold' on the front page of a newspaper, it had more impact than if it were buried inside. In the UK, you probably only had to look at a few newspapers lying on a table to be able to answer the question – the broadsheets *The Times* and the *Telegraph*, the *Guardian* and the *Financial Times*, then the *Daily Mail* and perhaps the *Daily Express* (the *Sun* always had excellent business coverage). In the US, the *Wall Street Journal* was the best outlet for business stories, as well as the key regional papers such as the *Washington Post* or the *New York Times*.

The question of the physical location of any article today is almost irrelevant, given the importance of online news. In the past, you might have strolled along to the offices of the *Sunday Times* on Friday night, and passed over an unmarked envelope with details of a story to be run exclusively in the next edition. The journalists were typically so grateful for exclusivity that they wouldn't run around asking challenging questions, and there was no one around on Saturday in any case. This method of placing exclusive stories now feels as antiquated as using a cleft stick to pass on a message.

Reputation is refracted through various fragmented media sources, from the online editions of the mainstream media to news-wires (such as Reuters or Bloomberg) and a plethora of new, online publications, from Huffington Post to Politico to Business Insider, Buzzfeed and Medium. It was noticeable that when in August 2015 the *New York Times* accused Amazon of 'shockingly callous working practices', Amazon responded not in the pages of the august *Washington Post* (owned by Amazon founder Jeff Bezos), but on the hyper-cool essay site Medium.[4] A loyal employee posted his own riposte on LinkedIn. Some of the new media is good, some awful, creating an unceasing 24/7 cycle of news and views that is exceedingly difficult to influence. People, young people in particular, will tailor their own news feeds from a variety of sources or get their news through Twitter, which is a wonderful way of wasting time staying abreast of what is happening on a second-by-second basis. There is also the phenomenon of 'citizen journalism', where people post blogs, tweets and videos of their experiences, without the mediation of editors. Any one of billions of smartphone owners has the technology to be a citizen journalist. This reportage is much appreciated by other social media users, and increasingly absorbed into mainstream media.

In the days when the authors were starting out, the life of a reporter was almost languid. You wouldn't get into the office until 10 A.M. There would be a news conference at 11 A.M., when the editors would start to think about the look of the next day's newspaper, then you might go out and meet a contact for lunch or a drink. There might be a press conference to attend as well. You could roll back into the office mid-afternoon and start thinking about today's article. Your work would get done in a frenzy of activity from 4 P.M. to 6 P.M., when the threat of a looming deadline would galvanize you into activity.

Now there are running deadlines and the journalist's output is subject to real-time metrics and interactive feedback. You dash something off and, within seconds, someone who knows infinitely more about the subject than you do has pointed out a spelling mistake or an error of emphasis. You have to enter into a conversation, correct the article if it is wrong, wrangle with the reader if you disagree with him or her. Analytics tell you how many people have read your article, how often it got reposted or retweeted, by whom and where in the world. In the old days, Richard Lambert (who was a distinguished editor of the FT) would call you into his office to tell you that Lord Weinstock had phoned to complain about the tone of your article ('Did you have a venom injection this morning?' Weinstock asked one time). More rarely, the editor would pass on some praise after having lunch with the deputy governor of the Bank of England who had liked your piece on monetary policy.

Buzzfeed provides a good example of how story has evolved in the age of new media. This is an organization founded only in 2006. In a decade when hundreds of newspapers have closed around the world or shut down their print editions, it generates hundreds of millions of dollars of revenue; it has 130 million unique users around the globe, two million subscribers on YouTube, and its quirky stories are liked and reposted around the Internet tens of millions of times. Its article about whether a certain dress was blue and black, or white and gold, has been viewed by more than thirty-two million people. Other classics include the listicles '27 Sandwiches That are Better than a Boyfriend' or '27 Signs You Were Raised by Immigrant Parents'. Buzzfeed is not strictly a news site: it provides social news and entertainment, so it is not seeking to compete with the FT, more with the Mail Online. But it is highly effective. Some seventy-five per cent of its traffic comes from social media such as Twitter and Pinterest.

And while the articles are written by human beings, what the humans write is heavily influenced by technology and analytics. Everything about the impact of Buzzfeed posts is studied. Publisher Dao Nguyen explains how the firm tracks all the posts that appear on its ninety Facebook pages. 'We can look at traditional things, like when is the best time to post? And how does using video for certain pages affect growth? And how the rates are different between pages. We can use that to optimize what pages we post videos on.'[5] Posts on the regular site are put into buckets, according to how many readers they attract. A good result is 100,000 to 250,000 shares, while some go viral (like the story of the blue and black dress) and get one million or more hits. The journalists on Buzzfeed are not slaves to the algorithm, they are imaginative and enterprising reporters who often publish many different versions of the same story to see which lands best with readers. The algorithms, in combination with humans, work out the very specific subject matter where people are strongly emotionally engaged, and tailor stories accordingly – a far cry from the reliable kingmakers of old media.

RAYMOND NASR'S CLOCK

To understand the role of media in story creation more broadly, we spoke to Raymond Nasr, the former director of communications at Google who now advises Silicon Valley companies including Snapchat and Twitter, and lectures at the Graduate School of Business at Stanford University. His CV includes spells at Apple, Sun Microsystems and Novell, and he is also a visiting fellow at the University of Oxford. (Something of a Renaissance man, he is also an entrepreneur and a qualified sommelier.) Based on his extensive experience of managing these gilded corporate reputations, he has developed his own take on the concept of the media cycle.

'The idea came during the early days at Apple where we were so high minded in our communications that we asked "What is the press really about?" recalls Nasr. 'We asked ourselves, "What gets written?" And we reduced it to only four things that the media likes to write about – companies that are at the top of the hill, companies that are perched for a fall, companies that are in the dumpster and companies that are engaged in the turnaround. We used the metaphor of a clock because time defines the flow of this narrative. Each of these sits within the quadrants of an analogue clock.'

The clock analogy is as simple as it is powerful. The four quadrants sit visually between 12 ('top of the hill'), 3 ('perched for a fall'), 6 ('in the dumpster') and 9 ('engaged in the turnaround'). And like a clock, time only moves one way. It is not possible for companies to move backwards around Nasr's media clock. Companies cannot be perched for a fall and then step back from the brink to once again be top of the hill. He believes that companies need to push on through the cycle, take their medicine, before they can regain the top spot.

'The top-of-the-hill story is one that the press loves because it speaks to the invincibility of these great franchises that as a consuming world we have come to adore. The big FANG – Facebook, Apple, Netflix and Google. Untouchable consecutive quarters of profitability, partners that are just loving them to death. Pope Francis is top of the hill at the moment,' says Nasr.

Top-of-the-hill companies are seemingly invincible. They have complete alignment of what Nasr calls 'the three Ps' – products, performance and partners. The company's products are selling strongly, and are seen to have a growth trajectory, a momentum behind them. The financial performance of the company is visibly strong as evidenced by the relevant metrics – it could be sales, profits or share-price performance. And the company has become a magnet for strong partnerships. The stars are aligned. Its brand is strong, and it can do big, bold and innovative things. Apple has been in this quadrant at least twice, first in the mid-1980s and then again in the late 1990s, and arguably a third time from 2009 to 2012. Google was in this quadrant prior to the listing of its shares in spring 2004.

In this quadrant, the types of story that you see are also distinctive. Typical stories will focus on metrics of success (for example, the number of CVs the company is receiving every week), anticipation about the next blockbuster product developments (for example, expected approvals of new drugs), or strategic enhancements (for example, being named as a probable consolidator in its sector).

Companies tend to move into the second quadrant almost without knowing that they have done so. It usually starts with one journalist who happens across some facts that they position as an 'emperor's new clothes' story – the type of story that suggests that all might not be as it seems at the company. 'The second quadrant is perched for a fall, and a really important element in this quadrant is the 3.30 story,' explains Nasr. 'Communications directors are really on the lookout for this story. An example would be a reporter who has evidence that a director is interviewing at a competitor, or that products are slipping in popularity, or that profitability is falling. These are "perched for a fall" stories.'

Nasr focuses on the 3.30 story because this is just when the cycle is at its most dangerous. The majority of the media has been writing about the company as a top-of-the-hill story, but there are now one or two stories that suggest there is trouble ahead. Most communications executives know this feeling only too well: a dread in the pit of the stomach. For when the media starts to sniff out a counternarrative, a story that runs contrary to the perceived wisdom, momentum can begin to turn in the wrong direction. Worryingly, it is often difficult to quickly establish the facts behind any rumours or allegations that are being put forward. And when the company has been riding high, it is also difficult to get executives to take suggestions of problems seriously. This makes the story doubly difficult to manage.

Hillary Clinton had been poised for a fall when it was discovered that she had written private emails on a non-protected home computer that may have been linked to her duties as secretary of state. Her failure to deal quickly with this issue and to be transparent about her motives resulted in her staying in the dumpster for much longer than necessary. Similarly, in the UK, Sir Philip Green, the billionaire retailer, was for years treated by the UK press as a pugnacious but loveable tycoon who had made billions by shaking up the high street. Then in April 2016 the department-store chain BHS collapsed into administration with debts of £1.3 billion and a £570 million pensions deficit. Some eleven thousand jobs were immediately at risk. A year before, Green had sold the company for £1, having paid out hundreds of millions by way of dividends to his family in the years of his ownership. Overnight he went from hero to villain, with MPs calling for him to pay up in order to save jobs and pensions, or be stripped of his knighthood.

Once you are in the second quadrant, you accelerate quickly through it into 'the dumpster', which is the third of Nasr's quadrants. Being in the dumpster is of course not a comfortable place to be for a company. The organization might be in full crisis at that point, finding it difficult to negotiate with its partners, retain its employees or even show a brave face to its customers. It is easy for a company to get trapped here, and the types of stories that get written do not help. They tend to reinforce the sense of crisis or hopelessness surrounding the company. Stories may focus on the reasons why an organization has arrived at this point ('it is easy to see why this happened'), the ongoing turmoil and infighting that has broken out ('management team defections') or the associated problems facing the company ('banks withdraw funding from troubled company'). These stories perpetuate a sense of gloom.

'In the dumpster is the place that you want to spend the least amount of time in your career, but everyone has to be there for at least a moment,' says Nasr. 'You learn an enormous amount from that moment. Great visionary founders and CEOs have all been in the dumpster. It sharpens your instincts, it teaches you the latest lessons and it prepares you for the turnaround.'

It takes decisive leadership to escape the dumpster, but once such a leader has emerged, this sets the scene for a period that communications professionals find energizing and fun: the turnaround. As Nasr explains, 'The turnaround story is a very interesting one. For listed companies, the quarterly earnings call is one of the most visible moments in this quadrant – and in terms of the narrative you have got to have your soundbites so well scripted that it foreshadows – credibly – where the company will be once it again becomes a top-of-the-hill story. This is a very important insight on the turnaround because, if this top-of-the-hill moment never arrives, your credibility as a CEO is impacted.'

There is a palpable sense of momentum when it comes to a turnaround, and the media are highly sensitive to anything that slows it down. Journalists are prepared to foreshadow a successful turnaround story, but don't want to be seen to have got it wrong or, even worse, to be 'in the pocket' of a company – after all, every story puts their own reputation on the line.

Nasr points again to 'the three Ps'. In this quadrant, you have to be sure that the turnaround is being evidenced by products that people are actually buying and/or using; by performance as evidenced by consecutive quarters of profitability or sales growth; and with partners who will testify to your resurgence as a company. Once you have the three Ps in place, you can safely climb back up to the top of the hill.

'The biggest mistake in this quadrant is to push a narrative ahead of the facts. There is so much attention on whether you can earn the right to be a top-of-the-hill story that the media is much more careful and much more cautious, picking over every aspect of your revival,' says Nasr. 'And also, being a top-of-the-hill story again is not easy either – you have to meet expectations, which get bigger and bigger as time goes on. You can be a 3.30 P.M. story again very quickly unless you manage things right.'

FAKE NEWS!

On Saturday, 21 January 2017, President Trump made a speech at the Central Intelligence Agency. In that speech, he took issue with reports about a 'feud' between himself and the US intelligence community, saying that the media had falsely and deliberately 'constructed' it, and also made comments about the size of the inauguration crowd on the day before in Washington. 'It looked honestly like a million and a half people, whatever it was, it was, but it went all the way back to the Washington Monument,' he stated.

Aerial photographs disagreed. In a series of photographs released by the *New York Times* (and others), comparisons with the Obama inauguration of 2009 clearly showed more people attending Obama's event than Trump's, and also directly contradicted Trump's statement that the crowd went all the way back to the Washington Monument.

Challenged about these discrepancies by NBC's *Meet The Press on Sunday*, President Trump's counselor Kellyanne Conway defended the comments by saying that the White House had put forward 'alternative facts' to the ones reported by the news media, leading to widespread controversy and derision.

Trump's rise to power reflects an understanding of the value of entertainment, rather than pure fact. In the modern age, all US presidents have sought a way to speak directly and intimately to the mass of the population – Franklin D. Roosevelt's fireside chats in the radio age come to mind, or Richard Nixon's prime-time TV addresses. But the amount of time allocated to presidents has dwindled in the age of mass media. Trump's experience as a gameshow host gave him an instinct for bypassing the mainstream media and reaching the mass market using the instrument of Twitter.[6]

For the voters who felt alienated by globalization and abandoned by the political elite, Trump's tweeted claims and post-truths seem to resonate. For them, the media are part of the problem. It is in this environment that technology companies such as Facebook and Twitter have been able not just to survive, but become information behemoths. A report by the Pew Research Centre and the Knight Foundation, released in May 2016, found that over forty per cent of American adults get their news from Facebook. This becomes even more significant when set against data published in Buzzfeed, which found that fake news on Facebook was read by more people than reports in the traditional news outlets, and that seventeen of the top twenty fake news stories were either pro-Trump or anti-Hillary.[7]

Welcome to the new world of fake news. So great is its perceived impact that the Oxford Dictionary made 'post-truth' its 2016 word of the year, describing it as 'an adjective defined as "relating to or denoting circumstances in which objective facts are less influential in shaping public opinion than appeals to emotion and personal belief"'.[8]

In a world where truth is relative, reputation – which relies on perceptions – has become even more important. In a post-truth world, what others say about you is paramount.

GUERRILLA CAMPAIGNING

Reputations don't simply grow out of your own interactions with the wider world – they can be created and destroyed by people with their own agendas or special interests. And there is a whole category of activists who specialize in using the threat of reputational damage to push for meaningful change.

Gary Alan Fine explains this in terms of highly incentivized 'reputational entrepreneurs'. 'They are people who have the motivation to engage in creating or destroying reputations,' he explains. 'In US politics, for example, we have this two-party division, which we have had for 150 years now, and it means that Democrats are always going to be looking to discredit Republicans and vice versa. We are all potential reputational entrepreneurs, but some of us don't have the incentives to do anything about it.'

Activists take many forms, and campaign on many different issues. Broadly speaking they can be categorized into four camps: environmental (such as Greenpeace); social (such as Global Justice Now); political (such as Amnesty International); and financial (such as the hedge fund Knight Vinke). In a broader sense, your competitors are also activists, stirring up trouble for you when you have a problem, seeking to snatch market share and influence journalists, regulators and politicians.

The impact of activism is that much greater in the world of 24/7 media, when the intervention of a motivated actor creates the kind of friction that engenders headlines. Knight Vinke may only have a handful of employees but, as a prominent shareholder taking on the immense HSBC, it attracted an extraordinary amount of press interest. There is a default tendency for the public to support an activist against a corporate Goliath, if only by giving airtime. The growth of public scrutiny of business and politics is a welcome trend, but it means that there is more for activists to get their teeth into: more information to scrutinize, with more failings to point out and more legitimate agendas for reputational contest.

Narratives are the key weapons in an activist's arsenal. Through the strategic use of story, activists generate momentum and support. This means they are often more interested in reputational impact than substance. 'Many activist groups see targeting an organization or a company or an industry as a means to an end,' says Professor Brayden King, also of Northwestern University. 'For them the end is: "How can we change public opinion?" The target itself is often a stage or a platform on which they can project their cause. So, do they go after the worst offenders? No, they go after the ones who are most likely to be noticed, then the ones who have the best reputations. They go after the ones who are trying to do things right, they are trying to deal with the issue because they are visible and also they are susceptible to campaigning.'

Focusing on these highly visible targets serves to prove the legitimacy of the activist, drawing in other interested parties who will join the debate one way or another. For NGOs, it also helps build their *own* reputation within their peer group. Visibility has become important in an increasingly competitive field for donors. As long as an organization has some form of vulnerability to the issue, that's good enough to make them a primary target. Professor King cites Apple as an example: a company with a great brand, known for trying to change the world in a positive way. Precisely this progressive reputation has made it vulnerable to activism. When it was discovered that Apple was using the controversial Chinese electronics manufacturer Foxconn as a supplier, as many others did, the iconic company became a very attractive target for activists who wanted to highlight the issue of labour conditions in manufacturing. Foxconn's workers were paid so poorly, and conditions were so bad, that there had been a spate of suicides at their plants. 'Whether Apple changed their policies or not is not really the point,' says King. 'The campaign against Foxconn chose Apple in order to increase public awareness of the issue.'

Although companies with strong reputations are targeted more frequently, they are actually less likely just to give in to activists' demands. Instead, they tend to find other ways to protect their reputational position. A highly reputable company that has been attacked may seek to deflect an activist onslaught by being overtly philanthropic or even by teaming up with NGOs. In fact, there have been some surprising outbreaks of harmonious relations between big companies and the organizations that were previously sworn enemies.

Greenpeace teamed up with global utility giant Enel in 2015 to tackle global warming. The two organizations had been at each other's throats, with legal claims swirling around the courts since 2012 when Greenpeace targeted Enel for its coal-fired plants. Greenpeace claimed that its emissions were enough to kill a thousand Europeans each year. Enel responded with a lawsuit that dragged on until 2015. When Francesco Starace took over as CEO of Enel, he decided on a different approach. As part of his work to transform the company into a champion of climate-friendly power production – mainly solar and wind – he was keen to engage in a more constructive dialogue with Greenpeace, who had many years of experience and expertise in the field. 'We have to acknowledge that the climate clock is ticking and time is of the essence,' commented Starace in an interview in 2015. 'Conventional fossil fuels and nuclear power plants are a trap,' he said. 'A trap for companies to die.'

Kumi Naidoo, until recently executive director of Greenpeace, agreed with Starace's analysis, and saw a real opportunity in engaging with a major utility to deliver meaningful action that would reduce carbon emissions. 'We thought that what Enel was doing was critically necessary and that we needed to acknowledge and encourage it,' he said. 'It was a first, and we welcomed their actions.' The reputational impact was hugely positive on two fronts. First, everyone from investors to regulators welcomed the end of the legal battle. Uncertainty like that is unwelcome at the best of times, and was seen as unproductive. And second, settlement was also a welcome reputational signal, showing how the new management team at Enel was going to run the company. And it was also a big reputational signal for Greenpeace, traditionally one of the most confrontational of activist NGOs.

King agrees. 'If you look at the increase in the number of environmental NGOs, you also see a shift in the centre of the market of NGOs where more and more of them are adopting a more collaborative approach. Even Greenpeace are doing this – they are working more closely with companies to achieve outcomes.'

The trend towards collaboration also extends to the work being done by competing NGOs. 'My data shows that disruptive tactics are going down, and collaborative tactics are going up,' says King. This kind of collaboration between former foes promises to create a more benign environment for companies, but it may lead to challenges for NGOs themselves. They now stand accused by their peers and supporters of being captive to big business. Most of the large NGOs rebut this. Organizations such as Save the Children and Oxfam have worked together with companies for many years, endorsing them when things go well, while being prepared to point out deficiencies when they don't.

'Any serious campaign or advocacy planning will include a thorough mapping of public perception of the target, their brand positioning and key influencers in specific markets,' says Thomas Schultz-Jagow, Amnesty International's senior director of campaigns and communications. 'This will lead to a decision on whether the strategy should veer towards a confrontational or collaborative approach. NGOs understand the value of an organization's reputation, and will reflect carefully on the different reputations that the organization has before making a decision about which aspect of their business to attack.'

Yet as the bigger and more established campaigning organizations are defanged, this creates opportunities for smaller, more confrontational activists to make their mark. For example, 350.org campaigns on environmental issues in 188 countries around the world, and Change.org has grown into one of the most important campaigning websites. 'These NGOs are not only more radical in their rhetoric, but also in the tactics that they use such as performance theatre, throwing fake blood on executives and so on,' says King.

COURTING CONTROVERSY

One of the most controversial propaganda campaigns in recent years has been that organized and run by Islamic State (IS). Its messages have had an extremely high impact with some of the more horrific acts of cruelty reaching a global audience; the production values have been highly professional; and it has succeeded in generating an active and motivated group of social media followers who themselves have helped spread the IS message. Abdel Bari Atwan, author of the incisive and authoritative book *Islamic State: The Digital Caliphate* (2015), states it clearly: 'Without digital technology, it is highly unlikely that Islamic State would have ever come into existence, let alone be able to survive and expand.'

Strategic use of narrative lies at the heart of IS's strategy: it is playing the reputation game in deadly earnest. Quilliam, a counter-extremism think-tank, in its October 2015 report 'Documenting the Virtual Caliphate' argues that 'it is in psychological terms . . . that IS has truly transformed the state of play. Its vast propaganda operation is unrivalled, involving devoted media teams from West Africa to Afghanistan who work relentlessly, day and night, in the production and dissemination of the "caliphate" brand.' Their research finds that IS produces on average thirty-eight 'individual batches' of information each day, including photos, video, audio, posters, theological essays and scripted articles. Theirs is a wall of narrative, a tsunami of content that leaves those fighting the propaganda reeling with the intensity of the campaign. IS has created an impressive and highly professional communications team to manage and plan the scope of its narrative activity. It has established several 'foundations' dedicated to media production, including the Al-Furqan Foundation for Media Production, which produces CDs, DVDs, posters, pamphlets, and Web-related propaganda products and official statements; the Al-I'tisam and Ajnad

Foundations, which specialize in the production of 'nasheeds' – vocal chants constructed without the use of musical instruments (which are forbidden in Islam); and in 2014 the Al-Hayat Media Center, which focuses on English, German, Russian and French language communication.

Atwan calls IS 'masters of the digital universe'. 'Most Islamic State commanders and recruits are tech-savvy,' he writes. 'Coding (writing software programs, inputting information in html) is as familiar to them as their mother tongue. Most of the digital caliphate's business is conducted online, from recruitment and propaganda to battlefield strategy and instruction. What the jihadis lack in the way of sophisticated weaponry they more than make up for with their online expertise.' Each IS fighter is 'expected to be his or her own media outlet, reporting live from the front line in tweets, offering enticing visions of domestic bliss via short films and images posted to JustPaste.it and Instagram, entering into friendly conversations via Skype, messaging on anonymous Android platforms, and posting links to the group's propaganda material and its infamous catalogue of videos', says Atwan.

Contrary to popular impression, the propaganda that these groups create does not just rest on brutal images: the Quilliam report identifies six 'non-discrete' strands to the IS communications message – mercy, belonging, brutality, victimhood, war and utopia. Its uniting feature is a narrative aimed at reuniting the global Sunni brotherhood in order to create a revived and dominant Muslim world. It is a strategy aimed as much at inspiration as it is at obedience and submission.

This helps us to put in context, and perhaps understand better, the strange allure of the IS message. Professor Shahira Fahmy of the University of Arizona spent a year seconded to NATO studying IS propaganda. Among the various media used by IS – which include several targeted at women – she researched *Dabiq*, a glossy magazine distributed by IS. Her research found that the number of images in the magazine promoting an 'idealistic caliphate' far outnumbered photographs of killing and torture. In fact, she found

that only five per cent of imagery produced by IS could be categorized as 'violent'.

A wider analysis of the propaganda distributed by IS shows a
broad communications strategy to establish legitimacy as a state.
Nowhere is this clearer than in the evolution of its chosen name.
The origins of IS are to be found in a mix of al-Qaeda; former
Ba'ath party members together with officers and troops from
Saddam Hussein's defeated armies in Iraq; and strict Salafists from
the region, including Kurdish separatists. This disparate group
came together to form Jaish Ansar al-Sunna under the leadership of
Abu Musab al-Zarqawi. It was al-Zarqawi who first espoused the
extreme violence that is today a hallmark of IS, and it was he who
personally beheaded the twenty-six-year-old American businessman Nick Berg in 2004, causing some in the group to distance
themselves from him.

In order to shore up support al-Zarqawi created a new
umbrella group of insurgent Sunnis initially called the 'Mujahideen
Shura Council'. Following al-Zarqawi's death at the hands of US
special forces, this umbrella organization was headed up by the
Iraqi exile Abu Omar al-Baghdadi and was renamed 'Islamic State
of Iraq' (ISI) in 2006, adopting the explicit aim of establishing an
Islamic emirate. But it was the contested and controversial 'merger'
of ISI with the Syrian jihadist rebels of the al-Nusra Front in 2013
that eventually created the much more deadly organization called
the Islamic State of Iraq and al-Sham (ISIS). Upon its declaration of
an Islamic caliphate in June 2014, the leadership now refers to itself
just as Islamic State (IS).

The evolution of its name follows the organization's search for
legitimacy. Western leaders have since sought to delegitimize IS by
referring to it by another name – Daesh – which has the advantage
of being derogatory, sounding like an Arabic word meaning 'one
who crushes something underfoot'.

Western audiences are divided over which name to use. Some
reject the name IS, believing it concedes too much legitimacy to
what they regard as a group of terrorists who happen to occupy, by

force, some territory in Iraq and Syria. The caliph of the newly proclaimed caliphate is Abu Bakr al-Baghdadi, whose intent through this name was to eradicate what he sees as artificial and externally imposed borders between modern-day Syria and Iraq. At its peak, IS controlled territory extended from northern Syria, just shy of the border with Turkey and Mosul in the north of Iraq, down to the area east of Damascus and all the way over to Baghdad. (Following the fall of Mosul in the summer of 2017 and other reversals, IS has lost virtually all its territory in Syria and Iraq.) IS has also created a broader 'statehood' narrative in support of its claims. In late 2014, it announced that it was creating its own currency system based on coinage used by the Umayyad Caliphate in the seventh century. IS stated that this was part of an effort 'to emancipate itself from the Satanic global economic system ... a strike against the Crusader coalition'. The currency would be overseen by a leadership council in the 'house of finance' and approved by the caliph himself.

None of these attempts to emulate legitimate statehood should understate the power of its brutal message strategy. Such messaging is by no means random – it is enshrined in a 2004 essay entitled 'Management of Savagery' authored by al-Qaeda ideologue Abu Bakr Naji, which draws on the work of the fourteenth-century Islamic scholar Taqi al-Din ibn Taymiyyah. In this essay, the author identifies three stages in the re-establishment of the caliphate. First, 'a stage of vexation and exhaustion' occurs whereby the superpowers are worn down militarily by constant pressure from jihadi activity. This military pressure will exert political pressure on weak Western governments who will find it increasingly hard to maintain support among their citizens, amid mounting economic costs. Indeed, this seems to be what happened with the Soviet Union in Afghanistan, and we have seen fractious debates over Middle East engagement in the UK and the US. The second stage identified by Naji is 'the administration of savagery', which is seen as a vital and highly powerful psychological weapon. According to Naji, this leads to the third stage, where people in areas afflicted by acts of

Figure 2 Infographic detailing total attack numbers by type (1434 H/2013)

savagery 'long' for someone to come in and restore some sort of order, leading to the establishment of the Islamic State.

Naji also emphasizes the need for jihadists to be personally savage. He cites early militants who 'burned people with fire even though it is odious because they know the effect of rough violence in times of need . . . they did not undertake it because they love killing: they were certainly not coarse people. By God! How tender were their hearts . . . The reality of this role must be understood by explaining it to the youth who want to fight.' The narrative of savagery also links back into the wider IS strategy of legitimization. In March each year since 2012 IS has produced an annual report of its activities, called *al-Naba* ('The Report'). It is typically over four hundred pages long, and includes a rundown of 'government' activities.

The Institute for the Study of War has analysed the IS reports. Its findings are of an organization using these reports to communicate a disciplined military command structure, a detailed process for assimilation of conquered territories (tactics, techniques and procedures), and a careful analysis of the different operating environments it faces in the territories it controls or seeks to control. Perhaps the most chilling aspect of the report was an infographic detailing the total number of attacks made by its forces, broken down by type of attack – including assassinations, roadside bombs, mortar attacks and kidnappings (see figure 2). In disclosing these gruesome key performance indicators, IS is engaging in a ghastly parody of corporate best practice.

THE ASYMMETRICAL POWER OF A BAD STORY

On 4 February 1981, Ray Donovan was appointed secretary of labour in the Reagan administration. Almost immediately, however, allegations of corruption and links to the Mafia started to surface.

Donovan was already president of the Schiavone Construction Company and a big shareholder. In 1978, Schiavone had been awarded a contract by the New York public works authorities to construct the East 63rd Street tunnel between Queens and Manhattan. Over the next six years, federal prosecutors worked with the Bronx District Attorney, Mario Merola, to investigate accusations of bribery and corruption. This eventually led to the indictment of Donovan and seven other executives involved in Schiavone or its subcontractors who were charged with scheming to defraud the New York City Transit Authority of US $7.4 million.

There had been previous attempts to link Donovan to organized crime, but they had been shaky at best. In 1982, a special federal prosecutor, Leon Silverman, had investigated Donovan and found 'insufficient credible evidence' that he had witnessed union payoffs or that he had links to organized crime. But that did not stop Mario Merola from including Donovan in his 1984 Schiavone charge sheet. The charges against him did not involve his Reagan administration position, but Donovan resigned anyway when he was ordered to stand trial. In the end, the trial proceeded and all eight defendants were found not guilty on all charges. Jurors were openly contemptuous of the fact that this case had been brought to trial in the first place, and the jury foreperson commented in an interview after the case that she thought that the case was at least in part politically motivated.

But it was the comment by Donovan, on the steps of the courthouse, that resonated. Standing next to his wife, Catherine, he said: 'It's a cruel thing they did to me. After two and a half years, this nightmare is behind us. Which office do I go to now to get my reputation back?'

When individuals are merely *accused* of association with the mob or of vile crimes such as rape or child abuse, their reputations collapse instantaneously, whether they are guilty or not. As the DJ Paul Gambaccini has testified, friends, professional contacts, charities he had worked with for more than twenty years, the Labour Party whom he had had supported for decades, all dropped him from the moment he was arrested at home and charged with child abuse early in the morning of 29 October 2013. He was unable to find work and his life was in effect destroyed. He was put on rolling bail while the police tried to substantiate the one allegation they had against him. Eventually, on 10 October 2014, he was told that he had no case to answer. He subsequently lamented to the *Daily Mail*:

'Great Britain persecuted me from 29 October 2013, to 10 October 2014. Its agents entered my home in the middle of the night, took away my possessions, arrested me on trumped-up allegations, disgraced me in the national media, deprived me of employment and kept me on bail for twelve months even though they knew they had no case against me. These are the actions of a totalitarian state.' He never received an apology. Others have received similar treatment, including Field Marshall Lord Bramall, who was accused of raping and torturing a boy on a military base forty years ago. The investigation was eventually dropped several months later and he received a grudging apology from the police. For Lord Brittan, who stood similarly accused, the apology came too late: the former politician had died before his name was cleared and Met Commissioner Sir Bernard Hogan-Howe delivered the apology to Brittan's widow.

Despite our long tradition of assumed innocence in legal matters, regulators and lawmakers increasingly use the single-minded and sometimes cynical tactics of activists. In this light, it is easy to see why leader of the Malaysian opposition Anwar Ibrahim is subject to persistent charges of sodomy, illegal in Malaysia, which have the dual effect of blackening his name and ruling him out of contention for leadership. But even in the UK or the US, allegations of wrongdoing are extremely difficult to contest. Once allegations have been made by government officials, there is a default assumption that there must be at least some level of underlying guilt – which is to say, there's no smoke without fire.

In the US, the Securities and Exchange Commission (SEC) is getting tougher. The SEC for decades had a process called 'neither admitting nor denying wrongdoing'. When they saw wrongdoing, they would look to achieve a monetary settlement that would deter others from the same behaviour. As a result, they were prepared to offer companies a settlement 'without admission of guilt'. But under Mary Jo White, who served as SEC Chair from 2013 to 2017, that changed. She signalled a desire to be tougher than her predecessors and she wanted to hold individuals to account rather than just corporations. She also insisted on a public admission of guilt as part of any settlement. This had far-reaching reputational consequences. No longer could companies hide behind the 'no admission of liability' clause when defending any settlement. And the SEC's counterpart in the UK, the Financial Conduct Authority (FCA), is now moving in the same direction. The SEC and the FCA know that the mere announcement of an investigation, irrespective of whether that leads to a formal case, has become an important reputational weapon.

'If you are representing some guy who engages in persistent criminal activity, he does not care about reputation because jail time is the cost of doing business,' explains Ike Sorkin, the veteran US defence attorney. 'But a normal "white-collar" professional does. He is respected, a pillar of the community – and feels viscerally that "if I am charged, I lose everything". Once charged, you become toxic . . . The reputational risk can be devastating.'

Reputation has been a very significant tool for the regulators. They know full well that if there is an investigation then people are likely to fall into line rather than risk a long and damaging court case. It's a wonderful tool for the federal, state and local prosecutors to hold out to force a settlement. In the US, the charges get more press than the results of the trial. 'There is something awesome about the term "grand jury charges",' says Sorkin. 'In fact there is nothing special about the make-up of a grand jury, which is made up of the same types of individuals who sit on trial juries.'

This leads us to an important mechanism of reputation: it is not always fair. When people hear the name Max Mosley, few think of his distinguished career in motorsport. Instead, he will forever be known as the man exposed by the *News of the World* for having what they termed a 'sick Nazi orgy with five hookers'. He disagrees with the Nazi allegations, but admits to a fifty-year interest in bondage, dominance and sadomasochism. In this context, reputation is asymmetrical: one startling attribute, the man's sexual peccadilloes, overwhelms considerations of his other qualities. Note that in this case, the reputational damage is to his character, rather than his competence as a businessman.

The specific problem was not so much the sex, though it was doubtless embarrassing; it was the alleged (and thoroughly denied) eroticization of Nazism. This allowed the press to make the link with his parents, the Nazi-supporting Oswald Mosley and Diana Mitford. Mosley's willingness to acknowledge sexual preferences he would rather have kept private does soften the reputational blow. Still, however unfairly, this is how he will be remembered, rather than as the extremely effective head of the Fédération Internationale de l'Automobile.

PATIENT ZERO

In March 2015, Monica Lewinsky walked into the spotlights above a circular stage at a TED event in Vancouver, Canada. She opened with the words, 'You are looking at a woman who was publicly silent for a decade.'

She spoke for twenty-two minutes about her notoriety and the events of 1998 that saw her branded 'that woman' by the most powerful man on earth. In her talk she speaks eloquently about the dangers of online harassment in a social media world where today anyone can say almost anything and get away with it. Her scandal, she says, 'was brought to you by the digital revolution'. The video has been viewed over 3.3 million times.

Today's social media titans did not even exist in 1998. Facebook was launched in 2004, Twitter in 2006, and Instagram and Snapchat in 2010 and 2011, respectively. In 1998, Amazon was four years old, eBay three years old and Hotmail two years old. In the same year, Google launched its now ubiquitous search tool, and Yahoo first started offering email. Online comment and news was, at the time, mainly provided by blogs and chat forums, with these mostly linked to the established media organizations in existence at the time. Hers, says Lewinsky, was 'the first major news story to be broken online – a click that reverberated around the world. I was Patient Zero of losing a personal reputation on a global scale almost instantaneously.'

People are a lot nastier to each other online than they would be in the flesh, particularly when hiding behind anonymity. It is an unpalatable fact that women, particularly intelligent and outspoken women, are often singled out for the worst abuse. For instance, the author Britni de la Cretaz posted an article for *Cosmopolitan* in which she said that eliminating 'obligation sex' had improved her relationship with her husband. Within minutes, she was subject to a torrent of abuse. ('I hope your husband cheats on you,' was one of the nicer comments on her Facebook page.)[9] Ella Dawson, who wrote for *Women's Health* about living with herpes, and Suzannah Weiss, who had the temerity to write a piece about choosing not to shave her legs, had similar experiences. Danah boyd, the tech blogger, wears a bracelet with the inscription: 'Do Not Read the Comments'. Her articles are engaging and thoughtful, and this is evidently too much for many readers. She has received death threats and is subject to malicious, sexualized comments on a regular basis. 'I get some very serious and unpleasant backlash, and I know I am not alone,' she says. 'The more visibility you get online, the more you get an onslaught that is sexualized or extraordinarily racist, depending on your social position. I live by a simple rule: don't feed the trolls.' She doesn't read the feedback and won't allow herself to get wound up by the abuse.

Today, people can post information about others online without context, evidence or consent. Childline, a UK charity that provides a private and confidential service for children and young people up to the age of nineteen, recorded an eighty-seven per cent increase in calls and emails related to cyberbullying between 2012 and 2013. Bullying and humiliation have always been damaging, but before the Internet they were a local, constrained phenomenon. At worst, cruel words could travel around a section of your personal network or contacts before fizzling out. Today, your reputation is potentially subject to global attention.

The psychologist John Suler labelled this the 'online disinhibition effect', a state of mind he attributes to the absence of authority online and the power of 'dissociative' anonymity (which means you are not empathizing with your victims), among other factors.[10] In a similar vein, Professor Judy Olsen at the University of California, Irvine, has found that people are willing to pass judgement when interacting online, irrespective of whether they have reliable information to support these judgements. Even if there are very few points of reference, people online will construct whole personality profiles from what little information is available. When we are talking about mistakes that we ourselves have made, we tend to blame other factors ('Sorry I'm late, there's been terrible traffic'), whereas when we are talking online about the mistakes made by others we tend to focus on their personality ('They would be late – it's typical of them!').

When especially unpleasant trolls are unmasked, there is online jubilation, as when the Reddit blogger Violentacrez was revealed to be Michael Brutsch, a middle-aged computer programmer living in Arlington, Texas. He had been posting pictures of underage, skimpily clad girls, attracting thousands of perverted followers, and set up Reddit forums on a host of unsavoury and provocative themes, from incest to Nazism. He was outed in October 2012 by a reporter from Gawker, and promptly fired from his job.

The use of humiliation narratives, according to Nicolaus Mills, a professor of American studies at Sarah Lawrence College in Bronxville, New York, has become so endemic as to have spawned a subculture of its own. He cites the ritual humiliation of contestants on TV shows such as *The Apprentice* or *Pop Idol*, and also within politics, where candidates try to humiliate their opponents as part of a wider political narrative strategy. One of the most objectionable forms of online humiliation is the phenomenon of 'slut-shaming'. Slut-shaming is 'the experience of being labelled a sexually out-of-control girl or woman (a "slut" or "ho") and then being punished socially for possessing this identity', according to Leora Tanenbaum, author of *I Am Not a Slut: Slut-Shaming in the Age of the Internet* (2015). The ubiquity of social media has dramatically increased the prevalence of slut-shaming. It has become 'normalized and omnipresent', and there seems little that women can do about it. Once the slurs have been made, the reputation sticks.

Narratives within social media have also had a significant impact on the reputation of large organizations. 'Boogergate' is the term now used for the 2009 scandal that saw two Domino's Pizza employees uploading a video showing them sneezing on pizza dough and sticking pieces of cheese up their nose before placing them on a pizza. The video was initially uploaded on an LGBT website called Good As You (G-A-Y) before being uploaded to YouTube by someone else. It immediately went viral, causing huge damage to the Domino's Pizza brand and prompting a major PR campaign designed to reinforce Domino's reputation as a responsible, clean and hygienic company. At the same time, it placed a burden of shame on the two employees, identified as Kristy Hammonds and Michael Setzer, who were working at the company's branch in Conover, North Carolina. It was noted that the pair would probably face criminal charges, and the company spent much of its response strategy isolating their behaviour and emphasizing the positive customer feedback and support it was receiving. That kind of distancing from the epicentre of a crisis is highly effective, but only when you are not considered a culprit – when you are, you don't want to be seen shirking your responsibilities.

In another example, musician Dave Carroll flew United Airlines from Halifax to Nebraska and, on arrival, found that his US $3,500 Taylor guitar was damaged. He recalled fellow passengers talking about how they had seen baggage handlers at Chicago's O'Hare Airport – where he'd made a transfer – throwing guitars between them when offloading baggage onto the tarmac, and he complained to United. His complaint was greeted with 'complete indifference', according to Carroll, with United responding that he was not entitled to any compensation as he had not filed his claim within the twenty-four hours maximum stipulated in the airline's policy. He negotiated, unsuccessfully, with the airline for nine months, after which he decided to write a song about his experience. The result – a song called 'United Breaks Guitars' – was posted on 6 July

2009. It was an immediate sensation, watched 150,000 times on the first day of its release. Within three days it had half a million views. It took seven months for the song to be viewed ten million times, and by the time of writing it had been viewed over seventeen million times. It was a reputational catastrophe for United. Within four days of the video being uploaded, United's share price had fallen ten per cent, wiping US $180 million off the company's value. Carroll went on to write and release two further songs about United, charting not only the events of that day but also United's response and the personalities of some of the people at United that Carroll had to deal with.

The Internet provided the network power that fuelled this reputation crisis – and it went viral when a motivated activist came up with a catchy narrative. Without social media, this would have remained a local story, if that. It highlights just how fast a crisis can escalate in the online world, and how broadly it can spread. For large corporations, with slow-moving chains of command, responding effectively and quickly enough to these sorts of narrative attacks is extremely difficult. This is the subject of the next section of the book, where we look at the ways in which reputations are contested, in times of crisis but also in everyday life.

PART II

REPUTATIONS
IN PRACTICE

5

MANAGING CRISIS

*It takes twenty years to build a reputation and five minutes to
ruin it. If you think about that, you'll do things differently.*
Warren Buffett

VOLATILE, UNCERTAIN, COMPLEX AND AMBIGUOUS

We disagree with Warren Buffett. As we have outlined earlier, reputation has two different dimensions – capability and character – and each of these has very different dynamics when it comes to how easy they are to lose and how long it takes to recover.

The key difference is this: capability reputations are extremely sticky, while character reputations are much more volatile. For example, once an oil company has developed a reputation for being able to find oil, based on a sustained series of discoveries over a period of time, it will take a large number of failures for that to erode. By contrast, a reputation for transparency will erode very quickly in the event that you decide to hide previously available information. Capability and character reputation dynamics are most clearly visible in a crisis.

Two things differentiate a crisis from your average week. In a crisis, we have much less time to react, and very little reliable information. The urgency and uncertainty have dramatic effects on behavioural signalling, network closure and the ability to create authentic narratives.

Time compression not only creates an environment where we have to make decisions at speed. The fact that we are being bombarded by highly relevant and often problematic information at speed from multiple different sources can overload us during a crisis. Information uncertainty compounds this pressure. So we have less time to consider information and act in a crisis, and the information that we receive tends to be incomplete and often unreliable. Even more confusing, the information that we hold to be accurate is more often than not simply the product of an overwhelming consensus. Taken together, this produces a dangerous environment where we are making instinctive decisions based on false or misleading information.

Daniel Kahneman, in his bestselling book *Thinking, Fast and Slow* (2011), explores this phenomenon, separating out our response systems into 'system one' (fast, instinctive and emotional) and 'system two' (deliberative, systematic, logical). While Kahneman's analysis was founded on behavioural economics, his findings are deeply relevant when considering the reputation implications of handling a crisis.

There is a horrible acronym used to describe the highly pressurized, time- and information-poor world in which companies operate: VUCA, which means volatile, uncertain, complex and ambiguous. Executives look back nostalgically to a time when all the necessary information was at their fingertips; when trust prevailed between different stakeholders; when they were not at risk from 'disruption', with complete outsiders reinventing the rules and making whole business models obsolete overnight; when a national champion was indeed a champion, protected from competition by a friendly government and regulators. One has to doubt whether this idealized environment ever really existed, but it is certainly true that the disruptive and dislocating forces on everyday business life have mounted.

In this section, we explore the way in which those involved in crisis navigate their way through the reputation game, the traps they fall into, and the ways in which they might rescue themselves and climb back up the ladders of the game. This section has to start with the defining crisis of our century so far, BP's Deepwater Horizon disaster in 2010, in which our three pillars of behaviour, networks and narratives are all at play.

TROUBLE ON MACONDO

'The whole experience of being hit by a bullet is very interesting and I think it is worth describing in detail,' wrote George Orwell. 'Roughly speaking it was the sensation of being at the centre of an explosion . . . I fancy you would feel much the same if you were struck by lightning.'

BP's Deepwater Horizon disaster in the Gulf of Mexico was the corporate equivalent of being hit by a bullet. It started with an explosion on the Macondo rig on 20 April 2010, with the tragic loss of eleven lives. The then CEO of BP, the hapless Tony Hayward, received a call over breakfast in London. It was Andy Inglis, BP's head of exploration and production (E&P), phoning from Houston, Texas, to say that the Macondo rig had exploded some three and a half hours before. Men were lost, the rig was blazing and oil was pouring into the Gulf. Very few facts were known and events were moving at extraordinary speed.

The first thing you realize, when you are caught up in a crisis, is the sheer speed at which everything happens. In a fast-moving situation such as Deepwater Horizon, no one has a handle on what is going on: facts and data are incomplete and contradictory, and yet you still have to make decisions. For large organizations with ponderous and bureaucratic decision-making processes, this is often a near-impossible challenge. If everyday commercial life is peacetime, you suddenly find yourself operating in the fog of war.

The BP crisis had a visceral and all-consuming impact on the company, its management and employees as well as the millions who had invested in its stock (it paid the biggest dividend of any UK-listed company and was therefore at the heart of many people's pension plans). It also ended lives and destroyed livelihoods in the Gulf, and the 203 million gallons of spilled oil had a profound impact on the environment. The accident and its aftermath cost BP half its market capitalization and required a provision of US $50 billion following intense and protracted media scrutiny. By the summer of 2016, the total cost to the company was $61.6 billion.

This was not just a crisis, but an unmitigated disaster. First and foremost, BP's *behaviours* were at fault. Following the Texas City Oil Refinery explosion in 2005 (in which fifteen people lost their lives and 120 were injured in fires and explosions at the BP-owned plant) and the Alaska pipeline oil spill in 2006, the company had sought to put safety at the heart of its operations. The company's record had attracted negative attention from US regulators, notably in the review carried out by James Baker III, former US secretary of state, on behalf of the US Chemical Safety and Hazard Investigation Board (CSB).[1] This was initiated when Lord Browne was still CEO, but its conclusions were published a couple of weeks before Hayward took over as his successor at the start of May 2007. It found that the Texas City incident was caused by 'organizational and safety deficiencies at all levels of the BP Corporation'. It identified five major safety failings in BP's US operations, including poor corporate culture, drawing comparisons with NASA's loss of the Columbia space shuttle. Following the report, BP was obliged to pay large fines, and Hayward vowed to focus like a laser on safety.

BP had been transformed from a regional player into one of the world's major oil companies by a series of bold acquisitions, notably the US $48.2 billion purchase of Amoco in 1998 and of Arco for $27 billion a year later. As a swashbuckling, entrepreneurial corporation, BP did not impose its own failsafe processes on the companies it bought. This contrasted with the approach taken by Exxon following its own environmental disaster in Alaska, when the Exxon Valdez tanker ran aground in Prince William Sound. After that catastrophe, in 1989, Exxon made it a priority to set the industry standard for safety. BP had a different philosophy, devolving considerable independence to its subsidiaries and working with third-party contractors who were not under its direct control. 'BP say they can deploy technology as good as Shell's in half the time at half the cost,' complained one competitor cited in journalist Tom Bergin's excellent *Spills and Spin* (2011). 'How can they do that? Only because they are prepared to tolerate a risk profile that we wouldn't.' Certainly, cost-cutting was endemic, in the Gulf of Mexico and elsewhere.

A balanced, sober analysis of Macondo would suggest that what happened was not solely the responsibility of BP's management: oil exploration is a dangerous and risky business and all oil companies have bad accidents from time to time. BP's internal investigation 'did not identify any single action or inaction that caused this accident. Rather, a complex and interlinked series of mechanical failures, human judgments, engineering design, operational implementation and team interfaces came together to allow the initiation and escalation of the accident. Multiple companies, work teams and circumstances were involved over time.'[2] But fair-minded analysis is in short supply during times of crisis.

The immediate cause of the accident was a failure to spot that pressure was building up in the well, and then to plug the hole. Standing twenty storeys above the ocean, fifty miles offshore, Macondo was absolutely state of the art, and should have been equipped for the highly complex technical challenge of extracting oil from thirteen thousand feet below the seabed in seas a mile deep. In fact, the rig had become known inside the company as the 'well from hell'. In March, there was a gas explosion a long way below the seabed, and the safety systems kicked in as they should, preventing oil rising to the seabed. There were then problems constructing the cement casing for the well, and safety corners were cut. On the morning of 20 April, tests showed that pressure was building up: the Transocean operators and their BP overseers convinced themselves that the readings were false. Later that night, the well blew as a toxic mix of oil, gas and slurry forced its way to the surface of the Gulf.

As a UK-domiciled but globally active corporation, BP found its reputation – literally, its licence to operate – determined by hostile forces operating in *networks* where it had little or no influence. It didn't help that its CEO was an English gentleman, whose foreign accent simply served to emphasize the company's isolation in the US. Hayward's heart was in the right place: someone had to front up the crisis, and he wanted to be the one on hand and on-site, echoing Lord Browne's response when he flew straight to Texas City at the time of the 2005 explosion. Yet Hayward was the wrong person: it needed to be someone with an American accent. (Eventually the New York-born Bob Dudley took a more prominent role.) The heads of the company's two main operating divisions were British. Its chief of media relations was Andrew Gowers, the British former editor of the *Financial Times*, who had plenty of experience of crisis communications, having worked at Lehman Brothers at the time of its collapse. BP's PR firm was Brunswick, also British, and its founder, Sir Alan Parker, spent much of the crisis on-site in Houston, impressing others in the war room with his ability to handle more than one epic situation simultaneously: he was advising the Greek government on its debt renegotiations at the time as well as a big transaction in Asia.

Although one-quarter of BP's production, nearly one-third of its reserves and more than half its refining capacity were in the US, it had limited political clout in this major market. BP was simply not well-enough connected. It had no reserve of goodwill with the White House. All the governors in the region were Republican and were keen to generate political capital out of the weakness of President Obama, who had authorized an extension of deep-sea drilling rights only weeks before the crisis struck. Obama's decision to call BP 'British Petroleum' at a key point in the disaster prompted a furious UK government response to what seemed like an attack on the reputation of the UK – but to no avail. The company became a lightning rod for anti-business sentiment in the wake of the financial crisis. Hayward and other BP bosses were summoned to the White House in mid-June and called to congressional hearings, their uninspiring performances taking some of the heat off Goldman Sachs, which was being hauled over the coals at the same time.

This was the first global corporate crisis to play out in the age of social media. *Narratives* – both those put forward by the company and those used by reputation activists – have more than any other factor come to define the crisis in reputational terms. There were ten thousand news stories a day for nearly ninety days in a row: the media treated the story as 'apocalypse now' (widespread and irrevocable environmental damage in the Gulf of Mexico), when in fact full-scale contamination of the Gulf never transpired. News and opinion were blurred as the story played out around the world, 24/7. Facts were basically irrelevant, especially for TV coverage that seized on any number of grisly images of turtles or pelicans covered in oil. There was always a jaded fisherman, near-bankrupt restaurant owner or local politician ready to go on air and denounce BP. And, from a few days into the crisis, there was a real-time feed of the oil gushing out of a hole in the ocean floor into the waters of the Gulf: unanswerable visual proof of the damage that BP was doing, and of its inability to 'plug the damn hole', in President Obama's memorable words. The saga became a national obsession, compounded by new media technology and unrelenting competition between different media channels. 'You don't manage the crisis,' comments one person who was close to events, 'the crisis manages you.'

To a large extent, it didn't matter what BP did or said to present its case: the company was presented as bungling at best and criminal at worst. Its own efforts to construct any kind of counternarrative were drowned out by media hostility and also by its inability to 'plug the damn hole'. That was the ineluctable fact that undermined BP's competence reputation, notwithstanding the unprecedented engineering and scientific talent gathered in the Gulf and at the company's control centre on the third floor of the 4 Westlake building in Houston. All sorts of ingenious plans were hatched, including drilling two relief wells and a 'top kill' operation (an unfortunate phrase, again showing just how tone-deaf BP's narrative was), which was an attempt to force mud down into the well to seal it up. It was a spectacular but ineffectual logistical and engineering response, with 31,000 people at work, 5,050 vessels and several supporting aircraft. Week after week, nothing worked. After the well was finally capped in July, there was grudging acknowledgement that BP had done as good a job as could be expected, given the extraordinary engineering challenges. That sort of understanding was in exceedingly short supply while the oil was still flowing.

BP made the situation worse with a series of communications cock-ups. The company's first response to the accident was to lay the blame on Transocean, which was operating the rig. 'It wasn't our accident,' Hayward told reporters in the early days of the crisis. But this wasn't a case of a rogue employee sneezing on a pizza: in light of the severity of the crisis, it looked like an attempt to pass the buck, as the company positioned itself for the inevitable litigation with its subcontractors.

The extraordinary time pressure is often why companies' first communications in a crisis come back to haunt them. The other reason is that the lawyers often do the scripting, and they typically have limited sensitivity to reputational aftershocks. As a communications strategy, passing on the blame was inappropriate for the highly charged atmosphere of the crisis. In this situation, companies need to ignore the lawyers, express sympathy for the victims and accept responsibility for what has happened. Before too long it dawned on BP that it needed to change its tune.

The second big narrative mistake was to play down the amount of oil flowing into the gulf. Throughout May, Hayward was telling the media that oil was spewing into the ocean at the rate of five thousand barrels per day (an estimate that in fact came from the Coast Guard). His message was that the volume was 'relatively tiny' and the environmental impact would be 'very, very modest'. 'The Gulf of Mexico is a very big ocean,' he told the *Guardian*. 'The amount of volume of oil and dispersant we are putting into it is tiny in relation to the total water volume.' In strict, scientific terms, that might have been true, but his audiences were not interested in such nuances. In June, not long after the company's top kill operation failed, a US government panel said that oil was leaking at the rate of *fifty thousand* barrels per day. A congressman cited BP's internal projections that it could flow at twice that rate. The company's credibility was savaged: how could anything it said be trusted, if it was apparently dissembling over such crucial facts? This is when Obama ramped up the rhetoric, stating: 'We will not relent until this leak is contained, until the waters and shores are cleaned up, and until the people unjustly victimized by this disaster are made whole.' He declared that he would keep his 'boot on the neck of British Petroleum'. (The company had dropped the 'British' from its name in 2000.) BP's share price collapsed, down seventeen per cent in one day, its credit default swaps suggesting that the company might go bankrupt. Overall, the stock fell fifty-four per cent between 20 April and mid-June, wiping nearly US $100 billion off its value. It was saved only on 16 June when Hayward went cap in hand to the White House to agree a $20 billion fund to meet damage claims: this served at least to plug the hole of BP's apparently limitless financial liabilities.

In late May, just after top kill had failed, Hayward gave a TV interview in which he gave a sincere apology for the accident. Then he blurted out the words that would come to define his incompetence as a communicator: 'No one wants this over more than I do. I want my life back.' Cue outraged statements from the relatives of those who had died. According to the *New York Daily News*, he was 'the most hated and clueless man in America'. It was a tactical error to make him the face of an ad campaign, promising to 'make this right'. But the bigger blunder was to head back to the UK for a weekend's recreational sailing. The media caught images of him sunning himself on his yacht at a time when fishermen in the Gulf could not leave the harbour. As White House Chief of Staff Rahm Emanuel told ABC News, 'I think we can all conclude that Tony Hayward is not going to have a second career in PR consulting.'

The well was capped on 15 July and, by the end of the month, Hayward was replaced by the American Bob Dudley. At the time of writing, BP has said that Deepwater Horizon is expected to cost it $61.6 billion.[3] Having sold off vast quantities of assets and depleted its reserves to meet its claims, BP is a much-diminished company.

What lessons can we learn? First, the roots of the crisis went back a long way. Like the explosion itself: you saw the flames and slurry on the surface, but the source was much deeper. Even before BP started making the communications gaffes for which Hayward would become notorious, the disaster can be explained in terms of legacy *behaviours* – chiefly around cost-cutting and tolerance of risk. There were other factors at work: there was an absence of leadership and a dysfunctional board. Chairman Carl-Henric Svanberg hired his own PR agency to protect his reputation, while the CEO employed separate spin doctors. Journalists love multiple sources of conflicting information, especially from inside an organization, so this fragmented messaging served to fan the flames of negative press coverage. It is the sort of situation journalists long for – the opportunity to triangulate the views of different BP executives, regulators, national politicians and oil major rivals to create a rich multi-dimensional picture of the factions at war.

BP failed in both its capability reputations and its character reputations. The failure to cap the well seriously dented its reputation for engineering excellence, and the way in which the company communicated and acted throughout the crisis sent very poor signals about the character of the organization and its leadership team.

In seeking to engage with its reputations, BP was hopeless in all three pillars of the reputation game. Its failure to address earlier warnings about safety led to the crisis and, when it came, the company was incompetent in its response. It offered an unappealing narrative by talking down the environmental impact and talking up the chances of a quick fix, and its networks were not equipped to deal with the scale of the challenge in the US market. In fact, BP was such a poor player of the reputation game, it seems the company didn't realize it was playing.

Was this all the fault of Tony Hayward, a geologist with none of the feline political instincts of his predecessor? Up to a point he was responsible, as he evidently saw Macondo as an engineering and logistical problem to be solved, rather than a reputational crisis. But laying Hayward's involvement aside, there was no organizational recognition that the company could face the risk of corporate annihilation as a result of this onslaught on its reputation. BP did not understand the politics of the world in which it operated, and it was not set up to deal with the real-time pressures of 24/7 media attention in an age when statistics about barrels per day are competing with vivid footage of gushing oil and dying pelicans.

In this, BP was not alone. As Michael Skapinker put it in the *Financial Times*, 'a Deepwater Horizon lurks in every organization.'[4] The proximate cause could come from any angle: financial mismanagement (Lehman Brothers); fraud (Siemens, Enron, Arthur Andersen, Ahold); poor culture and ineffectual business model (Deutsche Bank); technical failure (Toyota); horsemeat in the supply chain (Tesco); benzene contamination (Perrier); or cyanide poisoning (J&J in the Tylenol case); a mentally ill employee (Lufthansa). Other causes could be terrorism, NGO activism, litigation, a natural disaster or malfunctioning technology, or a fundamental breakdown in business model.

In the wake of Deepwater Horizon, many big companies with complex, global operations dusted off their disaster recovery plans and considered the implications for their own business. But how many are truly prepared?

SCHLAMASSEL

Schlamassel is a German word meaning 'a big mess'. It is a perfect descriptor for the VW emissions scandal that, at the time of writing, continues to engulf the company and the wider automotive sector.

There are no direct parallels between Deepwater Horizon and the VW emissions scandal. No one died as a result of the announcement from the US Environment Protection Agency in September 2015 that for years VW had systematically cheated emissions tests. Yet the financial and reputational implications for one of Germany's iconic companies are profound. If BP is central to the UK economy and stock market, VW is a pillar of Germany's most important sector, on which one in five German jobs depend. Along with BMW and Daimler-Benz, VW has a special status as one of the car companies that powered the *Wirtschaftswunder*, Germany's postwar industrial miracle. More recently, it has been at the forefront of Germany's export-driven success, becoming the world's second largest car manufacturer after Toyota, with annual sales of more than ten million units produced in a hundred locations in twenty-seven countries. The company employs nearly 600,000 people around the world, with brand names including VW, Audi, SEAT, Skoda, Bentley, Lamborghini and, more recently, Porsche.

On the one hand, it was a poster child for German industrial success. On the other, VW is *sui generis*, a very peculiar organization. Institutional shareholders are not as powerful as they are at comparable companies, and do not exert effective pressure to deliver profitability and transparency. Rather, it is a hybrid of government-influenced and family-controlled corporation, reflecting its historic roots. It was established in 1937 with the sponsorship of Adolf Hitler and the Nazi Party, who wanted a car for the masses. Ferdinand Porsche, the Czech engineering genius, designed a vehicle, but it was not until after the war that the VW Beetle was produced in large numbers. Its HQ is in Wolfsburg, a small city in the state of Lower Saxony, for decades right up against the border with East Germany and so cut off from the rest of the world. The Porsche branch of the family split off and established the sports car company in Stuttgart, as well as a massive car dealership in Austria.

To this day, the Porsche and Piëch cousins still control the organization, even after a painful takeover saga in which Porsche tried and failed to acquire VW, instead being swallowed up by its intended target. The perennially feuding cousins own just over fifty per cent of the company, while another twenty per cent is in the hands of the state of Lower Saxony, traditionally a bastion of the socialist SPD party. The State of Qatar owns seventeen per cent. Institutional investors own less than twenty per cent, but their interests come long after those of everyone else: the family, Lower Saxony, the unions and workforce all get special representation rights on the company's supervisory board.

It is a very German set-up, rooted in dynastic and local politics. Socialist heritage sits uneasily with the whims of warring billionaire family factions. Luxury cars meet job protection for German workers. The company is insular yet it has successfully expanded internationally. It understands global consumers, but critics have claimed it is inward looking and arrogant. It has long displayed 'corporate excess on an epic scale', according to TCI, the activist hedge fund that is agitating for major governance changes at the company. Managers almost always come from within – a classic example of a closed network: while its working practices might be made more efficient by this closure, new blood and a fresh, critical perspective are not encouraged.

The immediate cause of the crisis was the revelation by US regulators that so-called 'defeat devices' had been installed in 482,000 of VW's diesel vehicles sold in the US over the previous six years. This device is a clever piece of software that allowed the engine to detect whether it was being tested for noxious emissions, or whether it was out on the road. In the lab, the device would kick in and emissions would fall below the stringent levels set by regulators. Take the car out on the road again, and the device disengaged. It turned out that emissions could be as much as *forty times* the permitted level. VW later confessed that it had installed this software in as many as eleven million diesel cars around the world, including Audi models, from the year 2009.

The initial revelations triggered a BP-style collapse in share price, and frenzied press interest as journalists tried to work out what on earth had been going on – and for how long. Just as in the case of BP, the potential financial liabilities to the company were deemed imponderable but no doubt immense, estimates ranging from US $30 to $50 billion (though given the greater resources of VW, this has never been an existential crisis). Martin Winterkorn, the company's powerful CEO since 2007, resigned. In his apology, he added that he wasn't aware he had done anything wrong.

At the time of writing, no official explanation of what happened has been published. The company has insisted that very few people knew about the fraudulent software and it is thought that no more than ten engineers have lost their jobs. A plausible scenario is that, in the early years of the century, Winterkorn determined that VW needed to build a winning position in the US market, as Toyota had managed to do. The German company traditionally had a modest US market share, three per cent or less, and it is thought that despite years of expansion it has never turned a profit there. To build meaningful market share would mean producing the bigger cars that Americans like. The point of differentiation would have to be the company's diesel technology, which VW proclaimed as cleaner and cheaper than petrol alternatives.

Diesel engines are indeed more efficient than petrol, but more polluting. Rival companies could only meet the standards by introducing a filter using the chemical urea, which neutralized the noxious nitrogen oxide produced by diesel. This technology was costly, heavy (reducing the car's performance) and inconvenient, as customers had to go to a garage to get it filled up. Competitors scratched their heads and wondered how VW had managed to square the circle of meeting the US's stringent environmental standards while keeping costs down. 'The fact is that VW engineers could not meet the standards,' an adviser to VW told us. 'But engineers are used to solving problems, all kinds of problems. So they solved this problem with a brilliant piece of software engineering.' By cheating, VW's engineers could claim to deliver both lower costs and higher performance – the perfect proposition for the customer.

In essence, the reputational crisis was of course caused by VW's *behaviour* in installing the fraudulent technology. In a bizarre way, though, the company's *capability* reputation has not been called into question. Engineering is at the core of VW's heritage, identity and values: the famous slogan for its premier brand Audi is *Vorsprung durch Technik*, advancement through technology. In finding a fix to the emissions problem, VW demonstrated that it was smarter at engineering than its competitors. But this is true only in a narrow, amoral sense: being devious does not win the hearts and minds of customers or regulators. The reputational failing is principally one of *character* as VW's engineering expertise was put in service of a deliberate and sustained lie. 'This is like the barbarians entering the temple and breaking everything that is breakable – it is a real scandal,' comments one industrialist.

In German, they use the phrase 'drag someone over the table' to mean they have been cheated. VW has been exposed, dragging not just US regulators over the table but also millions of consumers around the world. As Damon Hill, former Formula One champion, said, 'I have one of these illegal VWs – a Passat with the two-litre diesel engine that doesn't meet emissions standards. You try to do something right for the planet by having something nice and efficient, and it turns out that it is the worst thing you could have chosen.'[5]

From now on, how can one take VW's clean diesel advertising at face value? It produced a famous commercial for the US Super Bowl showing its engineers turning into angels every time a car reached 100,000 miles: patently this company is not angelic! Why should you trust anything VW says, when it has proved itself to be institutionally mendacious? We have talked about the importance of authenticity in creating and sustaining reputations: being exposed in this way, being brought kicking and screaming to a grudging admission of guilt, shows that VW has failed an authenticity challenge on an epic scale.

In common with BP, the roots of VW's crisis go back a long way, the company's behaviours reflecting a tough corporate culture where people were expected to deliver results – in this case, increased market share in the US – without too many questions being asked about how those results were achieved. Showing the limitations of a closed network, there was clearly a governance failure. 'What happened is incredible,' comments one senior businessperson. 'It is difficult to believe that [the family owners] would have been so fascinated by their own power that they tolerated something like this.' The hedge fund TCI charges that management have long been paid too much and encouraged to take too big risks. 'The dirty secret of the VW group is that for years management has been richly rewarded with massive compensation despite presiding over a profitability and profit collapse,' TCI's Sir Chris Hohn told the *Financial Times*. 'We believe this excessive top management compensation ... has encouraged aggressive management behaviour contributing to the diesel emission scandal.'[6] The official investigation is still under way at the time of writing and there are many unanswered questions, not least – how many in the organization really knew what was going on? It beggars belief that only ten out of nearly 593,000 employees had an inkling of something that had such a material impact on the company's US business.

Another unfortunate parallel with BP is that communications gaffes have made the situation worse. The company is hugely adept in creating narratives to promote its range of cars, but less sure-footed when it comes to communicating on delicate corporate matters. Perhaps under the baleful influence of lawyers, and not helped by the need to translate from German, the firm seems incapable of issuing a straightforward statement, and has had to backtrack after making incorrect remarks – as when the new CEO Matthias Müller told an American TV station that 'we didn't lie.' That was soon retracted, as was another statement claiming that Audi had not installed any of the cheat devices. In late April 2016, VW announced it would buy back as many as 480,000 US cars equipped with the cheat software: the biggest car buy-back in history. It remains to be seen whether VW will be forced to do something similar in Europe and Asia.

VW is currently losing the reputation game and needs to relearn the rules if it is to rebuild the trust of customers and regulators around the world. (But there is not much point in launching a campaign to rebuild trust until the mass of litigation in the US is out of the way: hence perhaps its less than compelling explanations so far.) The broader question is whether the affair damages the reputation of German engineering more generally. There are parallels with the bribery crisis at Siemens, which culminated in 2008 with a US $1.3 billion settlement with US and German authorities. Again, that was a very large and *traditionsreich* (proudly traditional) German company where managers were put under extraordinary pressure to deliver results. A blind eye was turned to institutionalized corruption. So far, the spillover effect from VW to other companies and sectors seems limited, though Daimler has been obliged by the US Department of Justice to launch an enquiry into its own emissions testing, and indeed other companies are facing regulatory scrutiny, including Mitsubishi.

German engineers remain extremely competent and are beginning to think about the technology that comes after the combustion engine that their forebears invented at the end of the nineteenth century. But the VW affair reminds us there is no point in being capable if you don't play the game according to the highest ethical standards. One hopes that in Wolfsburg, and in boardrooms elsewhere in Germany, there is a realization that the VW affair has damaged their character reputation for years to come.

DENNIS KOZLOWSKI'S $6,000 SHOWER CURTAIN

On 17 January 2014, Dennis Kozlowski – once lauded as the highest-paid and most admired CEO in the world – was released from the Lincoln Correctional Facility in New York. Jailed for larceny relating to the payment of 'unauthorized' bonuses alongside charges of misuse of corporate assets, Kozlowski was granted conditional release early after serving seven years of his maximum twenty-five-year sentence. The trial provided a window into the lifestyle of the rich and powerful corporate elite, and has become one of the most infamous stories of corporate excess in modern business folklore.

For Kozlowski, it was the trial that forever tarnished his good name. He was transmogrified, overnight, from corporate titan to corporate villain, a label that has stuck with him pretty much to this day. 'My story is one of greed and avarice, maybe, but the criminality part I would debate with anybody,' he says when we meet.

Tyco was a US success story. Initially formed by an entrepreneur and investor, Arthur J. Rosenberg, the firm was built through a series of acquisitions in the security systems and semiconductor technology sector. By the time Kozlowski became CEO in 1992, the company had three divisions – fire protection, electronics and packaging. Kozlowski would, over the course of his career at Tyco, build the company into one of the most valuable companies in the US, partly driven by over one thousand corporate acquisitions. During the course of his trial, the prosecution paraded before the jury and the media evidence of his lavish personal lifestyle, funded, they argued, by the company's shareholders. Gleeful stories were told of a lavish party on the island of Sardinia, flights taken in the corporate jet and, perhaps most infamously, the expensing of a $6,000 shower curtain for his New York apartment.

Kozlowski has always maintained that he was both innocent and a scapegoat and that his payments – while large – were all fully authorized by the board. His view is that he was convicted at a time when 'superstar' CEOs were being targeted due to the collapse of a number of high-profile businesses, including Enron, due to accounting scandals. We spoke with him twice for this book – first in Oxford, where he was helping a group of academics studying the sociology of scandal, and later in the modest apartment owned by his third wife, Kimberley, situated opposite the UN in New York.

He highlights a number of important factors that affected his own reputation game. First, the role of *reputation activists* – in this instance a campaigning district attorney up for re-election and a journalist out to make his name. Ironically, Kozlowski was not the original focus of enquiry for lawmakers. At a time when the US was introducing the Patriot Act, the US district attorney's office in New York got involved in tracing the provenance of art that was imported from overseas by US citizens. Kozlowski had imported some art and he received a request for an interview from Robert Morgenthau, the US district attorney for the State of New York. Kozlowski and his advisers thought that it might be an investigation into the provenance of the art, but it soon became clear that the focus was in fact whether a sales tax had been paid. Kozlowski and his advisers were confused. He was the buyer of the art, not the seller. But Morgenthau continued to probe, and suddenly it became clear that he was after a 'big scalp'.

'Had I not been a high-profile CEO on a pedestal, I don't think that would have happened. I was a high-profile CEO and at that time there was a dot-com crash happening in the stock market and so people were looking for a scapegoat. The timing was perfect for Morgenthau, as all of a sudden people were losing money,' says Kozlowski.

In addition to Morgenthau, Kozlowski's high visibility and status made him a perfect target for a journalist out to make his name. 'In the world of business, the media loves to build you up as a superstar – and you love being put on the pedestal – but what you don't realize is that you are only going to be there a short while. The writer Mark Merrimont [who led the news reporting for the *Wall Street Journal*] was my own nemesis – he was looking for a Pulitzer Prize based on us.'

What happened next demonstrates the power of closed *networks* – in this case, power that worked very much to the detriment of Kozlowski. Several months before, Kozlowski had informed Patty Prue, Tyco's HR director, that he was considering leaving the company, having been offered a position at the Carlyle Group, a leading private equity company. Kozlowski's record in mergers and acquisitions, and his reputation within the business community for integrating these businesses successfully, made him a very attractive proposition for Carlyle, which was looking for exactly this set of skills.

Prue asked him whether there was a counter-offer that Tyco could make that would persuade him to stay. After all, Kozlowski had been with Tyco for twenty-seven years, and had been group CEO for ten. He had taken the company from making US $20 million in annual revenue to become a leading Fortune 100 company making over $40 *billion* in revenue. At its height, Tyco was worth a staggering $130 billion. To investors, he was a hero, and they did not want to lose him.

Kozlowski made a rough calculation of the amount that he would be prepared to stay at Tyco for, and replied that a sum of around US $300 million over five years was what it would take to retain him. 'I did not expect to get the $300 million that I asked for – there was a mathematical formula behind it. Tyco had offered me a factor of three times the best years over the next seven years and I said that I wanted it from the best years including the last three years, which had been very profitable, so that led to the $300 million,' he says. To his astonishment, the board agreed.

So when the issue of his investigation by the US district attorney emerged some months later, the Tyco board was unsettled. It had agreed to a remuneration package that would become the largest ever awarded to a senior executive in a US listed company – at a time when shareholders and the general public were looking for scapegoats to atone for the losses being uncovered in accounting scandals at Worldcom and Enron.

'The $300 million ask certainly had a bearing on the way that the board members reacted. They had to find a way for that payment to go away before they could deal with me. They had agreed to it, and that's the part that's crazy – this board would have given me anything I asked for. This was signed off by the directors,' says Kozlowski.

The board closed ranks. The directors hired the services of David Boyes, a corporate lawyer who was building a reputation for himself as a big shot within the ranks of the largest US corporates. 'Tyco closed the wagons and told everyone inside the company not to take my calls,' recalls Kozlowski. 'They hired David Boyes to investigate a payment that I had made to an investment banker – he was effectively running the company at that stage. He did more than anyone else on this to advance his own agenda and reputation.'

This leads us to the narrative element. Boyes persuaded the Tyco board to include in its quarterly financial report (called a 10Q) details of a corporate party in Sardinia that Kozlowski had signed off on, as well as the now infamous purchase of the shower curtain. 'It was on the moment of the publication of the 10Q in August 2002 – which had details of the Sardinian party and the shower curtain and all of that – that my reputation was destroyed,' Kozlowski says. 'The board were protecting their own reputations back at the country club. They separated themselves from me. And they were also scared of the legal situation too – John Moscow [deputy chief of investigations at the US district attorney's office in New York] was an attorney who had a dogged reputation for chasing people down and he threatened to indict lots of senior people on the board.'

Kozlowski had lost the support of the one group within the network who could have advocated for him most effectively – and whose testimony and recollections could have helped exonerate him from the charge of wrongdoing. But, crucially, Kozlowski was now faced with even worse – not just a board that would not advocate for him but a weak board that was motivated to act against him. This is how Gary Alan Fine's theory of contested reputations works in real life. The board now had clear personal reasons not to contest the allegations being made by the prosecutors. Kozlowski was on his own.

So what of Kozlowski today? This question is particularly pertinent as it sheds light on the vexed question of whether people who have been damaged by scandal can ever recover their reputations.

Kozlowski today is a man mellowed by his experience. Gone is his trademark brusqueness and impatience. Talking with him about his experience in jail, and the ramifications for his personal life, reveals a man who is reflective about what motivates our actions. He speaks with a wisdom that can only come from being forced to face himself in the most basic of contexts, stripped of the trappings of success.

On leaving prison, he understood clearly that he would not be accepted within most of the social circles that he had enjoyed before prison. He was also unwelcome in the charitable circles that had courted him when he was able to sign large corporate and personal cheques. But he has found that his specific reputation for deal-making has remained intact – his competence was never called into question – and this particular skill set holds value. He has set up a consultancy providing advice on mergers, and has been hired by a number of small to mid-size companies whose CEOs know Kozlowski has a valuable perspective to bring.

'For CEOs who have hired me since coming out of jail, they have had to do a sales job with their colleagues,' he comments when we meet in New York. 'I have also used a number of these people as references.'

For Kozlowski, there was a light at the end of the tunnel, but only in specific areas where he has an authentic edge. In February 2016, he was appointed chairman of the Fortune Society, which helps ex-offenders re-enter the community on release from prison, and also explores alternatives to prison. He has been active within the Fortune Society since getting involved in a work-release scheme organized by the charity from 2012 onwards, and he is absolutely passionate about it. 'I'm doing all I can to make a difference at the Fortune Society. And perhaps more importantly, I learned to enjoy the value of freedom and personal relationships,' he says. Although certain opportunities are now closed to him, his reputation has now begun to grow anew in a more positive direction.

THE PEOPLE'S POPE

Before his election in March 2013, Pope Francis had given perhaps four or five interviews in his entire career, and one to a parish maga-zine in his native Argentina. None of this suggested that Jorge Mario Bergoglio, the surprise choice as 266th pope, would display a genius for rebuilding reputation through word and deed. Those around him speak in awed tones of the Holy Spirit at work: the seventy-six-year-old Pope Francis proved instantly assured in transmitting a message of absolute humility.

Jorge Mario Bergoglio is the first non-European pope in 1,272 years and, as a Jesuit, the first from a religious order. The former archbishop of Buenos Aires, the lower-middle-class son of Italian immigrants, was the ultimate outsider, elected with a mandate for institutional reform and spiritual regeneration. The Church was mired in sex and financial scandals, its core teachings increasingly ignored, even by the faithful. Nearly eighty per cent of the 1.2 billion Catholics around the world support the use of contraceptives, and everywhere apart from Africa and the Philippines a majority of believers are tolerant of divorce and remarriage.[7] In May 2015, Ireland became the first country to legalize gay marriage by popular vote, an affront to Catholic teaching that was voted through by a resounding majority of a population disgusted by decades of sex abuse in Church institutions. The Church has a vigorous following in Africa, Latin America and the Philippines, but is moribund in its historic European heartland. In France, Ireland, Spain and even Italy, young men do not want to become priests and congregations have fallen dramatically. The tide of faith was going out, and Pope Francis was the man to stop it.

The first sign of the new pope's talent as a communicator came in the Mass to celebrate his election: standing on the balcony of St Peter's, going against convention, Bergoglio asked the crowds to pray for him, rather than the other way round. This was a revolutionary narrative gesture, signalling that the power of the pope, the ineffable magnificence of St Peter's and the Church at large, existed to serve the people. That first day, his narrative was strikingly informal. 'The same day the pope was elected, the first words he said were "Buona Sera",' comments Stefano Lucchini, a senior Italian businessman with strong links with the Vatican. 'Normally there would be very formal words like, "I am here with a very big task. I am here for you," and so on. Everyone was very surprised – he was using Everyman language.'

Lucchini highlights a critical initial behavioural signal – one that expert Vatican-watchers around the world found very significant: 'The second thing he did, which was a big behavioural signal, was to spend only a few minutes in the waiting room once he had been elected. Popes past have spent up to two days in that room, praying and thinking about the role that they are taking on. He spent just a few minutes. People found that very interesting and important – a signal of the type of pope that he would become.' He was signalling a more informal papal style than his predecessors, refusing to stand on ceremony or to keep others waiting.

With the Church divided and wounded, and the world hostile, this immediate behaviour, supported by his down-to-earth narrative, touched the hearts of millions, breaking down the barriers that separate the pontiff from the people. It was just what the Church needed after the previous pope, the cerebral Joseph Ratzinger, Benedict XVI, became only the second head of the Church in a thousand years to abdicate, in the wake of the so-called Vatileaks scandal, in which leaked documents exposed corruption and nepotism in the functioning of the Vatican Bank and the central bureaucracy known as the Roman Curia.

The overall message of humility was reinforced by his choice of name: he was the first pope to be named after St Francis of Assisi, a man of peace and poverty. As if allergic to the trappings of office, the day after his election, he turned up to settle his own bill at the *pensione* where he had been staying. He carried on wearing the comfortable, ugly black shoes he had always worn, rather than papal slippers. He went to the optician's to buy his own glasses. He travelled to official functions in a blue Ford Focus, rather than the official Popemobile.

His behaviour-led strategy continued. He chose to live in Room 201 of the Casa Santa Marta guesthouse adjacent to St Peter's, rather than the papal apartments where his predecessors held court. He later explained his decision in terms of wanting to remain close to people and to ordinary life, observing that the papal apartments were not as grand as might be expected, but were like an 'inverted funnel', very difficult for people to enter.

Then there were the official visits. Again, his actions sent clear messages about the type of pontiff that he aimed to be. His first official trip inside Italy was not to Milan, Venice, Florence or even Assisi, but to the island of Lampedusa off the south coast, so often the first port of call for literally shipwrecked humanity. He was reclaiming the role of pope as the spiritual shepherd of refugees, the poor of the world, the immigrants and outcasts. In this spirit, he sacked Franz-Peter Tebartz-van Elst as Bishop of Limburg in Germany, after the latter allegedly spent €31 million restoring his official residence. In Lampedusa, Pope Francis talked poignantly of a 'globalization of indifference', words that put him on the side of the losers in the globalized economy, rather than the rich, powerful and successful. In another interview, he explained that he sees the Church as a field hospital after a battle. 'The thing the Church needs most today is the ability to heal wounds and to warm the hearts of the faithful; it needs nearness, proximity . . . Heal the wounds, heal the wounds . . . and you have to start from the ground up.' This is the vivid language of the people's pope.

His first trip overseas was to Brazil, in July 2013, which culminated in an open-air Mass attended by an estimated 3.5 million people on the Copacabana beach. At one point, his car took a wrong turn in downtown Rio and he seemed to rather enjoy the resulting chaos as the car got stuck and he was mobbed. On the flight back to Europe he held an informal press conference with a crowd of journalists and uttered the remark that suggested the beginning of a new era of tolerance for the Church. What did he think of homosexuality, he was asked. 'If a person is gay and seeks God and has goodwill, who am I to judge?' he replied. It was immediately seen as a statement of tolerance and humility. On closer scrutiny, it was a reiteration of his long-standing position that being homosexual was not a sin, even if homosexual acts are sinful. Pope Francis had not declared himself a liberal, yet that is how his remarks were interpreted in many parts of the world. His statement expressed his belief in divine mercy and God's grace in a fallen world.

These early behaviours led to a surge in the popularity of the Church, as measured by the 6.6 million people who visited papal events at the Vatican in the first nine and a half months of his reign in 2013. This figure has dropped since his first year, but remains a spectacular improvement on the ratings of Pope Benedict, who had just 2.3 million visitors in 2012.[8]

The paradox is that although the pope is head of state as well as head of the Church, operating out of the most magnificent HQ in history, his executive power is constrained. Successive popes have struggled to impose their authority on the world around them, especially over Church bureaucracy.

While popularity does not keep him in office, it does buy him political capital. This is put to work behind the scenes in the exalted realm of international relations, where Pope Francis has the credibility to bring together heads of state from long-term enemies such as the US and Cuba, mobilizing a wide set of different global networks.

Both Barack Obama and Raul Castro have praised his influence in promoting the thaw in relations between these two countries. In receiving Queen Elizabeth II at the Vatican in April 2014, he helped smooth relations between the UK and Argentina, still at loggerheads over the status of the Falkland Islands (known as the Islas Malvinas in South America). He has also used his status to help broker a peace process between the Colombian government and FARC militants.

Network capital was also on display during Pope Francis's visit to the US in September 2015. He was met personally on arrival at the airport by President Obama and, over the course of the next six days, addressed the General Assembly of the United Nations in New York; served food to the homeless at St Patrick's Church, Washington DC; gave a speech to Congress on Capitol Hill; held an open-air Mass for hundreds of thousands gathered in

Philadelphia; and met with victims of sex abuse. He complemented this broad network strategy with a powerful narrative, delivering uncomfortable messages about the need to relieve debt and alleviate poverty, and annoying conservatives by suggesting that unfettered capitalism was not the answer to the world's problems. He argued that politics and economics had a sacred duty to serve humanity.

'Above and beyond our programmes, we are dealing with men and women who live, struggle and suffer, and are often forced to live in great poverty, deprived of all rights,' he told the UN. He argued for a minimum standard of living, not a minimum wage. 'This absolute minimum has three names, lodging, labour, land ... lodging, dignified and properly remunerated employment, adequate food and drinking water.' He spoke out on climate change, denouncing 'a selfish and boundless thirst for power and material prosperity'. (In June, he had published *Laudato Si'*, the first papal encyclical on the subject.) There is no one else in the world who could speak with such impact and authority on behalf of the downtrodden, and jolt the world's elite out of the state of globalized indifference he identified early in his tenure. He displayed an extraordinarily 'deft juggling of spirituality, politics and economics', according to David Smith, former White House correspondent.[9]

It is sometimes easier to achieve foreign policy successes than deal with intractable issues of domestic reform, but soon after Pope Francis's election, he took a series of measures to shake up the Curia and introduce transparency and professional best practice to the way the Vatican Bank is run, setting up a commission for addressing the economic and administrative structure of the Holy See (the COSEA). He also appointed a board for the handling of sex-abuse cases, which was designed at last to override the Church's default instinct to protect itself over the rights of the most vulnerable in society. This kind of work lacks the arresting impact of his pastoral outreach, but in focusing on this area he has understood that breaking up the historically insular and closed networks will be crucial to effecting reform and reputation recovery. It is also critical to the pope's competence reputation: an inability to get a grip on the administrative machinery of the Church was what brought down Benedict, after all.

Pope Francis's spirituality and genius for communication count for little against the resistance of Vatican bureaucrats, and he has suffered his own leak scandal. In November 2015, two books appeared containing scurrilous stories about cardinals living in opulent apartments, petty corruption among Vatican employees, money for sainthood and so forth. The books, written by Italian journalists Gianluigi Nuzzi and Emiliano Fittipaldi, were based on confidential documents leaked by members of the pope's commission.

The bizarre aspect of Vatileaks II, as this affair is known, is that the revelations were not in themselves shockingly new, but were flushed out as a result of Pope Francis's reforming zeal. 'For once, this is not a case of an institution trying to hide its dirty laundry,' explains Vatican-watcher John L. Allen. 'The commission whose documents were leaked was created by Francis in 2013 for the express purpose of documenting financial misconduct so that it could be remedied.'[10] Here was a case of reform causing a scandal, rather than scandal triggering reform. Three Vatican employees were arrested, including a Monsignor and the glamorous PR executive and former member of COSEA, Francesca Chaouqui. In October 2015, Pope Francis felt compelled to apologize for unspecified scandals 'in Rome or the Vatican'.

Another aspect of papal competence is the ability to prevail on matters of doctrine. Notwithstanding his theoretical infallibility in such matters, the process of getting the Church to embrace change is long-winded and highly political. Synods of cardinals and bishops need to be convened, and deeply held convictions overturned. The pope's position is not helped by the fact that senior clergy have devoted their lives to thinking about these issues, and have the benefit of a literal pulpit to make their views known. They enjoy considerably more independence than, for example, company executives standing in the way of a CEO's restructuring programme, or recalcitrant politicians in a government ministry. Executives can be fired, politicians ousted. On occasions, Pope Francis has resorted to similar tactics, for example demoting the outspoken US Cardinal Raymond Burke, but this kind of raw power is not inexhaustible.

One very specific issue where Pope Francis is profoundly at odds with conservative elements in the Church is that of communion for the divorced and remarried. For lay people and liberals, it seems a matter of basic human decency that those who have remarried should be able to participate in the central ritual of the Church. But this is contrary to Church doctrine, which does not recognize the legitimacy of divorce. So if you remarry you are actually adulterous and you must be denied the sacrament as you are in a state of sin. At a crucial synod when this issue was debated, Pope Francis fulminated against 'closed hearts that hide behind the Church's teachings'. It might be difficult for a liberal newspaper, or the authors of this book, to disagree with him here, but that is not how many Catholics think. His exhortation, *Amoris Laetitia*, the joy of love, could have been an opportunity to clarify matters: but when this was published in the spring of 2016, there was no abolition of ambiguity, just a coded reference buried in footnote 351. This pusillanimity in matters of doctrine where he is supposed to be all-powerful, and where he has strong convictions, points to the real constraints on his authority. As one Catholic journalist wrote, he looked 'less like a supreme pontiff and more like a prime minister who has failed to get a bill through parliament'.[11]

Another sensitive issue is the tolerance of homosexuality. This is an unusually delicate issue for the Church, given its historically static attitudes towards sexuality in general. It is Church doctrine that prevents priests being married, not the teaching of Christ, and it has led to an all-male hierarchy in which it is hardly surprising that homosexuality should be prevalent. This was confirmed in the spectacular 'coming out' of Krzysztof Charamsa, a Polish priest working in the Vatican, who chose the eve of Pope Francis's second synod on the family in October 2015 to tell the press that he had a boyfriend, and that many other priests did as well. Both Benedict and Francis have talked about a mysterious 'gay lobby' at work inside the Church. As one would expect, Francis has extended words of tolerance and empathy to gay people, but this does not amount to a change in the official Church position that gay sex acts are 'intrinsically disordered'.

If reputation were a simple matter of attracting bigger crowds, one might be tempted to say: job done, reputation restored. But the Church cannot judge its performance in this way. It is not a company measuring its success in terms of sales and profits, nor a government seeking to win votes. It teaches a body of doctrine that is held to be morally correct, even if uncomfortable or out of step with modern society; it sets out to be a rock of truth in an ocean of uncertainty and moral relativism. It is meant to be immutable, certain, coherent. Just because most Catholics desire a certain outcome, that does not mean the Catholic Church will overturn its teaching. Nor will the Church extend its blessings to homosexuals, just because liberal opinion believes this the warm-hearted thing to do. Its strict views on abortion are not for negotiation, either. Narrative consistency has always been central to the reputation of the papacy.

The Church has a 'perverse and idiosyncratic relationship' with believers, says Catholic author Peter Stanford, refusing to change its offering despite being out of step with the beliefs and practices of its spiritual 'customer base'. A supermarket would go out of business if it so consistently ignored what its customers want to hear. But the Church is in the business of saving souls, and no one has devised a key performance indicator to tell you how successful it is in achieving that goal.

The Church does not exist in a vacuum, however. Over the centuries, it has adapted to the changes in society around it, sometimes very slowly indeed – it took the Church more than 350 years to recognize the truth of Galileo Galilei's observation that the earth moves around the sun, rather than the other way round. In the Middle Ages, the teachings of St Francis led to spiritual revival; at the time of the Renaissance, the Church was able to re-energize itself with the Counter-Reformation, a renewal of the Church's spiritual and temporal authority in response to the rise of Protestantism. In the late nineteenth century, it came up with the doctrine of infallibility in matters of doctrine, at the moment that the temporal powers of the Vatican were most under threat. In the latter half of the twentieth century, the Second Vatican Council led to adjustment to the culture and values of the Swinging Sixties, if not outright accommodation. These are seismic shifts that take place over generations, their workings so complex and mysterious that it may be wiser to attribute them to the influence of the Holy Spirit than to the decisions of mortals.

So, Pope Francis's third strategy in playing the reputation game has been the successful use of narrative. It is worth noting that the Church has a powerful heritage in this regard – the story of Christ's birth, life, crucifixion and resurrection is perhaps the most compelling in history, shaping civilizations for two millennia. As Vicar of Christ, the pope has special storytelling powers. He is the custodian of the *magisterium*, the authority to give the true interpretation of the gospel, vested in Peter by Jesus, and passed down like a spiritual baton from pope to pope over the millennia. And this narrative strategy has the power of an unrivalled global network, one that provides the opportunity to reach out to the mass of humanity. He can communicate the old-fashioned way, his sermons and papal bulls read out in tens of thousands of churches around the world, reinforced by hundreds of millions of private conversations between priests and worshippers in the confessional. And he has at his disposal the apparatus of the modern media, for example TV, radio and the Internet. Like any modern corporation or government department, the Vatican has a website and employs seasoned PR professionals, including a former correspondent for Fox News (Greg Burke). It has a radio station and Twitter accounts in multiple languages. Pope Francis today is leveraging all of these network channels, realizing that he can be the ultimate network broker, using his status to reach out across network gaps to new, or lapsed, followers – and in doing so increase the power of the Church's reputation.

While Pope Francis has taken the use of social media to new heights of influence, the Church has in fact long been at the forefront of proactive communications: in 1622, Pope Gregory XV set up the Propaganda Fide, a PR department designed to promote the faith in the New World and fight off Protestantism in the Old. Last century, Pope John Paul II (Karol Wojtyla, the so-called Polish Pope, who reigned from 1978 to 2005) had an instinctive grasp of the power of the new technology of TV, travelling constantly, visiting 129 countries and covering 1.2 million kilometres or more, giving TV interviews wherever he went. He embraced modern media technology to promote doctrinal and social conservatism, while pursuing a selectively radical political agenda: he campaigned indefatigably against communism and he was arguably as much responsible for the fall of the Soviet Union as President Ronald Reagan. Even his death agony was turned into a TV spectacle. Pope Benedict XVI (2005–13) was the first pope to use social media, sending the first papal tweet from his iPad in December 2012 using the handle @Pontifex. 'Dear Friends,' he wrote, 'I am pleased to get in touch with you through Twitter. Thank you for your generous response. I bless all of you from my heart.' Though not a gifted communicator, the eighty-five-year-old pope soon had one million Twitter followers. 'The Internet . . . offers immense possibilities for encounter and solidarity,' Francis said in June 2014, reflecting an unusually thoughtful perspective on the purpose of social media communications. 'This is something truly good, a gift from God.'[12] With an estimated more than thirty million Twitter followers at the end of 2016, Pope Francis is one of the world's most influential global leaders on Twitter, each tweet being retweeted nearly ten thousand times. (There are some quandaries at this intersection of an ancient institution and the Web: if the pope makes a typo, is the typo infallible?)

Pope Francis's authority is underscored by his authenticity. His decision to live in a hostel and eschew the trappings of office is not an act: there is no dissonance between the way he is and the way he is perceived. This goes back to his early career in Argentina, where he spurned the official limousine and travelled on public transport. He lived in a modest apartment, even when made archbishop of Buenos Aires and then cardinal. He was nicknamed the Slum Bishop because of his engagement with the very poor. He washed the feet of prisoners and patients and slum-dwellers on Holy Thursday.

When asked who he is, Pope Francis invariably replies: 'I am a sinner.' He sees himself as a man who has made mistakes in life. Before his election, he had often been accused of being complicit in the arrest and torture of two Jesuit priests during Argentina's Dirty War (1976–86). The allegations were refuted, but he has always conceded that he could have done more to fight the murderous regime.[13] He has also owned up to other failings, not least being too dictatorial and divisive when put in charge of the Jesuits in Argentina at the age of thirty-six (a job he held from 1973 to 1979). He caused so much trouble that for a while he was in effect exiled from Buenos Aires to the city of Córdoba, and it was said in jest when he eventually became pope that the Jesuits had contrived the election to get him out of the country. Pope Francis considers himself touched by God's mercy, and mercy is at the heart of his mission. His papal motto is *Miserando atque eligendo* ('by having mercy and by choosing') and in December 2015 he declared a special jubilee year of mercy. For non-believers, there may be something patronizing in his wish to extend God's mercy to gay people and divorcees – to be a beneficiary of God's mercy you have to have committed a sin in the first place. But it implies tolerance and empathy, qualities not associated with more doctrinaire religious leaders.

So in evaluating Pope Francis's reputation, one has to ask: what is the reputation for, and who is it with? He has enhanced his reputation with liberal and secular society at the cost of his popularity with conservative believers. This is born out in poll data from the US, which shows the pope's popularity improving with non-Catholics, while declining with believers. Even practising Catholics are likely to approve or disapprove of reform, depending on whether they are liberal or conservative. If anyone can navigate these uncertainties, and juggle these multiple constituencies, it is Pope Francis, a man of humility with a genius for communication and empathy. With a little more help from the Holy Spirit, let's hope he will prevail.

BLAIR VERSUS CLINTON: REPUTATIONAL LEGACIES IN FOCUS

Once in office, the pope does not have to worry about fighting another election, and can focus on the core business of saving souls. By contrast, politicians in democratic societies are in the business of getting elected and, whatever else they may achieve, their competence reputation is critically dependent on their ability to win elections, time and time again.

Political reputations are notoriously fickle: Winston Churchill was a great wartime leader, but was voted out by a seemingly ungrateful electorate in 1945. Margaret Thatcher was a highly popular if divisive leader in her day, but died reviled by many. Jimmy Carter and John Major left office under a cloud of mediocrity, but their reputations recovered the longer they were out of office. Donald Trump took office as the forty-fifth president of the US amid an unusual degree of recrimination and division, millions gathering around the world to protest at his sexism and much else besides. His supporters, however, celebrated his election as a triumph akin to the second coming.

This reputational volatility reflects the special circumstances of politics, where the rules of the game are very different from business.

Tony Blair, prime minister of the UK from 1997 to 2007, and Bill Clinton, president of the US from 1993 to 2001, were remarkably competent politicians. Blair won three general elections in a row, the first two of which were landslide victories. This followed four successive electoral defeats for the Labour Party. He managed to unify the party, no mean feat in the light of its self-destructive, fissiparous tendencies. And he stepped down from office after ten years, at a time of his own choosing, without a knife in his back, handing over to his nominated successor, Gordon Brown. This was a rare achievement: even Thatcher, the dominant political figure of the 1980s, was eventually dethroned by her own party.

The tide has turned dramatically for Tony Blair: at the time of writing, he is a pariah in the UK, his interventions in the Brexit debate thoroughly disregarded.

Blair took power aged forty-three, Bill Clinton was first elected president at the age of forty-six, the third youngest in the history of the US. He won two elections, the first Democrat to pull this off since Franklin D. Roosevelt. Clinton presided over the longest peacetime expansion of the economy in US history. He spent the last three years of his second term fighting charges of obstruction of justice and perjury following his notorious liaison with White House intern Monica Lewinsky. He squeaked clear of impeachment after the Senate overturned the earlier decision of the House of Representatives. Thus dragged through the mud by his myriad political opponents, Clinton limped to the end of his presidency in 2001 in disgrace and with debts of $12 million after racking up enormous legal fees.

Since the two leaders left office, their fortunes have flipped. Clinton regularly polls as one of the greatest presidents of all time, the 'Big Dog' who is as popular as the pope or the late Nelson Mandela. Tony Blair is still admired outside the UK, especially in the US, and that is a nuance that we will examine in due course. But still the question that needs to be addressed is: how has Clinton played a brilliant reputation recovery game, while the formerly masterful Blair has bungled so badly?

First we have to understand that there are severe limitations on what politicians can actually do. The amount of raw power in the hands of the prime minister or president is constrained to prevent abuse of the position. It is not enough to declare that the economy should perform better or that the budget should be balanced or the National Health Service be reformed, or indeed that Vladimir Putin should behave in a more neighbourly fashion. (In fact, not even Putin can make his economy flourish when oil prices are low and Russia is subject to economic sanctions.)

A leader's authority to make things happen is bolstered by electoral success, which gives him or her control over the machinery of government, but even that is not enough to solve the intractable problems of modern economics or international relations. It is very hard to be the master of events: so many political leaders give the impression of being on the run, at the mercy of circumstance. Only once in a generation do politicians manage to break free of constraints and achieve something of real substance, such as Chancellor Kohl's success in unifying Germany, or, in Tony Blair's case, negotiating an enduring peace in Northern Ireland. One could argue that Mrs Thatcher's controversial and painful reforms of the economy have given the UK an enduring competitive advantage. For all Gordon Brown's failings as prime minister, his competence in arguing the economic benefits for the UK of staying out of the euro are plain for all to see.

Because democratic leaders' executive power is so limited, what comes to matter is how you talk about what you are doing, or are going to do. Great politicians are able to turn the sow's ear of reality into a silk purse of rhetoric. Narratives link the present with the past and the future. Typically, political stories appeal to their electorate by evoking shared experiences of hardship or collective aspirations of hope, stability and opportunity. A classic of this kind is Winston Churchill's famous 'never surrender' speech delivered to the House of Commons on 4 June 1940, after the disaster of the withdrawal from France and the relief at the Dunkirk evacuation:

> Even though large tracts of Europe and many old and famous states have fallen or may fall into the grip of the Gestapo and all the odious apparatus of Nazi rule, we shall not flag or fail. We shall go on to the end, we shall fight in France, we shall fight on the seas and oceans, we shall fight with growing confidence and growing strength in the air, we shall defend our island, whatever

the cost may be, we shall fight on the beaches, we shall fight on the landing grounds, we shall fight in the fields and in the streets, we shall fight in the hills; we shall never surrender.

These words spoke to the passions of the moment. They were authentic, direct and inspiring, as were his two other famous speeches in those perilous months for Great Britain: 'Blood, Sweat and Tears' and 'This was Their Finest Hour'. When asked years later what exactly Churchill did to win the war, his cabinet colleague and Labour leader Clement Attlee answered: 'talk about it'. Storytelling, rather than military strategy, was Churchill's great contribution, to the extent that he declared, 'History will be kind to me, for I intend to write it.'

A political leader needs a *master narrative*, a simple but inspiring framework that explains his or her fundamental political agenda. Think of 'Make America Great Again', a slogan so successful in Ronald Reagan's 1980 presidential campaign that it was borrowed by Donald Trump for his 2016 campaign. Ronald Reagan was a genius in this respect: he talked convincingly about the Evil Empire and his words led to the fall of communism. (When you think about what Reagan actually *did* in the foreign policy sphere, invading Grenada, investing in a missile shield, and overseeing the Iran–Contra scandal do not suggest a hyperactive agenda: but his rhetoric was still highly effective.) In Bill Clinton's case, the message was delivering prosperity and well-being for middle-class Americans. His mastery of his brief earned him the sobriquet Explainer-in-Chief.

Tony Blair sought to deliver social justice and improved public services, while balancing the nation's books, being friendly to business and appealing to middle-class voters whose aspirations had long been ignored by the Labour party. 'A day like today is not a day for soundbites,' said Tony Blair on 7 April 1998 as he was about to announce the Good Friday Agreement ending the conflict in Northern Ireland, 'but I feel the hand of history upon our shoulder with respect to this, I really do.' Excusing the element of inadvertent self-parody, this was Blair the communicator at his finest.

Politicians need to be able to utter the memorable phrase that can be translated into a newspaper or television headline.

Like classical orators, politicians also need to project *ethos*. Personal credibility comes from having something in common with the voter. In this respect, Clinton was especially effective, with a roguish appeal for many Americans. Despite philandering and allegations of corruption (as evidenced by the Whitewater scandal dating from his time as governor of Arkansas), his own story was of a poor white boy made good through hard work, guile and command of policy. This was a version of the American dream that resonated with tens of millions of voters, especially the Black and Hispanic communities.

Perversely, the impeachment attacks from political opponents increased his popularity, as significant numbers of Americans felt that he was being victimized and subjected to double standards. He also exercised a disarming personal charm that worked on political opponents as well as fans. One senior American businesswoman recalls being presented to the president at the White House at the height of the Lewinsky scandal. 'I was determined to be stony-faced and cold in his presence,' she says. 'I was there for professional reasons but there was no way I was going to like him. But after he had spoken to me for a moment or two, I melted, I was like putty in his hands. He had the ability to make you feel you were the only person in the room.'

Blair's personal narrative was also authentically in tune with the times, albeit in a different context. Here was a Labour politician from a privileged background (public school, Oxford, the bar) who was not going to be an enemy to the middle classes. Far from it, he was one of them, who shared many of their aspirations, not least a healthy respect for making money and a taste for luxurious holidays in Tuscany. The film star Michael Caine, a millionaire from a working-class background, has said he voted for Tony Blair because Blair was a right-wing Labour politician, just as he voted for David Cameron because Cameron was a left-wing Tory. Millions of other voters felt the same.

We can take networks almost for granted: politicians have instant access to the world's political, business, cultural and media elite, their words and actions attracting a disproportionate share of attention. This gives politicians an unrivalled opportunity to disseminate their stories to vast audiences. Even though many ordinary people find politics quite tedious, the press and politicians have a mutual interest in turning politics into a form of showbusiness. In the US of Donald Trump, like the Italy of Silvio Berlusconi, there is increasingly little distinction between politics and soap opera: one reason for Trump's stunning electoral victory was his celebrity as a former reality TV star and instinct for a headline. 'This gave him a direct reputation with the American people that bypassed the usual channels,' comments Ed Reilly, a veteran political campaigner and now Washington-based chief executive of FTI Consulting's Strategic Communications business. 'None of us [in the political establishment] thought he was a known commodity and we grossly underestimated him as a result. In fact, American people know his character and his behaviours and were prepared to forgive his rough edges. Donald Trump is everyman's version of what a rich and successful businessman should look like. He looks the part to the working class.'

Certainly, politicians themselves devote an obsessive amount of attention to the media, seeking to ensure that their own actions are conveyed in as positive a light as possible. It was only later in Tony Blair's political career that he started disregarding what appeared in the morning's press, and began to have an almost messianic desire to pursue what he was convinced was the right course of action, whether or not it proved popular with the public.

Spin occurs when the story told begins to diverge too far from the reality. It's a particular occupational hazard for politicians. Since it is so hard for politicians to deliver tangible results, they have so much more incentive to exaggerate their achievements, to build castles in the air as they promise more than they will ever be able to achieve. The electoral calculus is finely balanced, and there is a default assumption that it is worth fighting for every headline, on the basis that a positive or negative interpretation is going to sway a marginal voter one way or another. A culture of spin, combining aggressive and adversarial press briefings, is part and parcel of politics at all times, but was especially acute in the era of Tony Blair and his successor, Gordon Brown. Spin doctors briefed against the opposition, but like the rival factions in Clarence House and Kensington Palace when the marriage of Prince Charles and Princess Diana was falling apart, they also briefed against each other, with gusto. These were the modern PR equivalent of ancient *flyting* competitions, when Scottish bards would compete to deliver the most elaborate and wounding insults.

This dynamic creates a reputational paradox: the qualities required to be a competent politician tend to leave you with a poor character reputation. Or as Niccolò Machiavelli put it five hundred years ago: 'Princes who have achieved great things have been those who have given their word lightly, who have known how to trick men with their cunning, and who, in the end, have overcome those abiding by honest principles.' A politician almost certainly has to lie and cheat to get elected, and then once in office he or she has to lie or cheat some more. As one former close adviser to a British prime minister explains, you get elected by 'erecting a totem pole with a bunch of different symbols hanging from it with the aim of getting as many people to dance around as possible'. You cannot make appeals only to people from your own tribe. That was Tony Blair's electoral genius, his true competence as a politician: to extend the appeal of the Labour party from its working-class heartlands to the mass of the middle class. Subsequent attempts to reverse this New Labour strategy have proven disastrous for successive leaders, from Gordon Brown and Ed Miliband to Jeremy Corbyn – though the latter was surprisingly successful in broadening the appeal of his left wing policies in the UK general election of June 2017. By definition, if you are seeking to appeal to a coalition of people who will not naturally agree with one another, you have to stretch the truth – to trim, to use clever, ambiguous formulations that are acceptable to the broadest possible group of people.

Once you get voted in, there is no let-up: the dodging and diving has to continue. As Otto von Bismarck, the great Prussian chancellor, remarked – no gentleman should know how laws or sausages are made. One might go into politics with the best intentions, but along the way one is inevitably forced to make messy compromises that undermine one's ideals. Sometimes these flip-flops of principle lead to enduring political power, but they can undermine you for ever – as in the case of Liberal Democrat leader Nick Clegg's betrayal of his pre-election promise that people should not have to pay tuition fees for university education.

Under these circumstances, it is no wonder that voters have a fundamentally cynical and untrusting view of politicians. The Germans have a lovely word to describe the state of disillusionment with politicians and the political process: *Politikverdrossenheit.* This prevails in most modern democracies, from the US to Germany, France and the UK, and is driving the popularity of extremist parties at both ends of the political spectrum. Large numbers of eligible voters express their contempt by simply not turning up to vote, while those who do hold their leaders in low regard. Every now and again, new leaders emerge who hold the promise of a change in spirit and substance. Part of Donald Trump's appeal to wide swathes of the US electorate was his promise to 'drain the swamp' of Washington politics: whether he does represent a substantive break with the past remains to be seen.

President Clinton left the White House in January 2001 with big personal debts and a reputation tarnished not merely by his near impeachment, but also by the long-standing Whitewater case. Ex-presidents typically establish libraries and foundations, and in his early years as a private citizen, he did the same from his new base in Harlem. There were charitable initiatives to fight HIV/ AIDS, obesity and other conditions, a climate change programme, and a magnificent library in Little Rock, Arkansas. Despite the overhang of ill-will, Clinton retained extraordinary charisma and appeal, as much with the rich and powerful of the world as with ordinary people.

The vehicle for the transformation of Clinton's fortunes, in all senses of the word, was the Clinton Global Initiative (CGI), established in 2005 alongside his charitable foundation. The CGI did not dispense charitable donations; rather it brokered deals between big companies and governments to achieve very specific objectives, for example to finance clean water in India, small business development in Africa or boosting production of rice in Mali. Before (in late 2015) the Clintons announced that it would be wound down, it was at the heart of what one critical journalist has described as a 'sprawling philanthropic empire like no other'.[14] Detractors pointed to a lack of transparency, and to dealings with dictators and unsavoury billionaires, and to a blurring of philanthropic objectives with personal enrichment. Incontestably, the CGI did a great deal of good in the world, securing pledges of US $85 billion between 2005 and 2013. It also made Bill Clinton very rich: he earned US $103 million in speaking fees between 2001 and 2013. But it was also controversial and Hillary Clinton's ready association with the rich and powerful confirmed her reputation with ordinary Americans as a quintessential member of the remote and uncaring elite – one factor behind her electoral defeat.

In the US, making money is self-evidently a worthwhile objective; that is not the case in the UK, as Tony Blair has found. It is now forgotten that when Tony Blair finally stepped down as leader in 2007, he was given a standing ovation in the House of Commons. He was held in higher esteem than most leaders at the end of their term. Six years later, more than half of UK citizens thought he was a war criminal (according to a YouGov poll),[15] and he could barely appear at a book signing without being pelted with rotten tomatoes or threatened with a citizen's arrest. He and his wife, Cherie, have received death threats. Like Bill Clinton, he is a highly paid speaker on the international lecture circuit, and acts as an adviser to a clutch of corporations and countries around the world. But despite his Brexit interventions, his political influence at home is less than zero. He was welcomed by students at Yale, but it is impossible to imagine the students at the London School of Economics allowing him onto the premises, let alone listening politely to a disquisition on world politics. How can we explain this spectacular domestic reputation reversal?

The first point is that he lost political allies within the Labour Party at precisely the time when he needed them to engage with detractors in support of his reputation. He lost his access to the political and business elites who would have previously defended him in any reputation contest. His own party lurched to the left following its disastrous performance in the UK general election of 2010, first under Ed Miliband, who led the party into its second defeat at the polls in 2015, and subsequently under Jeremy Corbyn, who pursued policies very much at odds with the centre-left policies pursued by Blair. The result of this has been a Labour Party long seen as unelectable by many, but also one that is seeking to return to its historic left-wing values. Until the 2017 election, it seemed that the party valued authenticity over electability. Either way, the reputational cost for Blair is high. Blair, and Blairite views, are in the political wilderness, and as a result he has lost the vocal support of his political party. Timing is an inestimably important factor in politics – and in the making and unmaking of reputations.

The second factor is context change. The British people now hold him personally accountable for the disastrous medium-term consequences of the second Iraq War. The central promise made by Blair, in supporting George Bush's invasion of Iraq, was that it would make the world safer. It has achieved the reverse. The overthrow of Saddam Hussein created a power vacuum in Iraq and destabilized the entire Middle East. Already deeply unpopular in 2003, the War on Terror begat more terror. Ordinary Britons who once voted for Tony Blair do not need a sophisticated grasp of the Sunni–Shiite conflict to know that hundreds of thousands have died as a consequence of policies championed by Blair. The creation of ISIS, the increase of terrorism in Europe and elsewhere, the failure of the Arab Spring, the millions of desperate refugees, are all part of the complicated legacy of Blair's blunder into war. Even Blair himself has acknowledged, in an interview with CNN TV in October 2015, that things did not turn out as expected.

This perception is made worse by the circumstances surrounding the 'dodgy dossier' of intelligence presented to Parliament as the basis for taking the country to war.[16] The long-awaited Chilcot Inquiry found that the case for war was deficient, that the legal basis was shaky, preparations inadequate and the UK's ability to influence the US tangential at best. Critics also denounce Blair for being too close to President Bush. 'I will be with you whatever,' he told Bush eight months before Parliament approved the invasion. 'Getting rid of Saddam is the right thing to do . . . his departure will free up the region.'

In popular perception, the invasion was a crime and a blunder. In one sense, the former premier's political competence was extraordinary: he turned out to be eminently capable of making the war happen despite the normal checks and balances. His mastery of this form of political competence, cajoling and manipulating Parliament and the people to back an unpopular course of action against their better judgement, is rendered catastrophic by the passage of time. But despite his competence, he was deficient in character, ignoring the reservations of his party, the UN and the public at large, who mounted the largest mass demonstrations in history.

Blair's reputation with the British people has taken a battering, but with the international elite it could not be higher. 'I think Blair is far more highly regarded in America than he is here,' comments the chancellor of the University of Oxford and former statesman Lord Patten. 'But that has started to be affected by his conspicuous consumption – by his enthusiasm for being paid large amounts of moolah . . . Americans are very critical too of Clinton for being an avaricious bugger, but he was just such a spectacular politician.'

The fact that a former Labour leader should have made such a fortune since he left office is the final twist of the knife for the Labour faithful. At a time of austerity and growing inequality, Blair's triumph as a businessman was seen by many party members as proof that he was a man of weak character. It follows that, for many years, there has been no one in the Labour Party prepared to speak up for him or his legacy: on the contrary, his name has become a rallying cry to his opponents. (It is no accident that Corbyn helped establish the Stop the War campaign in 2001.)

Blair has hardly helped himself, by spending so much time out of the UK and nursing a barely disguised contempt for the media he denounced, in one of his final speeches as prime minister, as feral. Even when, for example, he gave the substantial proceeds from his autobiography to charity, this was interpreted as a gimmick designed to curry favour, reinforcing just how rarefied a life the former Labour premier was now leading, light years away from the experience of Labour voters struggling to live on a minimum wage.

Perhaps a forthright apology would have done the trick? As we see in the next section, this can make all the difference.

GETTING BACK IN THE SADDLE

When Sir Howard Davies was appointed chairman of Royal Bank of Scotland in autumn 2015, there were many appreciative assessments. Sir Howard, an owlish intellectual with a razor-sharp mind honed at Manchester Grammar School and the University of Oxford, took on this challenging job after a distinguished career working at the interface between the private and the public sector. The articles recounted his early jobs at the Treasury and the Foreign Office, followed by a spell at McKinsey, before becoming deputy governor of the Bank of England and the first chairman of the Financial Services Authority regulator. As a consummate 'safe pair of hands', he was also brought in by the government to conduct a review of the complex and politically sensitive question of the UK's airport capacity.

Barely mentioned in these encomia was the one incident in this glittering career where it could all have gone horribly wrong: his resignation in March 2011 as director of the London School of Economics (LSE). He resigned to protect the LSE's reputation after it emerged that the prestigious university had become too close to the Libyan regime of Colonel Muammar Gaddafi. Before Davies became the university's director, the dictator's son Saif al-Islam had been accepted first as a graduate student, then as a PhD candidate; shortly after he was awarded the higher degree in July 2009, Gaddafi junior made a £1.5 million donation to the LSE. The school also won a £2.5 million contract to train Libyan civil servants. At the Foreign Office's invitation, Sir Howard himself became economic envoy to Libya and was appointed to the board of the Libyan Investment Authority, the country's sovereign wealth fund.

Such are the treacherous, shifting sands of international geopolitics that it is easy to forget that, at the time, it was official British government policy to support normalization of relations with the former pariah state. This was the context in which Saif was taken on as a student, in the hope that his work on philosophy, policy and social values would help the Gaddafi family's stated objective of reforming the country. It also explains why Sir Howard took on the role of adviser to Libya. The UK government paid for his one and only trip to the country, and he was chaperoned by the British ambassador. He was asked to join the board of the Libyan Investment Authority by the UK government, his fees paid directly to the LSE rather than to him personally. There were many in the UK and elsewhere who hoped that if Libya pursued reform with sincerity, the country could evolve into a sort of Norway for North Africa – a bastion of peace, prosperity and democracy.

Of course, that proved to be a pipe dream, as circumstances changed dramatically in early 2011 with the outbreak of armed rebellion in Libya. In late February, Saif was pictured on TV waving a machine gun. His studies forgotten, he declared that he would 'fight to the last bullet' and that rivers of blood would run through the country. His prediction proved gruesomely right: his father was brutally killed later in the year. He himself was betrayed as he tried to escape the country and he is held to this day under sentence of death. As Libya descended into increasingly violent civil war, the LSE's close links to the regime became a matter of public embarrassment.

Had the LSE bent the rules to admit Saif as a student, and then awarded a PhD, in order to curry favour with the regime and benefit from its financial largesse? It later emerged that when the Foreign

Office sounded out the University of Oxford as to whether it might admit Saif, Oxford had simply said no, he didn't have the academic credentials for arduous postgraduate study. The LSE, however, agreed to take him, and appeared to benefit institutionally and financially as a result. At least, that's what it looked like to the media, when the tide had turned.

Sir Howard sat at his breakfast table at home reading the news, asking himself whether his own position was tenable. He quickly reached the conclusion that it simply wasn't – which in reputational terms has become one of the most important decisions he could have made. Within days of Saif's sanguinary TV appearance, Sir Howard had gone.

'I realized that I had made enough personal errors to make it very difficult for me to articulate a persuasive defence of the LSE's engagement with Libya,' he reflects. 'There was no venality here, no personal gain, and I didn't approve Saif as a student or evaluate his PhD, and I didn't ask for the money. But I was implicated, there were errors of judgement. The process of resetting the school's reputation would have been beyond me.'

As he explains it, the central error was not to question the decision to take money from Libya. 'I could have stopped it,' he says. 'It was going to fund a conference to promote democracy in North Africa, which was a worthy cause, but a more sensible risk assessment would have said that the upside was modest but the downside risk was huge.' He defends the programme to educate Libyan civil servants. Lord Woolf, who later produced a report on the school's Libyan connection, found that the LSE was lacking in the sort of risk-assessment policies that would be normal in the private sector, and had drifted into an ever deeper relationship with the regime without stopping to evaluate the implications.[17]

It was not easy for Sir Howard to resign. Elements of the LSE hierarchy put pressure on him to stay, a delegation suggesting that if he went, he would enjoy a day's gratification, but an eternity in the wilderness. 'I'll take my chances,' Sir Howard decided. His resignation statement made it clear that he had made mistakes, and that it had all happened on his watch. 'The short point is that I am responsible for the school's reputation, and that has suffered,' the statement said.[18]

There was a frenzy of press coverage as Sir Howard's distinguished career appeared to reach, if not an end, at least an intermission. Behind the scenes, Morgan Stanley and the Government of Singapore Investment Corporation considered whether to keep him on their boards, and decided after reviewing the facts that he should stay. He seemed to disappear to Paris to take up a teaching post at Sciences Po, one of the elite French universities mentioned earlier. Sir Howard didn't actually move to Paris, but he spent a few days a week there as he took on his new responsibilities. Being out of town for a while helped with the process of rehabilitation.

In the event, the speed and clarity of Sir Howard's decision stood him in good stead, as did the candour with which he addressed his own failings. It was not an explicit apology, but it had the force of one. And crucially, the speed at which he fell on his sword, accepting the blame for something that clearly was not his direct decision, testified to his strength of character. And critically, within his own elite circles, everyone understood that he had 'done the decent thing' to protect the reputation of an important institution. His character reputation was firmly on display, and the circles in which he moved would not forget it.

Had there been any suggestion of delay or personal consideration, the process of getting back into the game might have been complex or even impossible. Had he hummed and havered, he probably would have been forced out in the end anyway. But in fact, his judgement here proved spot on. As a result it was only a matter of months before the headhunters started ringing, and the big jobs started coming his way again.

Admitting fault might seem, at first glance, to signal an acceptance that you have a flaw in your competence or character (or both). But it also signals that you are actively working towards consistency and authenticity in your behaviour. On Pope Francis's first official visit to Bolivia in July 2015, he issued an historic apology to the native peoples of the Americas for sins committed by the Catholic Church during the conquest. 'I humbly ask forgiveness, not only for the offences of the Church herself, but also for crimes committed against the native peoples during the so-called conquest of America,' he said to a crowd that included many from Indigenous groups and the country's first Indigenous president, Evo Morales. 'I also want for us to remember the thousands and thousands of priests who strongly opposed the logic of the sword with the power of the cross. There was sin, and it was plentiful. But we never apologized, so I now ask for forgiveness. But where there was sin, and there was plenty of sin, there was also an abundant grace increased by the men who defended indigenous peoples.'

Pope Francis knows how to make an apology. He combined clarity – there was no doubt that he was apologizing – with sincere humility. There was also a reminder that not all priests supported the logic of bloody conquest, and some stood up for Indigenous peoples. And, like Sir Howard Davies, he got the timing right, apologizing as soon as was feasible.

History is littered with examples of apologies that have failed. What makes a good apology? Does it always lessen the damage, as intended, or does it sometimes expose us to more visibility and risk? Nicole Gillespie, of the University of Queensland's Business School, and Graham Dietz, formerly of Durham University's Business School, over many years have researched the impact of apologies. They have found that successful apologies go a lot further than saying sorry. Other elements include expressions of regret, acknowledgement of responsibility and offers of reparation – as in a practical 'making good' that goes beyond mere words. You need to say and do things that actively demonstrate benevolence and integrity. Do this repeatedly, clearly and consistently, and you can foster a sense of 'hope, faith and assurance', thus resetting the basis of the relationship with the people to whom you are apologizing.

Apple provides a halfway good example of this wider, contextualized apology. CEO Tim Cook issued an open apology to Apple's customers following the emergence of serious problems with its Maps app. Here are highlights of the text:

> To our customers,
>
> At Apple, we strive to make world-class products that deliver the best experience possible to our customers. With the launch of our new Maps last week, we fell short on this commitment. We are extremely sorry for the frustration this has caused our customers and we are doing everything we can to make Maps better [. . .]
>
> There are already more than 100 million iOS devices using the new Apple Maps, with more and more joining us every day. In just over a week, iOS users with the new Maps have already searched for nearly half a billion locations. The more our customers use our Maps the better it will get and we greatly appreciate all of the feedback we have received from you [. . .]
>
> Everything we do at Apple is aimed at making our products the best in the world. We know that you expect that from us, and we will keep working non-stop until Maps lives up to the same incredibly high standard.
>
> Tim Cook
>
> Apple's CEO

The apology contains an expression of regret ('We are extremely sorry') and an acknowledgement of responsibility ('we fell short on this commitment'). But it does not include any offer of reparation, and it also includes a bit too much self-promotion ('more than 100 million iOS devices using the new Apple Maps, with more and more joining us every day'). The last paragraph degenerates into vacuous corporate-speak, which should be avoided in all effective communications.[19]

Gillespie and Dietz's model provides a useful framework for understanding the best timing for an apology. The first of four stages is the *immediate response*: if an organization has done something wrong, it needs to acknowledge that straight away to everyone affected. This first response 'needs to be well considered, timely, and credible', they write.[20] They acknowledge that it is often difficult for organizations to have credible information early on in a crisis, but point out that silence is worse, and reflects badly on your character.

'Not offering any communication conveys a lack of concern and integrity, as well as incompetence,' they argue. 'Such "reticence" has proven ineffective for trust repair. For example, Exxon's "no comment" stance immediately after the 1989 Exxon Valdez oil spill alienated employees, communities, and the media, damaging its credibility further.'

Silence also creates a vacuum of information, which in the whirlwind stages of a crisis will most likely be filled by those who are worst affected. Not speaking up to offer some form of context or comment will at best be seen to be a signal of confusion or disorganization, and at worst a sign of indifference – or capitulation to the lawyers, who generally advise that an organization should say as little as possible.

The second stage of the process is *diagnosing the problem*. Here, there is a trade-off between timeliness and credibility. Of course, the sooner a proper explanation of what has happened is made available, the better. But if it is rushed, it just won't be believable. On balance, the greater danger is waiting too long, as organizations risk being seen as dragging their heels. It is also worth bearing in mind that the accuracy of evidence erodes quickly over time, as witnesses forget details and trails disappear.

The third and fourth stages in their model – *reforming interventions* and *evaluation* of the outcomes to ensure that they have been effective – can both be done over time. The critical thing here is making sure that they are done well, rather than quickly.

A final question: is it ever too late to apologize? We think not. In addition to Pope Francis apologizing for the actions of Catholics five hundred years ago, we saw UK Prime Minister David Cameron apologizing for the actions of British troops in Derry in 1972, a sign that the government knows it has not always been on the right side of history. This is vastly preferable to refusing to acknowledge fault, but when so much time has elapsed, the apology needs to be underpinned by an authentic narrative that shows you have learned the appropriate lessons.

THE TWELVE PROFUMO YEARS

On 13 June 1975, amid the hundreds of businesspeople and establishment worthies recognized in the Queen's Birthday Honours List, there was one name that dominated the headlines: that of John (always known as Jack) Profumo, the former government minister whom the queen made a Commander of the British Empire (CBE). Twelve years before, Profumo had been at the centre of a sex and spying scandal that had helped bring down the Macmillan government.

In early July 1961, Profumo was a guest at Lord Astor's estate at Cliveden in Buckinghamshire, when the nineteen-year-old Christine Keeler emerged naked from the swimming pool. Profumo, a married man, was then secretary of state for war in Harold Macmillan's cabinet, a man of wealth and exotic aristocratic antecedents. Though married to the actress Valerie Hobson, a great beauty who starred opposite Alec Guinness in *Kind Hearts and Coronets*, Profumo's head was turned by Keeler – just as the young woman was impressed by him (and the fact he was married to a famous film star). They met again the next day at what Lord Denning described as a 'lighthearted and frolicsome bathing party'. He asked for the girl's phone number and soon began an affair that lasted several months. This erupted into a full-blown scandal a few months later.

At the same time as pursuing her liaison with the dashing politician, Keeler was sleeping with the Russian naval attaché Yevgeny Ivanov. When Profumo was given a warning that Ivanov was probably a spy, he broke it off with the teenage model and showgirl: quite apart from the basic impropriety of the affair, this was the height of the Cold War and it was an obvious security risk for a minister to be having sex with the same person as a Russian agent.

Who knows what secrets could have been passed from pillow to pillow?

Today, in the age of Twitter, it is unlikely that it would take long for such salacious stories to surface in the media, but the rumour mill used to take a little longer. Keeler was friends with the osteopath Stephen Ward, who had a cottage on the Cliveden estate and introduced young women to his friends and clients in high society and politics: through this insalubrious network, lots of people knew what was going on, but it took nearly two years before the story broke into the open. In early 1963, a Labour MP got up in Parliament and asked the home secretary to deny that there was any connection between Profumo and Keeler.

'Look Jack, the basic question is, "Did you fuck her?"' was how Profumo's indelicate colleague, Iain Macleod, put it to him in private. In public, Profumo answered the question everyone was asking with a bald lie: on 22 March, sitting next to the prime minister in the House of Commons, he stated that there had been 'no impropriety whatsoever in my acquaintanceship with Miss Keeler'. Many people, including the garrulous Stephen Ward and his clients, knew the truth. For just over two months, Profumo tried to brazen it out, fending off media reports and intensifying Westminster gossip. But at the end of May, Profumo went on holiday to Venice, and confessed to his wife that he had had the affair. She urged him to return to the UK and admit the lie. On Wednesday, 5 June, he resigned his ministerial post and his House of Commons seat, and issued a public apology in an open letter to the prime minister:

> I misled you, and my colleagues, and the House . . . I did this to protect, as I thought, my wife and family, who were equally misled, as were my professional advisers. I have come to realise that I have been guilty of a grave misdemeanour.

He denied that there had been any breach of national security. 'I cannot tell you of my deep remorse for the embarrassment I have caused you . . .'

With this statement, Profumo's political career was over. At the age of forty-eight, he was cast out of the inner circles of power, his political disgrace complete. He resigned as a privy counsellor, too ashamed to visit the queen at Buckingham Palace to hand over his insignia, as was the custom. He refused to give interviews and disappeared from public view. The next year the Macmillan government fell, having never recovered from the revelations of sleaze surrounding the affair to which Jack Profumo gave his name.

The Profumo affair sees both character and capability reputations at play. It is the job of a politician to exercise good judgement. Profumo's actions during this scandal ultimately indicated that he simply did not have the capability to be the political leader he so clearly wanted to be. There can be no doubt that he also failed the character test. Lying to Parliament indicated a serious degree of arrogance or disdain for his colleagues, and became one of the principal reasons behind his ejection from the elite political networks he had inhabited.

So how did Profumo get back in the reputation game? How did he get one of the highest honours that can be bestowed in the UK by the monarch after such a fall from grace? The answer lies in his elite networks and in leveraging the uncontested parts of his reputation in a new area. It lies in the rebuilding of a different competence reputation, carefully crafted over many years.

Profumo had been educated at Harrow and Oxford, where he shared a house with the Duke of Wellington and was a member of the notoriously exclusive Bullingdon Club. He became the sixth Baron Profumo, an Italian title bestowed on an ancestor by the King of Sardinia. He had also served with distinction in the Second World War, rising to the rank of brigadier, and, when first elected to Parliament at the age of twenty-five, was the youngest MP in the House of Commons. By the time of the louche house party at Cliveden, he was forty-six, impeccably well connected and with the best of his public career ahead of him. He was a member of the political establishment as well as Britain's aristocratic establishment, both tight, closed networks.

Despite being ejected from the political elite, Profumo continued to enjoy the support of the aristocratic elite, albeit in a much quieter capacity. He remained welcome at private dinner parties, testament to the humility he showed and the efforts he made to rehabilitate himself in a different setting.

In 1975, when Profumo did make the visit to Buckingham Palace to collect his CBE (second only to a knighthood), it was noted simply that the award was granted for 'services at Toynbee Hall'. To this day, Toynbee Hall is an outpost of charity in London's East End. Located in Whitechapel, near the Petticoat Lane market, it was established in 1888 as the first of the so-called University Settlements, where principled graduates of Oxford and Cambridge could come to live and work amid the poverty of the East End. From the first, it was intended that graduates would do practical good in the community. They would carry out social work and help educate the poor but intellectually curious, who flocked to hear lectures. At the same time, these young men would derive spiritual enrichment and political understanding through association with less privileged members of society.

Days after his fall from grace, Profumo contacted the director of the settlement and offered his services as a volunteer. Reports that he started off cleaning the lavatories exaggerate the extent to which the millionaire denizen of Cliveden was prepared to stoop in his personal quest for redemption. He began by washing dishes, helping to collect rents from the old people living on the site, chatting to meths drinkers and digging in the garden. In time, he put his formidable book of contacts to work to help raise money for the charity. The settlement expanded to provide youth clubs and homes for vulnerable locals, and linked with a nearby polytechnic to provide adult education. 'You see, we're not just do-gooders,' Profumo said. 'We're looking for ways to benefit society. We don't get any money from the government. We believe it is important to be independent.' All told, it was these actions that displayed a soundness of underlying character and rescued his reputation within the elite social circles he operated in, despite his political circles being shut.

Profumo himself disappeared almost completely from the limelight. He never sought to explain himself or give an account of the circumstances surrounding his downfall, giving only a handful of interviews in the decades he spent at Toynbee Hall, and then only to promote the charity. Even before Profumo's rehabilitation was completed with the award of the CBE, there were signs that he was being brought back into the fold. Labour Prime Minister Harold Wilson visited Toynbee Hall, and made a point of being photographed with his former political opponent. Profumo received an invitation to a Royal Garden Party, though it was said he did not meet the queen on that occasion. But the monarch did attend a film premiere in aid of Toynbee Hall, and very much later, when Profumo was entirely respectable again, she sat next to him at Lady Thatcher's seventieth birthday party. He served Toynbee Hall for forty years, rising to be chairman and president, and, largely through his efforts, the charity became a national institution, providing a rare template for private-sector engagement with the poor and disadvantaged, filling in the gaps left by the welfare state.

So, the defining feature of Profumo's story is that while he lost his political (and in some sense his public) reputation, his private social standing was not damaged at all. He was a rich and charming man, welcome at the Queen Mother's dinner table, or for tea with his chum the Duke of Wellington, even if he could no longer set foot in Parliament. His reputation with his immediate peers was, if anything, enhanced by the sanctity of his new vocation as a social worker.

It was Profumo's determined focus on rebuilding perceptions of his capability in a different sphere of activity that saved him. The fact that this new-found capability was in an area of social justice also clearly helped. Had he simply become a very rich banker or businessman one doubts that he would have recovered his esteemed position in society. His success with Toynbee Hall indicated that here was a man with underlying character and integrity – and his clear humility also helped. But ultimately it was his decision to move into a different world that allowed him the freedom to re-establish his capability reputation and, through this, rebuild his character as a tireless social worker, a champion of the underprivileged. Decades of selfless work in the East End made amends for his political violation, and his good name was restored.

THE TRIALS OF BIG PHARMA

Over a century and a half, big pharma (as it is now somewhat pejoratively known) has brought enormous benefits to humanity: drugs that have tamed pain and disease, given women control over their fertility and men control over their virility. Hardly a month goes by without news of a breakthrough in the treatment of cancer, an illness that was once a death sentence, but can now frequently be cured. Other illnesses and conditions, from schizophrenia to infertility, can now be treated thanks to the tremendous inventiveness of the big pharmaceutical companies.

Despite these achievements, the industry does not have a great reputation. It bumps along as the seventh out of eight industries in Edelman's Trust Index, behind tech, food and drink, consumer goods, telecoms, automotive and energy, ahead only of financial services. One factor may be the legacy of the thalidomide scandal, which had a terrible human cost. But there is a welter of other reputation issues weighing down on the industry: dubious ethics in paying scientists; publishing biased research; alleged profiteering in the developing world (John Le Carré's *The Constant Gardener* is a notable demolition job); rapacious pricing in the developed world.

Inevitably some would prefer that companies simply gave new drugs away. But pharmaceutical companies have to invest hundreds of millions of pounds to find new drugs that are clinically effective, and, when they finally bring their discoveries to market, they need to charge high prices, while the drugs are protected by patent so they can make a profit. For many companies, the challenge of doing original research is too great: it's far simpler to grow by merging and acquiring than to pursue independent research and development. And the industry is tarnished by hard-sell marketing tactics, as for example in 2012 when the venerable British company GlaxoSmithKline paid a record $3 billion fine for illegal promotion of its drugs in the US and, two years later, a further $489 million for bribing doctors in China.

Against this backdrop of fierce competition, high costs and close scrutiny from society at large, what sort of reputation should a pharma company aspire to achieve? One possible answer is the path of US–Canadian Valeant Pharmaceuticals International, until recently a poster child for stock-market success. Another is the approach taken by Hoffmann-La Roche, the Swiss giant founded in 1896 and celebrated for introducing the tranquillizer Valium in the 1960s.

If at the beginning of 2015 you had asked stock-market analysts for a list of the top pharma companies, Valeant would have been among them. With the burly Mike Pearson at the helm since 2008, Valeant had come from nowhere to achieve a market capitalization of US $90 billion, a stunning ascent by anyone's measure. Pearson followed a simple playbook: buy established pharma companies, ones that had built up a research and development pipeline, then sack the scientists (and as many other people as possible) and close off the research and development (R&D) spend. During Pearson's tenure, R&D fell from fourteen per cent of sales to three per cent, saving hundreds of millions in short-term costs. At the same time, the company priced newly acquired drugs aggressively, hiking the life-saving heart drugs Nitropress and Isuprel by 525 and 212 per cent, respectively. Since patients need the drugs to stay alive, they had little choice but to find the money, so the value of Valeant's sales increased. To add still more juice to the earnings machine, Valeant geared itself up, taking on as much debt as it could afford – some $30 billion at the time of writing.

The result of all this was sensational profit growth and a high stock-market rating that, thanks to the alchemy of corporate finance, allowed the whole procedure to be repeated over and over again. There was something old-fashioned about this kind of 'roll-up strategy', as it was known: it echoed the way asset strippers used to go about their business in the 1980s. But it worked. Pearson joined Valeant after a long and successful career at McKinsey, the doyen of management consultancies, and this is what he had told all his clients to do when he was their adviser. How gratifying, then, to be at the helm of his own company and put what he preached into triumphant practice. And how delightful to become a paper billionaire.

For many years, Mike Pearson and Valeant were winners of the reputation game, in the narrow sense that they were very highly regarded by financial market analysts, big investors and the Wall Street community, who extracted hundreds of millions of dollars in advisory and underwriting fees. Third-party endorsement came from Bill Ackman of Pershing Square Capital, a legendary hedge fund investor, who spent billions acquiring a nine per cent stake in Valeant. In May 2015, he said that Valeant was 'the next Berkshire Hathaway'. Comparing the company to Warren Buffett's fabled investment vehicle was high praise indeed. Fellow hedge fund managers piled in and, at one point, owned nearly thirty per cent of the company.

But other constituencies were not so impressed. For one, scientists were not enamoured of a company that put a very low value on their work, and ended many careers in the name of short-term earnings. And then there were the patients: ordinary, ill people, who saw the price of the drugs they depended on skyrocket. If you suffered from migraine and had been prescribed Valeant's DHE 45, you would have weathered four separate price rises from January to July 2015. In that time, the price of ten vials went from just over $3,000 to $14,120.

When the forces of mighty Wall Street are weighed up against the interests of scientists and the sick, one might expect Wall Street to prevail: certainly that was the default assumption of Pearson and the rest of the company's management team. But it was a miscalculation, as big in its own way as BP framing the Deepwater Horizon spill as an engineering problem, or Goldman Sachs delivering big bonuses in 2009 after the financial system had been brought to its knees. Ill people mobilize themselves on social media and they write to politicians seeking office. Even those who are not yet ill worry about how they might afford future bills under the US's ruthless health system. Regulators, who patrol this industry especially carefully, get twitchy. Valeant's inherent complacency was exposed in September 2015 when Hillary Clinton, in a tweet, condemned 'outrageous price gouging'. At this point, she did not mention Valeant by name, and indeed there were more extreme examples, such as the charmless hedge fund manager Martin Shkreli, who increased the price of Daraprim, a drug used in the treatment of AIDS, from $13.50 per pill to $750, a hike of 5,556%. (He was dubbed 'the most hated man in America' and subsequently arrested on securities fraud charges.) But Clinton's comments turned up the political heat on drug pricing in the US, and the Valeant story began to unravel.

When sorrows come, they come not in single spies, but in battalions. Certainly, the misfortunes piled on thick and fast after that tweet, and Valeant's decline had the unrelenting pace of Shakespearean tragedy. Having attracted hedge fund cheerleaders, Valeant now found itself the target of specialist activists called short-sellers, who look for reasons why a share price is too high, bet against the company, and then tell everyone who will listen. They alleged that there were accounting irregularities at a company called Philidor, a specialist pharmacy controlled by Valeant but supposedly operating at arm's length. The amounts of money were not huge, but newspapers began to draw parallels with Enron. The share price dropped by fifty per cent in one day. Meanwhile, the investor Bill Ackman gave a four-hour press conference in which he explained why the stock was undervalued, yet its slide continued. In November 2015, Goldman Sachs demonstrated its usual lack of sentimentality by making a 'margin call' on a $100 million personal loan it had made to Pearson in 2013, secured against Valeant stock. Since Pearson didn't have the money to repay the loan, Goldman dumped the shares it held as security, precipitating another twenty per cent drop in the share price.

In early 2016, while Pearson was in hospital with pneumonia, his former chum Bill Ackman led a boardroom coup and by the spring, Pearson was out. Hillary Clinton started singling out the company at her campaign rallies. Valeant is a morality tale for our times: the company's fate shows gratifyingly that it is not a valid long-term strategy to care only about what financial markets think. At the time of writing, the shares are down a staggering ninety-six per cent from their peak.

Our counter-example is the Basel-based Hoffmann-La Roche. This is a company formed 110 years before Valeant, with a long track record of excellence in research and a near thirty-year run of delivering annual increases in dividends, showing that there is no essential conflict between profit and commitment to R&D. When Valeant's share price was at its peak in early 2015, Roche's market capitalization was a little over half that of Valeant. Such valuation anomalies take place all the time, but it is gratifying for the Swiss company that the natural order of things has been restored: it is now worth about four times the US company, and is the third largest pharma group in the world.

Talking to André Hoffmann, the representative of the family owners, one seems a world away from the culture that created Valeant. Fluent in several languages, Hoffmann is in his mid-fifties, very tall and has the quiet, commanding presence of the head one of Europe's last great industrial dynasties. One crucial difference between this company and most others of its size is that Hoffmann and his siblings are firmly in control. They are the great-grandchildren of Fritz Hoffmann-La Roche, the company's founder, and they own a majority of the voting stock. (One imagines that the relevant bearer shares are hidden away under some especially inaccessible Swiss mattress.) While no family member has worked in the day-to-day business for two generations, André sits on the board and takes a very active role in overseeing the company's reputation. The ownership structure has parallels with the Porsche and Piëch families at VW, but at Roche, Hoffmann has taken care to bring world-class outsiders onto the board, including for example the CEOs of

Shell, Nestlé and Lufthansa, to provide a bracing and challenging external perspective: opening up the network rather than closing it down.

Anyone who has ever faced a serious illness knows how dehumanizing it can feel. After the preliminary small talk, one is poked and prodded by the experts, and then the patient is often ignored by the doctors as they focus on tests and treatment. Of course, the patient is delighted to be healed, but cancer patients in particular often feel passed from medical pillar to post. Surely the patient should also be treated as a person?

Unprompted, this is how Hoffmann defines the purpose of the company. 'We cannot be entrusted with looking after the health of society at large, if we do not respond to the demands of people who are ill,' he says. 'You've been to hospital. Once you enter, you are a number, you are a bed, you are a case. Our industry tends to look at diseases as if they are just a set of parameters, but in fact a disease affects a patient and a patient is something quite different from a bunch of physiological symptoms. We need to see the patient as a human being who breathes, who loves and hates and feels. Our industry is tainted because we have traditionally ignored all this.'

Roche has developed the model of personalized healthcare, where big data and genomics are deployed to provide an increasingly tailored medical solution. The ultimate goal of personalized medicine is to develop a reliable biomarker-based test, known as a 'companion diagnostic', which helps predict which patients will respond to the targeted therapies. 'We want to provide patient medicines that give the best therapeutic outcome, are safer and ultimately also more cost-effective,' he explains. 'How? Through diagnostics, by better understanding the genetic differences in patients before prescribing the drug. If you understand the patient you can assign him or her the right treatment. You can work out who is more sensitive to one molecule than others. Molecules have a big effect on some diseases, on others none at all! Selling the same molecule to everybody is a scam.'

While no defender of Valeant-style 'price gouging', Hoffmann insists that drug prices have to be high enough to generate profits over the short period of time that they are protected by patent. 'The Soviets thought they had found an alternative system, but it didn't work,' he quips. For all the famously capricious results of private-sector drug discovery – no one can guarantee what drugs will be winners, or when, or for how long – it is the best system that the world has come up with so far. But there are changes afoot: the era of the blockbuster pill such as Valium or Viagra is no more. A drug is considered a blockbuster now if it generates sales of just $1 billion, compared to the tens of billions generated by the big sellers of the past. Many of the specialized cancer medicines that Roche and its Basel neighbour Novartis are making fit into this new category. Pricing also increasingly reflects efficacy: if the drug really works when it hits the market, Roche can reasonably charge more.

'Having a good reputation is very important to us as a business,' Hoffmann says. 'If you want to be part of the solution as a company you need to be recognized as a trustworthy partner. We need the licence to operate and we need to be able to earn the right to provide these drugs because we have played the game and we have been part of the system.' As Hoffmann explains, there are four specific ways in which Roche's reputation matters.

First, Roche needs to be known as a great place to work. 'We are incredibly active in that. We have attractive salaries, a code of conduct, good working conditions . . . We really try to answer the demands of current and future employees to be a decent business.' In attracting and keeping research scientists in particular, it helps that family ownership means the company has a very long-term planning horizon. 'We tell research people to come to us as we are a stable organization. We are not focused on the next quarter earnings, or at least we are not only focused on that: in ten, twenty, thirty, maybe even a hundred years we will still be owned by the same family.' There is a multigenerational perspective, in keeping with the long-term nature of science. This, then, is the absolute opposite of Valeant's approach to employees, who were regarded as a cost to be trimmed.

Second, sustainability is more than a pious phrase. Roche can demonstrate to the rest of the industry and the investment community that it is a good and careful manager of resources. 'For the past seven consecutive years we have been sustainability champion in the Dow Jones sustainability index for pharma,' Hoffmann says. 'We don't do it just because of the index but, to be honest, if there wasn't an index we probably wouldn't be so focused: it gives us a framework.'

Third, it is important that the patient understands that the drugs he or she is receiving come from a good and ethical company. 'It's vital we can demonstrate to our eighty-five thousand employees that we are doing the right thing, it gives the right framework so they can be proud of Roche. It's also vital that we reach the patient, that he or she is treated with drugs manufactured by Roche, a company proud to be a world leader.' Again, the patient is not an inconvenient afterthought to be gouged, but at the centre of the company's strategy.

Hoffmann explains, delicately, that the family does not have any pressing need for the money that the company pumps out, quarter after quarter. (The dividends are deployed to a variety of charities.) He says the family is highly sensitized to reputational cock-ups, citing the company's role in the early 1990s as ringleader of a price-fixing cartel in the market for vitamins. This cost Roche hundreds of millions in fines around the world and put it in the reputational doldrums. 'It happened on my watch,' Hoffmann acknowledges. 'I spend an inordinate amount of time making sure something like that could never happen again.'

This is very different from the perspective of a normal, stock-market listed company, which is naturally much more vulnerable to the assaults of activists and the ups and downs of short-term performance. It is a form of paternalism, perhaps the very definition of Rhenish capitalism, appropriately enough given Roche's heritage on the banks of the Rhine in Basel. According to this model, companies are in business for the long term, owners are kindly, and the vagaries of the financial markets are secondary to the needs of employees and customers. It would be difficult if not impossible to transfer this model directly to the market-driven cultures of the UK or the US, but it is still a winning strategy in the reputation game, from which we can all learn.

The Valeant approach and the Roche approach highlight the way that multiple reputations interact. Valeant chose to prioritize its reputation for financial performance with Wall Street at the expense of other stakeholders. Roche did something different, focusing on its broader responsibilities to a wider group of stakeholders and positioning itself as a force for good. The company has been able to gain reputational advantage through authenticity and network ties to politicians, scientists and other employees, patients and society at large. This speaks to a system of governance that allows Roche to focus on its longer-term capability reputation, while having the resilience to fend off assaults on its character that are inevitable for any big pharma corporation.

Each strategy can be defended, but it is interesting to see how differently the two businesses are now perceived and valued. To give the last word to André Hoffmann: 'I'm a great believer that business can improve the state of the planet, not in terms of creating wealth but in terms of making a net contribution to society. In my position, you should not just be someone who increases the shareholder value of your company, you also need to go where society has a need. If Roche is run according to sound principles, the company can make a net positive contribution to the state of the planet, at least as potent as that of NGOs or other international organizations. It is a contribution that is sustainable, ethical and of which we as owners can be proud. Business can and should be a force for good.'

THE LIFE OF AN OLIGARCH

If you have ever wondered how to become an oligarch, the second richest man in Russia has given a candid explanation of how to go about it. In an address in his home town of Lviv in western Ukraine,

Mikhail Fridman said that the most important factor was time and place: ideally, you should have been present in Moscow when the Soviet empire was falling apart, ready to seize commercial opportunities amid the chaos. In the early to mid-1990s, when the Soviet Union was indeed crumbling, Fridman and others were able to take advantage of President Boris Yeltsin's privatizations to create the bedrock of their immense fortunes.

The second factor is to have an entrepreneurial outlook. Having started out selling rugs and theatre tickets, he set up the Alfa investment company in 1989. He told the story of how, in his mid-twenties and by now in Moscow, he rented an office in the same building as the Institute of Chemical Physics, one of the elite schools for Russian scientists. The cleverest graduates went there. Fridman tried to get some of them to join his fledgling business, but they raised all sorts of objections: lack of capital, the danger of rackets and gangsters, uncertainty around how the government might behave, the risk of jail . . .

All these concerns were absolutely rational, yet the Institute of Chemical Physics collapsed and Fridman went on_to become a billionaire many times over. 'We had no answers to their questions, but we did have an internal conviction that we would win through.'

Perhaps the most pertinent quality identified by Fridman was a determination to stand up for your own interests very firmly. This might mean making friends with yesterday's enemies. It means embracing conflict, which runs counter to the natural human tendency 'to be friends, reach agreements and talk in polite tones'. It means being prepared to be fierce. 'I think that, of all the types of human activity,' Fridman continued, 'entrepreneurship is in some sense the closest to war. Corporate wars reflect the level of tension in battle, the rigour and the lack of compromise. If someone is, in principle, prepared for this kind of war and can live with the idea of conflict, then he or she will probably be successful in business.'[21]

As these comments imply, Russia is a rough and tough place to do business. The economy went from communist central control to unbridled capitalism in a few years. As entrepreneurs fought for control of Russia's strategic assets, conditions were brutal: in the so-called aluminium wars of the early 1990s, murder was commonplace. Bankruptcy law was primitive and it was difficult to establish and hold on to ownership of assets. To this day, international businesses active in Russia often complain of a discriminatory legal system, corruption, harassment and all-round bully-boy tactics extending to beatings and corporate raids.[22]

Entrepreneurs such as Fridman, Vladimir Potanin, Oleg Deripaska, Mikhail Prokhorov, Alisher Usmanov and Roman Abramovich prospered amid the chaos. They are all tough, extremely smart and uncompromising, and have managed to navigate the brutal realities of Russian business as well as the politics of the Kremlin. Others, like Mikhail Khodorkovsky or Boris Berezovsky, were not so deft: Khodorkovsky was jailed and had his fortune largely confiscated, and now lives in exile in Switzerland; Berezovsky died in exile in the UK.

For as long as Russian businesses confined their activities to the home market, one can imagine that a reputation for bellicose behaviours was quite helpful: there would be no advantage in conveying a willingness to compromise. With no disrespect to the talents of Russian businessmen, there is a parallel with the 'bad' reputation enjoyed by the Mafia: the tougher you are perceived to be, the warier others will be around you, and the more likely you are to get your own way.

Of course, the very richest oligarchs soon wanted to expand beyond the domestic market. Some did this by spending part of their fortunes on sports clubs: Chelsea and Arsenal are both owned by oligarchs, as is the Brooklyn Nets basketball team. Others, including Mikhail Fridman himself, are building international business empires, a sensible diversification given the risks of commercial life in Russia.

It is here, in a milder business environment, that what is called toughness at home can appear more sinister. It is all about balancing what Fridman calls 'Russian realities' against the need for an adequate reputation in the West. 'As the Russian economy becomes more globalised, the question of reputation becomes more important,' Fridman told the *Financial Times*. 'Foreign companies want to deal with [those Russian companies] that have a good reputation.' Fridman was about to experience an opening of his networks and, with that, both opportunities and risks. He would have to play a different game.

In the early 2000s, Fridman's Alfa-Bank (by this time the largest privately owned bank in Russia) found itself blacklisted by the European Bank for Reconstruction and Development (EBRD), a multinational institution that supports investment in central and Eastern Europe. The reason: reports of criminal activities allegedly carried out by Alfa and its associates in Russia. Such stories might have been tolerated in Russia, but now they inflicted reputational damage with a real commercial price. The EBRD refused to have commercial dealings with Alfa, and the Export–Import Bank of the United States blocked a US $500 million loan guarantee to Alfa's oil and gas subsidiary TNK. This in effect stymied Alfa's international diversification plans.

Alfa's first response was to cry foul. Peter Aven, the bank's president, visited the EBRD and protested that the ban was based on malicious press reports stirred up by competitors, a practice called *kompromat* (compromising materials). But merely claiming that 'there are Russians and Russians, not all are Mafia,' was not enough to change the EBRD's mind. To succeed in the open networks game, they had to go one step further: they needed to engage more widely and persuade independent and vocal third parties that the damaging allegations were false.

Alfa commissioned a reputational audit from Kroll, the US-listed corporate investigation and business intelligence firm. Tommy Helsby, who is chairman of the firm's operations in Europe, the Middle East and Africa, explained to us the scope of this exercise: 'If you have a reputation as a wife beater there is not much we can do for you if you are in fact a wife beater. In that case, you need a confessor, a therapist or a PR man. If you are not a wife beater but still you are being accused of being one, people will say of course he would deny it. If you are going to persuade people you are not, you need to have the facts. You need facts to prove the contrary, but you can't do it yourself: you need to borrow someone else's credibility.'

In effect, the Kroll proposition was: we will investigate you and make our own independent assessment about the truth of the allegations. The firm was trading on its own reputation and credibility as a corporate investigations expert: its conclusions would carry weight. Kroll took a fee of US $500,000 (paid upfront) to assess the core allegations made against the firm, ranging from drug trafficking to arms dealing, bribery and fraud, not to mention connections with Mossad, the Israeli intelligence agency.

'We sat down with Mr Fridman and we went through each allegation one by one,' Helsby recalled. 'We said, "We need to hear your version of the story, and we need to know who is independent and can corroborate what you are telling us." Then we went out and we verified what we had been told.'

There was one story that bank president Peter Arven was an agent of Mossad, under the direction of his brother who was said to be representing the interests of Israel's security council. This one was easy to disprove: Arven doesn't have a brother and the allegation was an anti-Semitic slur. Another was that Alfa had been involved in drug smuggling in Siberia. There were stories in the Russian press dating back to the mid-1990s, when the company was active in importing sugar, that there had been a train crash near the city of Khabarovsk, and that the sacks of sugar that fell from the train were in fact full of heroin. There were, according to these lurid reports, multiple cases of heroin poisoning in local hospitals as a result.

'The fact is these stories are paid for,' Fridman told Helsby. 'Everyone in Russia knows the story is daft ... we were in dispute with another party and black PR was used against us as part of the dispute.' Helsby went to see the original publicist, who admitted planting the false story. But seeing that he could have been bought off, Helsby went to Siberia to check out the stories on the ground.

'There was a derailing but no reports of heroin poisoning,' the investigators concluded.

Kroll did find that TNK had used 'highly aggressive' commercial and legal tactics in a dispute with BP and others over a company called Chernogorneft, in which the British oil major had a ten per cent stake. Its creditors included the EBRD. '[TNK] was deliberately unconcerned with the interests of BP and the EBRD,' the report found. But it cleared the Russians of all criminal allegations, opening the way for the EBRD to reverse its ban on doing business with Alfa and its subsidiaries. 'There is a big difference between drug trafficking and sharp commercial practice,' Fridman told the *Financial Times*.[23]

This strategy of *narrative rebuttal* signals that you are confident you have your own facts straight. If accusations can be credibly disproved, as they were in this case, you can recover your reputation overnight. But it's not enough to fight back by yourself: reputation is driven by what others are saying.

6

ADVANCED TECHNIQUES

Take from a man his reputation for probity, and the more shrewd
and clever he is, the more hated and mistrusted he becomes.

Cicero

THE REPUTATION-BORROWING ECONOMY

Steve Stoute's book, *The Tanning of America* (2011), opens with a story about Run-DMC, a 1980s rap group, playing to a crowd of twenty thousand people in New York's Madison Square Garden. Having played at LiveAid, the group – Joseph 'Run' Simmons, Darryl 'DMC' McDaniels and Jason 'Jam Master Jay' Mizell – were on their way to becoming what Stoute describes as 'the first true superstars of hip hop'.

Stoute, a genial, barrel-chested man in his mid-forties, was a teenage kid from Queens at the time of the Madison Square Garden gig, and was not lucky enough to get a ticket. An avid hip hop fan, he became a senior record executive at Sony Music's urban label Def Jam Records before setting up his own marketing company. His purpose in writing his book had nothing to do with reputation or its dynamics. The narrative of the book in fact charts how hip hop set in motion a transformation of modern America – a 'tanning' – producing a rich and important cultural exchange that connected people of all races and socio-economic backgrounds. His ultimate goal in writing *The Tanning of America* was, as he puts it, 'to put an end, once and for all, to the boxing of individuals based on colour'.

One month earlier, Run-DMC had released their first single from the album *Raising Hell*, a track called 'My Adidas'. It was this track that tells the story of one of the most remarkable brand reinventions in recent history – that of Adidas sneakers in the US.

Adidas was, at that time, struggling as a brand in the US. Nike had come out strongly with its Michael Jordan line, and Reebok was doing well thanks to the fitness and aerobics craze in the US at the time. Adidas had, in the mid-1980s, only three per cent of the US sneaker market. It was a brand in decline, losing its relevance and appeal. While associating itself with an edgy movement like hip hop was brave, 'it was more risky for Adidas to just retain the status quo,' says Stoute.

Russell Simmons, Run's brother, saw what was happening with 'My Adidas', and took a gamble. He persuaded a group of senior Adidas executives to fly over from Germany for the show. He hoped that they would see the potential in working with the band. 'There was one particular executive who had the cultural curiosity to research and find the relationships that would help rebuild the brand,' says Stoute in a separate interview. 'He realized that it was hip hop and that it was culture being formed, and that if Adidas took their global cachet into this emerging subculture then they had something magical.'

Up to that point brand sponsorship deals had been the preserve of elite athletes and football stars. Urban rappers were not even in the frame. It was a bold vision, and one that paid off. According to Stoute, the band launched into 'My Adidas' and the crowd chimed in with them. But as they were into the final verse of the track, Run suddenly reached down and took off one of his Adidas sneakers, brandishing it high above his head like a sword, and started chanting, 'My Adidas'. The crowd went wild, and started removing their own sneakers and shoes, likewise holding them up 'so that it looked like a pulsating sea of black triple-striped Adidas emblem on white leather waving in unison over the heads of everyone at Madison Square Garden.'

It was an electric moment for the band, but perhaps even more so for the Adidas executives. One of them grabbed Run as he left the stage, immediately offering him his own Adidas line. Further discussions ensued – including a deal whereby Run-DMC would endorse the company's sneakers – and an unprecedented US $1.5 million deal was signed, making the rappers the first non-athletic endorsers of an athletic shoe. It also transformed the fortunes of Adidas in the US, making the shoe an emblem of cool and a must-have product for young urban Americans. 'Madison Square Garden was the lightbulb moment where the executive knew something that the company did not yet know,' says Stoute. 'But there was something that tipped into that – he knew, based on data, that there was something going on in the market that made the connection possible.'

Having a connection is critical to the success of the reputation lending and borrowing economy. According to Stoute, 'shared values are a critical part of how these things create new reputational capital. Whenever you try to do things without shared values it does not work, the public sees it, and it looks like money is driving everything. When reputation borrowing or lending takes place it only works when the impression created is that no money is being exchanged. People have to believe that it is being done with goodwill, that it is being done for the right reasons, and not because of commerce.'

The Run-DMC/Adidas deal was a two-way reputation exchange. Run-DMC became one of the most talked about and promoted hip hop brands in the world at a time when hip hop was still only a subculture. Other hip hop artists and their promoters jumped on the bandwagon, seeking out and securing major corporate sponsorships and helping to lift hip hop into the mainstream. As Jay-Z explains: 'Hip hop resonated around the world because it made people realize, "Oh shit, I don't need to be ashamed of where I come from, or my parents' meagre beginnings."' And Adidas became associated with one of the coolest young movements of the time, reinventing its image and its fortunes: Adidas's footwear market share grew from 3% in the mid-1980s to around 15% by the early to mid-2000s. By 2015, it had risen to 22.9%.[1]

Run-DMC turned out to be masters of collaboration. On the same album, they released their iconic remake of Aerosmith's 1977 hit 'Walk This Way'. The idea to cover the song was the brainchild of their legendary producer Rick Rubin, and they recorded it together with Aerosmith's lead singer Steve Tyler and guitarist Joe Perry. Released on 4 July 1986, the Run-DMC version was the first hip hop song to hit the top five on the Billboard Hot 100, the US singles record chart. It was also one of the first big hip hop singles to make it in the UK, reaching number eight in the UK charts that year.

Not only did the song introduce rock lovers to hip hop, it was also the catalyst for the successful relaunch of Aerosmith's faltering music career. Other music industry legends have similarly reinvented themselves by reputation borrowing and lending. Sir Tom Jones, one of the legendary names in the music business, relaunched his singing career with the 1999 album *Reload*, a collaboration with some of the most popular artists of the moment including The Cardigans, Stereophonics and Robbie Williams.

Reputation borrowing and lending lies at the heart of most sponsorship and endorsement deals. It is a cornerstone of marketing strategy, a way of connecting brands with aspirational people, and connecting talented people with visible or up-and-coming brands. But not everything can be borrowed or lent. 'First of all you have to have a reputation to lend. Any brand can do it, but for it to be successful the brand has to really understand which ingredients of their reputation are transferrable and which ingredients are not,' says Stoute.

We spoke to Rachel Botsman, one of the leading thinkers on the shared economy, who has been credited with coining the phrase 'collaborative consumption'. She is currently teaching an MBA course on the collaborative economy at the University of Oxford's Saïd Business School. She believes we are just at the beginning when it comes to the power of reputation. 'Reputation is becoming a currency that will be more powerful than our credit history in the twenty-first century,' she says. She believes that reputation will transform how we think about wealth, markets, power and personal identity in the twenty-first century.

'People realize that the reputation they create within one marketplace has value beyond that marketplace. You hear stories now of Airbnb hosts using their reputation as a way of getting a lease. And insurance companies tell me that this sort of information is a great predictor of the way people will behave in the future – that it is a great way of seeing the whole person rather than the way they behave in just one dimension.'

Reputation has become much more important as the connections between companies become more frequent and more strategic. The collaborative economy movement – what British Prime Minister Theresa May, in a speech in early 2017, called the 'shared society' – depends on reputation as its engine. Firms will collaborate with many more organizations and individuals based on their reputations, and these relationships will work better because of the power of reputations in keeping these relationships honest.

Mike Barry, head of sustainability for Marks and Spencer, agrees that collaboration is an important frontier. 'No single business, however large, can become sustainable alone. Sustainability has become about developing partnerships where we can win together; for example, through the Consumer Goods Forum or The World Economic Forum. These initiatives bring, for example, Pepsi and Coca-Cola, Unilever and Procter & Gamble, Carrefour and Wal-Mart to the same room. All of these companies are naturally competitive, but are increasingly suspending the sense of "we must win alone" to focus on "we must win together" when it comes to sustainability.'

The connectivity that exists within and between networks today is down to the advent of the Internet.

CONSIDER SNAPCHAT

Deepak Ravindran is a college dropout who is now one of India's most exciting young tech entrepreneurs. Initially from Kasaragod in Kerala, south-west India, Ravindran enrolled at Lal Bahadur Shastri College of Engineering, before dropping out of college to pursue his dream of setting up his own company. The result was Lookup, a messaging app that connects shoppers with local businesses.

'Today, it is very easy to find and buy products online. However, when you want to buy something offline, we still end up picking up our phone and dialling local shops or running around. We want Lookup to be the Google equivalent for finding products and services offline. For this, we hyperlink every local store near you with a simple chat app that gives you synchronous connection to the verified vendor,' says Ravindran. Launched in December 2014, Lookup claims to have over one million registered users, and the site sends and receives over a hundred thousand messages every day. The queries that come through the site range from food and groceries to medicines and electronics.

Critical to the success of the venture was the early involvement of some of the tech world's biggest names. In September 2015, Ravindran raised US $2.5 million in Series A funding. The funding round was led by Sun Microsystems co-founder Vinod Khosla, Twitter co-founder Biz Stone, and Infosys co-founders Narayana Murthy and Kris Gopalakrishnan.

These are huge names in the tech industry. Endorsement from them, especially when accompanied by a personal investment from them individually, is invaluable. Other backers flocked to the company, including New Look fashion chain founder Tom Singh and venture funds from Switzerland to Silicon Valley.

Margit Wennmachers, a partner at leading Silicon Valley venture capital firm Andreessen Horowitz, agrees that having big names behind you at an early stage creates momentum and is a platform of opportunity for a start-up company in a very competitive marketplace. 'The value of our name as a pre-series A investor is huge. We see letters from our entrepreneurs who, in the first paragraph, write that they are an Andreessen Horowitz-backed company – before they even say what they do as a company. And, in a very crowded market, if you are the CIO of a start-up bank these things matter as a way of getting you in the door.'

Tim Pollock, Farrell Professor of Entrepreneurship at Pennsylvania State University, has researched how social and political factors such as reputation, status and social capital influence the performance of firms when they first raise funding from the public. In a 2011 paper,[2] he and his co-authors studied a sample of venture capital-backed initial public offerings (IPOs) between 1990 and 2000. They found that the reputation of the VC backers has a marked impact on the way financial markets value an entrepreneurial venture. This is of particular importance in the technology world, where early-stage companies often make losses in their first few years as a public company. Persuading investors to back a loss-making company on the basis of expectations about the future is therefore of critical importance.

Consider Snapchat. The messaging app was launched in 2011, has minimal revenue, and has yet to make a profit. Yet its valuation, following its recent IPO, is around US $28 billion.[3] Smart investors are betting that Snapchat will be one of the winners in the tech race. And the fact that it was backed by high-reputation tech investors such as Lightspeed provided a critical springboard for its success.

Mike Abbott is one of the most highly regarded venture capital investors in Sand Hill Road, the now famous location for investors in tech start-ups in Silicon Valley.[4] He is a general partner at Kleiner Perkins Caufield & Byers, one of the best-known names in the sector. Before that, Abbott was vice president of engineering at Twitter. He told us that having a general reputation for being able to fund success stories is of secondary importance to having a reputation for providing advice and guidance. In the tech world, starting up is hard. Entrepreneurs need to navigate many different challenges as they scale up their business – and not many have the skill set to do this successfully. Scaling up demands new skills involving legal contracts, HR issues, capital investment decisions and so forth. The real reputation value of an investor, according to Abbott, is the value that they bring beyond money.

'Money is the biggest commodity out here. If anything, $5 million from KP [Kleiner Perkins] is no different from $5 million from some other firm. But what is different is the motivation behind that $5 million. How are they going to be helpful beyond the money? Can they bring empathy to the journey that they are embarking on? That's what I aim to bring. I have been in their shoes so I can ask questions, but it's their company and they have to come up with the solutions,' says Abbott.

'I would say that the name of the individual partner is more important than the name of the funding institutions. There are two big areas in which VCs can help entrepreneurs – the first is recruiting, and the other is partnerships and business development opportunities. But it's about trusting the person. Firm reputations can change, but the reputation of the individuals tends to persist,' says Abbott.

Success breeds success. Successful reputation borrowing and lending is a virtuous circle. And, as Abbott says, it's not about the company or the money at its disposal: 'In this space, it's all about the entrepreneur. They are the ones who matter.'

CHASING STATUS

Status is simply a position in a hierarchy. You are either high or low status relative to a group of others. Reputation adds a third dimension. It is easy enough to think of people who have high status but poor reputations, and vice versa: you only need to glance at the day's news. Prince Charles, for instance, has colossal status, but has not been immune to reputational setbacks. And grass-roots local funding initiatives, such as those promoted on Change.org or Just Giving, offer examples of groups that lack status but have positive reputations.

Status is created and sustained in two distinct ways. First, it can be earned. Take Robert Downey Jr as an example – he is a hugely successful actor with a very high status. Immediately, you can see that this high status does not equate automatically to a good reputation. His personal life made him for a while one of the most ridiculed stars in the film industry.

The sustainability and environmental initiatives promoted by Unilever and Nestlé have given them high status within that (very active) community. Nestlé's Creating Shared Value Forum each year brings together organizations and individuals who are more used to being combatants in the sector, and is a model that has been admired and copied by others. This has helped overcome the Swiss company's formerly dominant reputation (in the 1970s) as an unprincipled seller of powdered baby milk to the developing world.

But status is also conferred through association with others. Why else do we frame a picture of a meeting with someone of importance – political, cultural or perhaps royal – and place it on a mantelpiece? If you have met someone like that, and have a picture to boot, it strangely finds its way into a frame, or onto a profile picture. Why do we do this? We do not really know these people. The answer is that we seek, through positioning ourselves along-side high-status others, to say something about our own status. For organizations, status can be achieved by association through spon-sorship, becoming a member of an industry association, or taking on an unprofitable but high-status client – Coutts was happy to be the bank of the Queen Mother, despite her account running into overdraft by more than £4 million. These actions are all about creating and sustaining status by association. That is one reason why ex-chancellor George Osborne has found willing employers in both finance and the media: companies want to buy some of that status for themselves.[5]

For players in the reputation game, status can be either an asset or a liability. Players can advance faster with status than those who lack it. It is like strapping a rocket to your feet. But like a rocket, status can be unstable. Expectations accelerate when you have status. High-status actors, for example, are held to higher standards of behaviour than the extras. Becoming higher status therefore also adds risk to your reputation, making the fall harder and longer for those who fail to meet the expectations that come with high status. In that respect, status is also linked closely to visibility and sometimes celebrity, two other dimensions of our game.

'I'M A BUSINESS, MAN!'

'Your reputation precedes you, right,' says Jay-Z when we meet up to talk with him over a cigar and a glass of Yamazaki 18-Year Single Malt in the early summer of 2016. 'For the most part people know what type of business you do, what you have a reputation for, and for the way you carry yourself.'

Jay-Z is one of the most recognizable names on the planet today. He is, first and foremost, one of the most successful hip hop artists of all time, having been ranked number one by MTV in their list of 'The Greatest MCs of All Time' in 2006. But he is much more than a 'big noise' in the world of hip hop. He is also one of the world's best-selling artists of all time across any genre, having sold more than 100 million records during the course of his two-decade career. He has received over twenty Grammy Awards for his musical work during that time, and has partnered and collaborated with most of the biggest names in the industry, including The Notorious B.I.G., Mariah Carey, Drake, Dr. Dre, Eminem, R. Kelly, Lenny Kravitz, Frank Ocean, Nas, Rihanna, Justin Timberlake and Kanye West.

But Jay-Z's reputation transcends even this wider musical background. Today he is known in many fields, not just as a rapper and record producer but also as a successful entrepreneur. He co-owns the 40/40 club, a chain of sports bars; co-founded Roc-A-Fella Records, which is now part of Universal Music; founded Roc Nation, an artists' management company operating across music, sports, film, television and the literary arts; co-created the Rocawear clothing business; and co-owns the music streaming business Tidal.

In a court case that he was party to in October 2015, he was asked what he did. 'I make music, I'm a rapper, I've got a clothing line, I run a label, a media label called Roc Nation, with a sports agency, music publishing and management. Restaurants and nightclubs . . . I think that about covers it.' Asked to confirm by his lawyer that he also had a music streaming service, he replied, 'Yeah, yeah. Forgot about that!' Married to Beyoncé, another iconic name in the music industry, Jay-Z is now estimated to be worth somewhere north of US $500 million. As he himself put it, 'I'm not a businessman – I'm a business, man!'

Jay-Z sees himself, first and foremost, as an entrepreneur who happened to find his route through music. But while the music may be what he is best known for, Jay-Z sees his music more as an authentic expression of his lifestyle. 'I guess the ability [to port reputation] may be specific to the lifestyle,' he says. 'The lifestyle [of hip hop] is an expression of words, an expression of fashion, an expression of ideas. And it was always forced to be very entrepreneurial because of what it is. The spirit of hip hop has always been entrepreneurial, right from the beginning. You did not have the clubs. You had to go out with your turntables, plug them in, and play from the streets.'

He recalls how it all started. 'In Brooklyn we had a gift for rapping. So I put together a demo, and shopped it to every major label and they all turned it down – because I was speaking in a language that was coded to the streets. It was a specific conversation that only the people living that sort of lifestyle understood. So it was either like give up or start your own thing. So we pressed some records ourselves, took them to a record store, gave it to them on consignment, and had to wait until they gave you some money before you made some more.

'It was that spirit. I never had a plan. But I never had a choice – it was either that or nothing. So we would pull up in cars and play the music really loud, and have records in the trunk. And people would come by and ask what is that saying, and so we would say you can buy it right here. Three dollars.'

As it became clear that his music was gaining traction, Jay-Z took his first record to Rick Rubin and Russell Simmons's Def Jam records. They recognized that Jay-Z had something special. 'Def Jam had a soundtrack contract for *The Nutty Professor* movie, and they took my first single to use on the soundtrack,' he recalls. 'And from there we created a co-venture with them as they had seen our work. We were able to negotiate a 50:50 deal and we went from there.'

It is these entrepreneurial roots that explain how Jay-Z has been able to port his stellar reputation within music into other related ventures. His entrepreneurial energy was initially expressed and channelled through his music, but it soon also found an expression in other outlets. For him, it was a natural evolution. 'Do you get brand and reputation contagion [on the downside]. Yes, of course,' he says. 'But not if it's honest. For example, we started the 40/40 club for people who genuinely liked sports. It was an honest idea, an extension of ourselves. The idea came about when we were sitting around just like this and we said would it not be cool to have some place that we could just sit around and talk sports and have a big TV and big back rooms that we can hang out in. So we did just that. We did not have a business model in mind, we just did it. It was a good idea.

'It was the same thing with the clothes. We wanted to wear Iceberg. We wanted to wear clothes from these fashion houses and we could not wear them. Either we could not fit them because they were too small, or they did not want to be associated with hip hop.'

Are reputations portable? Can you bring your most valuable reputations with you and leave other less desirable ones behind?

It seems clear that under certain conditions they are portable. Most of us are lucky to achieve success in one area of business life. But for those who do achieve it, we can come back to the underpinnings of capability and character. Jay-Z is as capable as it gets as a musician. His tough upbringing combined with natural talent gave him unsurpassed authenticity. Failing initially to get a record deal, he co-created Roc-A-Fella Records with two friends as an independent label for his first album. While that album, *Reasonable Doubt*, was a slow burner, it created a network for the artist within the emerging hip hop community, including an important early collaboration with The Notorious B.I.G..

So Jay-Z's capability opened up broader network connections – from these early stages of his career, he was a network broker, bridging the holes between different networks within the hip hop scene, starting with New York hip hop, developing bridges into the wider urban music community, and then connecting more widely with the music industry, perhaps most notably with the hit 'Encore', in collaboration with Linkin Park, one of the biggest rock bands of the time. It was this ability to spot, and bridge, the gaps between the urban music scene and emerging trends that set Jay-Z on his broader entrepreneurial path.

Today, he hobnobs with some of the most powerful people in the world, counting former President Obama among his contacts (having performed at rallies for both his presidential election campaigns). Not bad for a boy raised by a single mum in Brooklyn's Marcy Houses Project, who had started out selling crack cocaine and being shot at.

Evidence from the stock market also strongly supports the view that reputations are portable, especially in the early stages of a CEO's tenure, where there is most uncertainty and few real facts acting as early warning signs of future success or failure. The market does not know for sure whether a new CEO will do a good job. That will depend on any number of factors, including the CEO's own motivation, whether he or she is able to navigate the new workplace and motivate others, and whether his or her skills are compatible with the new business. Yet stock markets respond immediately to new appointments, adding or subtracting sometimes billions of dollars of value on the promise of a name. What lies behind this? The answer is reputation – more specifically, expectations about the portability of the CEO's skills and expertise and a belief in their ability to create value.

Three Harvard Business School professors studied this phenomenon, writing up their findings in a 2006 *Harvard Business Review* article entitled 'Are Leaders Portable?'. Their conclusion was that the stock market certainly thinks so. They studied a selection of senior hires by companies out of General Electric (GE), still widely considered to be one of the world's best training grounds for senior executives. What they found was that the hiring company's stock price instantly spiked:

> We studied twenty former GE executives who were appointed chairman, CEO, or CEO designate at other companies between 1989 and 2001, and with only three exceptions, the hiring announcement provoked a positive stock-market reaction – an average gain of about $1.1 billion across the group. When, in 2000, Jeffrey Immelt signed on to replace Jack Welch as GE's own CEO, two rivals were almost immediately lured to other companies – James McNerney to 3M, which right away saw its market value increase more than $6.5 billion, and Robert Nardelli to Home Depot, where shareholder value jumped almost $10 billion. Such leaps in stock price reflect a favorable opinion of the way GE develops managers, a bet that GE executives will replicate GE's success, and an assumption that an executive's skills can be readily transferred from one setting to another.

When you're lower down in a business – a GE employee, or a musician – it can be harder to mobilize that specific reputation for another purpose. But the higher up you rise, the more portable your reputations for leadership or entrepreneurship, and the easier it gets to become your own business.

SPILLS AND SPILLOVER

Proximity also creates the potential for reputation 'spillover' – when one firm's reputation 'spills over' to reflect on its associates. We are, after all, judged by the company we keep.

This can be positive – being registered as a charitable organization lends some positive reputational capital, irrespective of your specific aims and objectives – but spillover is most commonly thought of as 'being tarred with the same brush'.

During the night of 2–3 December 1984, water found its way into a tank containing pesticide chemicals at a Union Carbide production facility in Bhopal in India's Madhya Pradesh. The introduction of water set in motion a chain reaction that led to the release of around thirty metric tonnes of toxic gas into the air over the next hour. It was catastrophic for the local population. The government of Madhya Pradesh confirmed a total of 3,787 deaths related to the gas leak. Other unofficial estimates put the death toll closer to 8,000, and a government document in 2006 stated that the leak caused 558,125 injuries, including 38,478 'temporary partial injuries' and approximately 3,900 'severely and permanently disabling injuries'. Bhopal was, and remains, the world's worst industrial accident.

The disaster at Union Carbide terrified executives at the world's largest chemical companies. 'Bhopal was the wake-up call,' said Dow Chemical Vice President David Buzzelli in a later interview. 'It brought home to everybody that we could have the best performance in the world but, if another company had an accident, all of us would be hurt, so we started to work together.'

There are many other examples of reputation spillover. We saw that Deepwater Horizon was a disaster for BP, but it affected popular perception of the oil industry more broadly, and competing firms from the industry sent executives to Houston to work with BP executives across the many technical and organizational issues that emerged as the crisis unfolded. Similarly, the entire automotive industry has found itself firmly in the regulatory spotlight after the revelation that VW had falsified its emission data in certain diesel models. And of course the global investment banks still remain firmly in the reputational dock following the revelation of LIBOR rigging, the recent scandal in London whereby traders at different banks colluded to fix the rates at which their banks could borrow from one another on a short-term basis.

When faced with information about an organization in crisis, we naturally look for reference points. We engage in a sense-making process, where we seek to put emerging information in the context of what we already know or understand. Proximity to the focal organization therefore becomes a major reputational liability, and explains why organizations develop sophisticated ways of distancing themselves from the source of the trouble.

BEATING STIGMA

The word 'stigma' was first used in ancient Greece where it referred to a physical brand, mark or scar inflicted on an individual by others to signify their inferior moral status. It was used to brand liars, cheats and others whose behaviour was deemed to be immoral.

Stigma differs from reputation and other constructs in important ways. While reputation can be defined as a signal of expected future behaviours based on perceptions of past behaviours, stigma is 'a label that evokes a collective perception that the organization is deeply flawed and discredited'.[6]

There are, broadly speaking, two types of stigma. First, there is the stigma that you have no actual control over. This type of stigma is typically *physical*, based on some form of ailment or imperfection. Examples of these would be people living with HIV/AIDS, or those with physical or mental disability. This type of stigma usually generates concern or pity rather than any more acute negative sentiment.

The more damaging and problematic stigmas are those over which you do indeed have a degree of choice. These are described as *conduct* stigmas and are based on the actions of individuals or firms. Examples of these would be scandals or deliberate actions such as choosing to run strip clubs or sell tobacco.

For advanced players of the reputation game there are two main strategies when it comes to dealing with stigma. The first is to defend your activities. Arms manufacturers, for example, adopt this strategy stating – accurately – that the right to defence is enshrined in international law and that therefore their activities are both legitimate and moral. The payday loans sector, and more recently the medical marijuana sector, have both likewise sought to defend their activities by calling for renewed regulation – a form of reputation borrowing and another advanced move in the reputation game.

Probably the best example of this has been the ongoing reinvention of Wonga, the UK payday loans business that suffered significant reputational damage in 2012–13 when it emerged that it was charging its most vulnerable customers an annual rate of interest of 5,853%. The backlash was severe and immediate, with politicians and consumer groups branding the company irresponsible – and worse. Even the archbishop of Canterbury got in on the act, condemning Wonga for 'usury' and vowing to put it out of business through the dual sword of education and the development of a more responsible Church of England credit line.[7]

Wonga responded with wholesale changes to its senior management and its strategy. Andy Haste, the highly respected former CEO of Royal Sun Alliance, was appointed group chairman and he quickly brought in a new management team who set about professionalizing the systems and creating the ability to engage in much more responsible lending, focused on what the customer could afford. They set out six clear priorities for the business focused on affordability, transparency, flexibility and additional governance controls; crucially, they worked with the UK government and welcomed new regulations aimed at capping the amount of interest and fees that could be charged, and limiting one-off charges for payment defaults.

Their strategy was to seek to drive a reputation 'wedge' between the responsible and irresponsible companies in the sector, thus defending their own reputation while distancing themselves from other less-responsible players. Martin Wheatley, who was head of the Financial Conduct Authority at the time the regulations came into force, commented publicly that he expected 'only four or five' of the four hundred or so firms operating in the payday loans sector to survive.[8]

The second strategy is to divest of stigmatized activity, or to seek to dilute the visibility of stigmatized business within the overall mix of activities that you are known for. Probably the best corporate example of this was Philip Morris International, parent company for a swathe of well-known tobacco brands including Marlboro, which in 2001 announced that it was changing its name to Altria Group. The process of discussion about this change originated in the late 1980s when executives became concerned that the dominance of one set of products – tobacco – adversely impacted their ability to compete and grow in their other sector – food (Philip Morris had an eighty-four per cent stake in Kraft Foods at the time). Internal documents from the time included a quote from brand consultants the Wirthlin Group who were hired to work on this project: 'The name-change alternative offers the possibility of masking the negatives associated with the tobacco business,' they stated. Several years later, in 2007, Altria conceded that the Kraft business was still held back by stigmatized perceptions relating to its tobacco activities, and it therefore decided to spin off its Kraft Foods business into a separately listed company. While this finally solved the problem, it highlighted that ultimately stigma is hard to shake off and that the strategy of dilution is at best a temporary one.

WHAT'S IN A BRAND?

Forbes produces a World's Most Valuable Brand list that includes some eye-watering numbers. Apple's brand is valued at US $145 billion, Microsoft and Google at $69 billion and $65 billion respectively. Successful brands create real advantage in terms of sales and marketing, ability to attract talent and so on.

David and Victoria Beckham have built 'brand Beckham' and have achieved fame, notoriety and commercial success on the back of it. But the Beckhams have suffered the ups and downs of fortune in the reputation game despite their brand success. Brand confers value, but it is different from reputation. Brand expresses what an organization or individual wants to stand for, particularly with regard to customers. Unlike reputation, a CEO has all the levers for building a brand under his or her own control – advertising spend, product name, colour and texture of packaging, price point and so on. Brand is an element of reputation, but reputation relies on more than brand. 'Reputations are earned, not bought,' says Ian Davis, the chairman of Rolls-Royce. 'You can buy brand but you can't finagle your way to a good reputation.' Brand is episodic, while reputation goes much deeper.

'Branding' has been around for a very long time. The earliest brands distinguished themselves through the use of trademarks, the earliest example of which is thought to be Roman swords, which carried a mark identifying the blacksmith. When, in the early 1300s, Genghis Khan's Golden Horde swept across thousands of miles of steppe to invade Europe, the Mongolian tribes applied brand marks to their cattle so they could tell them apart. These brands became the *tamga*, the battle insignia of the different tribes. One of the oldest commercial trademarks is Löwenbräu, which has used its Lion trademark since 1383, and in the UK, trademarks were written into law in 1266 by King Henry III, who demanded that all bakers use a trademark to help customers identify the bread that they bought.

Brand, at the start of its life, was concerned with products, not with companies. But by the early 1970s, management scholars began to argue that brands were relevant and powerful for the corporation, not just the product. Firms quickly cottoned on to the idea that brand was an integral part of competitive strategy, deeply connected to identity and values. There was a tendency to wrap brand and reputation together and think of them as the same thing. But established and powerful brands could still suffer reputational hits, and there were plentiful examples of individuals and organizations with great reputations, but no brand.[9] We can think of brands as being what we *want* to be seen as, and reputation as how we are seen in reality. Good branding succeeds in getting us to think of a company in ways that are consistent with its brand identity – Apple, Coca-Cola and Disney excel in this.

Innocent Drinks started life as a hardscrabble entrepreneurial company founded by three idealistic University of Cambridge graduates who wanted to take on the big drinks conglomerates. Adam Balon, Jon Wright and Richard Reed started the company in 1999 after selling their smoothies at a music festival and asking liggers to vote on the quality of the produce. 'We put up a big sign asking people if they thought we should give up our jobs to make smoothies, and put a bin saying "Yes" and a bin saying "No" in front of the stall. Then we got people to vote with their empties. At the end of the weekend, the "Yes" bin was full, so we resigned from our jobs the next day and got cracking.' This story is great brand positioning: it speaks to a commitment to doing good, an entrepreneurial spirit, a sense of fun and a commitment to giving customers what they want. It was a very successful formula and, ten years after they started, the founders sold a big stake in the company to Coca-Cola. Despite becoming a major company, the brand positioning remained deliberately low key, entrepreneurial and folksy. Innocent has achieved the holy grail of corporate branding, retaining a reputation that is consistent with its original mission to create 'delicious, healthy drinks that help people live well and die old'.

Compare that story with the brand positioning of BP under CEO Lord Browne. In 2001, BP rebranded the entire company under the slogan 'Beyond Petroleum'. This was designed to emphasize the company's commitment to moving away from fossil fuels, embracing instead alternative technologies such as solar. The campaign was initially praised for its ambition and the intent that it signalled. A celebrated series of articles in the *Financial Times* dubbed Lord Browne 'the Sun King'. Lord Browne's personal reputation was exalted. BP's eco-credentials soared and the reputation of the company started to move ahead of the pack of other oil companies, which were increasingly positioned as old and inflexible. Competitors gnashed their teeth, knowing that most of BP's business remained as dirty, dangerous and unsustainable as their own. But customers were also rightly cynical. Energy is expensive, and customers respond first and foremost to competitive prices – to draw attention to BP's branding, and by extension its business activities, only served to highlight inconvenient truths. It soon became clear that the logo and brand position was incompatible with the harsh fact that the majority of its activities were anything but 'beyond petroleum'.

By 2008, BP's credentials as a green champion were in tatters, and the company had moved away from the branding that had once created such excitement and heralded such promise. The inconsistency between its brand ambition and its reality left it open to charges of 'greenwashing', using its purported commitment to environmental causes as a fig leaf to disguise its activities.

Climate-change science has now reached an overwhelming consensus, and even once highly sceptical oil majors such as Exxon acknowledge that they need to plan for its real impact on their industry. So with hindsight, Browne's branding initiative looks farsighted, though Browne himself admits that he went too far and that the branding was aspirational, rather than a reflection of reality.

Majken Schultz, a professor of marketing at Copenhagen Business School, highlights an important point. Brand management has historically been the responsibility of the marketing departments, especially given that the origins of brand were in product marketing rather than corporate strategy. 'Many organizations that have formalized their corporate reputation and corporate brand management practices have assigned responsibility for branding to the marketing function, while corporate reputation is most often the responsibility of corporate communication along with media relations and reputation tracking,' she concludes. 'Even when both sit within the communication function they are often assigned to different groups.'[10] This silo mentality has contributed towards a general misunderstanding about the difference between brand and reputation. Brand was linked to marketing strategy, and therefore within the control of the organization. It became all too easy to see reputation simply as a reflection of brand.

Equally, having 'reputation management' located within the communications department did not help. Many CEOs struggle with the idea that reputation is not the same thing as 'media relations' (as in talking to journalists), and many a communications director has been hauled in to see the boss and given the instruction to 'fix our reputation', without attention to the underlying causes. 'Why are we getting killed in the press?' is a familiar refrain, of the sort that might have been shouted at the press people at Lehman Brothers in the months before the bank failed. The real answer is often that the company is doing something bad, which journalists are entitled to highlight.

The media are crucial in forming or destroying many different reputations, with customers, regulators or employees. Having things written about you in the media certainly brings visibility, and it can contribute towards a good reputation, or amplify a bad one. Bungling your communications with journalists can exacerbate reputational harm. But when it comes to reputation, media engagement is a means to an end, rather than an end in itself, and it is a gross oversimplification to imagine that positive headlines translate automatically to good reputations.

7

LEGACY

Most reputations are not ruined but forgotten.
                    Mason Cooley (1927–2002), American aphorist

RHODES MUST FALL

It is one of the peculiarities of the reputation game that it carries on even when you yourself are not around to play. That is because reputations are determined by other people, and if they continue to hold strong views on your past behaviours, you can find your reputation modified – sometimes for better, but usually for worse – after the event. So in this final section we look at the way players posthumously win or lose the game.

Most of us will lose our reputations when we pass on: it is vanity to imagine that we will be remembered for anything at all once we are dead. Yet for a very few individuals, reputation lives on after death, and remains hotly contested for generations.

We have to remind ourselves what they have reputations for, and with whom: in Henry VIII's case, it is for marrying six times and chopping the heads off so many of his spouses, as well as for a certain regal swagger. We remember Richard III for killing off his nephews in the Tower of London – or as the victim of a Tudor-inspired, Shakespeare-abetted campaign to besmirch him, depending on who you believe. For most people, Hitler is the archetype of evil, as we discussed earlier, but it is more complex with Stalin. He was a genocidal monster, forcing tens of millions to their deaths:

235

hardly evidence of an upstanding character. But as the man who brought Russia into the modern era and fought off Nazi Germany, he was terrifyingly competent. For historic reputations, competence seems to prevail over character.

There is an important distinction between reputations that are fascinating in historical terms (Richard III, Henry VIII) and those whose lives illustrate debates, issues and themes that are still topical. Taking a stance on a figure such as Chairman Mao plunges you into contemporary politics, even if the language is coded: the man's reputation is charged and challenged in today's networks and evaluated against the behaviours of his Communist Party successors. Christopher Columbus is another good example of a highly contested posthumous reputation. Italian by birth, he operated under the auspices of the King of Spain, completing four voyages across the Atlantic. In the context of trade wars between European monarchies in the fifteenth century, his proposal to help the Spanish Crown enter the spice trade by sailing to Asia through a new westward route saw him 'discover' the 'new world' in 1492, arriving in the Bahamas, rather than Japan as he had originally intended. Celebrating this momentous event, Columbus Day has long been a major national holiday in the US, Spain and several Central and South American countries. But its existence, and what it celebrates, has become a subject of fierce controversy. The reputation of Columbus and his achievements is now hotly contested.

In 1992, five centuries after his arrival in the Bahamas, plans were made to celebrate the five-hundredth anniversary of the founding of America. These plans, however, rapidly became subject to intense criticism and debate. Critics reminded people that the voyages were accompanied by acts of brutality and genocide. Today, four states – Hawaii, Alaska, Oregon and South Dakota – do not recognize Columbus Day at all, while others choose to call it a 'day of observance' or 'recognition', avoiding the use of the Columbus name. The outcry against a five-hundredth anniversary celebration made it impossible for the US government to mark this event in any unified, national way. As Professor Gary Fine of

Chicago puts it, 'The absence of consensus on Columbus's reputation made any large-scale collective commemoration problematic. Whereas Lincoln and Washington bring Americans together, Columbus pulls citizens apart. Columbus's voyages are seen as offensive to Native Americans, rather than legitimizing for Hispanic Americans. Columbus is seen as Italian more than his voyages are seen as Spanish.'

A similar problem faced Andrew Jackson, seventh president of the United States, whose reputation is subject to historical contest. Jackson's face has adorned the front of a US $20 bill since 1928. On 17 June 2015, the Obama administration announced that the face of a woman would feature on the front of a US $10 bill from 2020, replacing Alexander Hamilton, a founding father, aide to George Washington and the country's first Treasury secretary. But immediately there were calls for the slave-owning Andrew Jackson to be done away with instead: Jackson broke up the second Bank of the United States, which he called a 'monster institution', and restricted the use of paper money, laying down the conditions for the panic of 1837, one of the most severe depressions in US history.

Perhaps more damaging for Jackson's reputation were his actions in evicting Native Americans from their land. His Indian Removal Act paved the way for the forced removal of the Cherokee nation from lands east of the Mississippi River to an area in what is now present-day Oklahoma. The Cherokee people have since called this journey the 'Trail of Tears', because of its devastating and lasting effect. Jackson, once regarded as a hero of the early American settlements, found few willing to back him in this contemporary reputational contest, and the US government had a change of heart. Jackson will be replaced on the front of the $20 note by Harriet Tubman, the former slave and abolitionist, who will become the first African-American to appear on the front of a US bank note, and the first woman in over a century. Jackson will be on the reverse. Hamilton stays on the front of the $10 bill, while a variety of women and civil rights leaders will feature on the back of $5 and $10 notes. This is the most significant remaking of the US currency since 1929, and these reputational reorderings reflect modern values and preoccupations projected back onto the historic personalities of the past.

A classic example of the same phenomenon is the 'Rhodes Must Fall' protest movement, started by students in Cape Town, South Africa, in March 2015. There can be little doubt that Cecil John Rhodes was a bigot and a racist. The mining entrepreneur and adventurer initiated the policy of enforced segregation in South Africa and openly proclaimed the superiority of the Anglo-Saxon race. He famously said: 'I contend that we are the finest race in the world and that the more of the world we inhabit, the better it is for the human race.' (Rudyard Kipling agreed, writing of the 'white man's burden', the destiny of the Anglo-Saxon race to rule over the 'lesser breeds without the law' – repugnant sentiments in this day and age.) But in Rhodes's day, the magnate had a whole country named after him, and he was considered a heroic, inspirational figure. He inspired great loyalty from a wide group of people at the time, and even subsequent to his death. His will requested that his bones be buried on a hilltop in what is now Zimbabwe. Local tribal leaders agreed, and attended his burial service in honour of his positive influence. The temptation might be to say that they knew what was good for them, but when Zimbabwean government officials, following independence from Britain in 1980, tried to exhume Rhodes's grave and erase all memory of him, local tribal leaders again rallied in support of Rhodes and succeeded in preventing the exhumation.

The 'Rhodes Must Fall' campaign launched with the goal of getting his statue taken down from the campus of the University of Cape Town, on the basis that 'the fall of "Rhodes" is symbolic for the inevitable fall of white supremacy and privilege at our campus.' Two and a half weeks later, following a takeover and blockade of one of the main university buildings by students, the university's senate capitulated and announced that the statue would be removed. Within a month of the launch of the campaign, the statue was gone. The movement then turned its attention to other institutions with connections to Rhodes. In May 2015, the governing body of Rhodes University in the Eastern Cape responded to pressure from its own newly formed student activist group, approving plans to formally begin the process of changing the name of the university; in November 2015, the University of Stellenbosch approved plans to change the language used in the university from Afrikaans to English; and in January 2016 the University of Oxford's Oriel College, where Rhodes had studied briefly, announced that it had removed a plaque in honour of Rhodes and that it was launching a six-month consultation on whether to remove a small statue of Rhodes on the front of the college building itself.

As our societies evolve, so too do our views of what is acceptable and what is not. Should Rhodes's reputation be seen in the context of views that are acceptable in today's society, or should one take into account the prevailing narrative of the time? In that context, his white supremacist views were not unusual. Understanding the past demands that we recognize and account for the prevailing economic, political, cultural and societal context. Only then can we make sense of the contradiction that we see in Nelson Mandela – one of the main victims of Rhodes's apartheid policies – supporting the educational work of the Rhodes Trust. Some argue that racism and bigotry is just that in whatever age it takes place, and that such behaviour should be called out for what it is at any time. It is hard to argue against that, living as we do in a society that finds these things abhorrent. But there was a consistent and vocal commentary defending the existence of the Rhodes statue in Oxford from people across the political spectrum. While none defended Rhodes's values, they did defend the right for history to exist and not be subject to narrative revisionism on the basis of modern thought. After all, where would such revisionism stop? Would we tear down Churchill's statue because of his racist views? In a statement to the Palestine Royal Commission in 1937, Churchill stated: 'I do not admit for instance, that a great wrong has been done to the Red Indians of America or the black people of Australia. I do not admit that a wrong has been done to these people by the fact that a stronger race, a higher-grade race, a more worldly wise race to put it that way, has come in and taken their place.' In the end, the consultation at Oxford concluded that the statue of Rhodes should stay on Oriel's walls.

At the same time as the Rhodes debate was raging, ISIS was destroying historic sites of interest where temples and artefacts suggest there is more than one god. ISIS viewed such sites as pagan and idolatrous, and called for their destruction. A video, posted by ISIS in 2015, shows the destruction of ruins in the Iraqi city of Nimrud. In it, an ISIS soldier explains, 'Whenever we take control of a piece of land, we remove the symbols of polytheism and spread monotheism in it.' One of the latest acts of destruction at the time of writing was that of the historic Temple of Baalshamin, the centre-piece of an ancient city that was 'an oasis of date palms and gardens' in the Syrian desert and that had become known as the Venice of the Sands.

The historian Niall Ferguson deplores this iconoclasm. He identifies a tendency throughout history to destroy historical refer-ences that offend at times when it seems acceptable to do so because of the context in which that destruction takes place. The destruc-tion of the Berlin Wall, widely regarded as a good thing, and the toppling of the statue of Saddam Hussein following the fall of Baghdad, are but two examples. Ferguson and others have called for the addition of context, rather than the removal of history, when it comes to reputational narratives. London's Parliament Square – home to statues of six British prime ministers – is a testa-ment to this approach. Nelson Mandela now stands in the square meters away from Jan Smuts who was a vocal supporter of segrega-tion of blacks from whites in South Africa.

THE REAL CALIGULA

Helen Mirren once memorably described *Caligula*, the 1979 US–Italian movie bankrolled by the Penthouse organization, in which she had a part, as an 'irresistible mix of art and genitals'. The film is so awful that it is a classic: you have to look carefully to find the art, but there are genitals everywhere, most memorably when the emperor allows himself to be pleasured in his swimming pool. Caligula engages in bisexual orgies, sleeps with his beloved sister Drusilla, consigns the wives and daughters of the nobility to a brothel within his royal palace, turns himself into a god, declares his horse a senator, and generally behaves in a monstrous way until he is murdered, along with his wife and baby daughter, by his traitorous Praetorian guards. The murder took place in a corridor of his palace and was a fitting ending to his short and ghastly reign. The soldiers put the stammering Claudius on the throne, where he survived until the ripe old age of sixty-four. (The BBC TV series *I Claudius* went even further, portraying Caligula killing his pregnant sister and eating the foetus that he ripped from her womb, a scene so horrible it was banned in the US.)

The film served to reinforce the truly dreadful reputation of Caligula, otherwise known as Gaius Caesar Germanicus, who occupied the throne for just four years from 37 to 41 CE. 'It is almost superfluous to enumerate the unworthy successors of Augustus,' the eighteenth-century historian Edward Gibbon wrote in his *History of the Decline and Fall of the Roman Empire* (1776– 89). 'Their unparalleled vices, and the splendid theatre on which they were acted, have saved them from oblivion. The dark unrelenting Tiberius, the furious Caligula, the feeble Claudius, the profligate and cruel Nero, the beastly Vitellius, and the timid inhuman Domitian, are condemned to everlasting infamy. During four-score years ... Rome groaned beneath an unremitting tyranny, which exterminated the ancient families of the republic, and was fatal to almost every virtue, and every talent, that arose in that unhappy period.'

But were the emperors really that bad? There were fourteen of them in the 180 years from the death of Augustus to that of Commodus, assassinated in AD 192. There were some upstanding rulers, including Trajan, Hadrian, Antoninus Pius and the philosophical Marcus Aurelius, but plenty of debased and psychopathic

241

ones, including of course Nero, who famously fiddled while Rome burned around him. Was poor Caligula (his nickname signifying 'little boots' after the sandals he wore as a child soldier out on campaign with his father) really anything like as mad or bad as his reputation, or the films, might suggest? Although contemporaneous accounts do refer to his cruelty, love of luxury and capricious manner, the main source of lurid stories about Caligula and the other debauched emperors was Suetonius, writing almost a century after his death.

According to the historian Mary Beard, later accounts of the lives of the emperors would be conditioned by two enduring political themes. The first was the perspective of the senatorial class, who found many of their historic privileges rubbed out with the end of the Republic, and were naturally inclined to portray all emperors in a bad light. Most of the salacious stories that trickled down to Suetonius over the generations probably reflected this bias. The second and more important issue was regime change. The Romans never developed a workable system for imperial succession, and as a result three emperors were assassinated (Caligula, Nero and Domitian), while for the others succession almost inevitably meant political instability, violence, score-settling and vicious rumour. Livia, for example, was said to have poisoned her husband Augustus by smearing all the figs on a tree with poison, and the supposedly reluctant leader Claudius was rumoured to have been poisoned by his much younger wife Agrippina, sister of Caligula and mother of Nero.

Caligula's reputation is enduring and memorable, reflecting the power of lurid story to capture our imaginations nearly two thousand years after the events supposedly took place. Emperors who came to the throne through assassination had a strong interest in playing an uncompromising set of moves in the reputation game. The objective was to blacken the name of their murdered predecessor for all time, telling stories so grotesque and horrible that their murders looked excusable by contrast. As Mary Beard explains: 'It is hard to resist the conclusion that, whatever kernel of truth they might have, the stories told about [Caligula] are an inextricable mixture of fact, exaggeration, wilful misinterpretation and outright invention – largely constructed after his death, and largely for the benefit of the new emperor, Claudius ... To put it another way, [Caligula] may have been assassinated because he was a monster, but it is equally possible that he was made into a monster because he was assassinated.'[1]

THE ROLE OF STORYTELLER

To help us understand the way in which historical reputations are created, we spoke to Hilary Mantel, the author who has written many historical novels, including the Man Booker-winning *Wolf Hall* and *Bring Up the Bodies*, the first two of a planned trilogy centred on the life of Tudor statesman Thomas Cromwell. Mantel's novels portray Cromwell in a sympathetic light: while we are led to understand that he had ruthless and unpleasant characteristics, these are mitigated by his great intelligence and surprising sensitivity and loyalty to those around him.

Cromwell's reputation has fluctuated over time. He was a hero to the Elizabethans and a villain to the Victorians – the latter saw him as the destroyer of quaint medieval picture-book England through the dissolution of the monasteries. More recently, he has been seen portrayed (for example in Robert Bolt's play *A Man for All Seasons*) as a brutal fixer for the king, a foil to the supposedly benign Thomas More (whom Mantel portrays as a torturer).

There was a divide between what the public knew of Cromwell – not much, but they thought he was a bad man – and the way he was treated by academic historians, for whom he was not obscure at all. After the great historian G. R. Elton placed Cromwell at the heart of his work, Cromwell became the focus of intense and continuing debate.

'But I found the portrait of Cromwell in popular history was founded on repetition of unexamined tropes and a handful of factoids,' Mantel told us. 'People really do confuse him with Oliver

– or perhaps with Vikings – and believe that Henry VIII sent armed bands around to ride into churches and smite off monks' heads. No wonder they believe it – they've seen it on TV. In this respect the Cromwell problem is just part of a wider problem – there's a type of history out there that's big, bold, highly coloured and wrong. Mainly in fiction and drama. Though I think that TV factual history could be a bit more searching at times. It seems to be mainly about condescending to the past.'

Mantel knew that she was challenging the received version, particularly the image captured by Hans Holbein in his famous portrait of Cromwell. 'Holbein did him no favours,' reflects Mantel. 'Probably the portrait is responsible for our quick take on him as dour and thuggish. Whereas if you look at what his contemporaries say about him, you realize he was a very charming thug. The evidence cuts against the popular perception. But one image does more than a library.'

Early in Mantel's career, she wrote *A Place of Greater Safety*, a novel about the French Revolution. She compares the portrait of Cromwell to the varying portraits of Robespierre: 'No one ever reproduces the salon portrait of 1790. It's always one of the 1793 portraits, where he has aged ten years and looks pinched and cold. I think for the French it's a matter of where you stand politically. Here, it's just the same sort of ignorance as with Cromwell – once someone is cast as the bad guy, it's hard to shake.'

Thus imagination and literary panache help us to challenge received wisdom and the prejudices of influential experts and artists. Having a great novelist on your side is a certain way to see a historic reputation remade.

THE POWER OF EPITHET

Ivan the Terrible has probably one of the most famous names in history. This cognomen, as the one-word epithet applied to his name is known, is an English translation of the Russian word *grozny*, which means terrifying, dangerous or inspiring fear. This was the name that he was known by during his lifetime, a name that reflected his regular outbursts of incandescent rage, his obvious mental illness and stupendous brutality. The name proved highly valuable as a reputation tool in keeping dissent to a minimum domestically, and preparing the ground for territorial conquests. Originally grand prince of Moscow from 1533 to 1547, he created an empire spanning over a billion acres of land stretching from the Gulf of Finland in the north to the Caspian Sea in the south, and from the Polish border of today in the west to modern-day Siberia in the east. His epithet was helpful to him when he was alive, and has continued to define his reputation in history after he died.

Epithets have been in use a very long time. Homer uses them extensively in the *Iliad* and the *Odyssey*, referring to Athena as 'the grey-eyed goddess'. Various objects, too, have epithets such as a 'long-shadowed spear', 'fertile land' and the 'wine dark sea'. This is a form of rhetorical shorthand whereby one or two powerful, memorable words are attached to a person or object. Such phrases probably helped the bards to remember the story in the days before it was written down. Cognomens are a subset of epithets: names that are added either before or after a person's name. Examples of this include William 'The Conqueror' or Alfred and Alexander 'The Great'. Initially used in ancient Rome, cognomens were nicknames used to help identify the individual at a time when there were a limited number of names in common use. One such example would be Leo II, called Leo 'The Little' by dint of the fact that he became Caesar and then emperor when he was six years old (and was poisoned and died shortly afterwards). These cognomens subsequently became used as honorific titles, conferred by a grateful public or senate on military commanders who had achieved great victories for the Roman Republic. While this practice originated in ancient Rome, it was also adopted by many later empires, especially the Napoleonic, British and Russian.

'In Rome, rather like in the House of Lords, you could either be granted a name in recognition of something that you did that was great (an *agnomina*) like conquering a country, or simply call yourself something,' explains Dr Chris McKenna of Oxford University.[2] 'Examples of those granted titles include Scipio "Africanus" (the African, after his successful African military campaign against Hannibal), Pompey "Magnus" (the Great), Sulla "Felix" (the Lucky). And once you had earned that cognomen, you could pass it on to your family. So, Tiberius Claudius Drusus Nero Germanicus Britannicus Caesar Augustus had inherited most of those titles except "Britannicus" which he was awarded for his successful campaign in Britain. But people like Caesar (meaning "hairy") and Cicero ("chick-pea nose") had family names that they were simply carrying on. Moving into more recent history, you still see epithets in use,' says McKenna.

His favourite is, of course, 'His Excellency, President for Life, Field Marshal Al Hadji Doctor Idi Amin Dada, VC, DSO, MC, Lord of All the Beasts of the Earth and Fishes of the Seas and Conqueror of the British Empire in Africa in General and Uganda in Particular', who also claimed to be 'the Last King of Scotland'. This would suggest that epithets are created by the recipient as well as conferred by others. Conferring a name on yourself becomes a behavioural signal – a sort of personal branding, and a sign both of how you want to be seen and your self-esteem. Having an epithet conferred on you is a more direct reputational mechanism, reflecting the views and opinions of those surrounding you in the context of the society that you inhabit.

Throughout the ages, kings, queens and other leaders have also been subjected to epithets. Examples include Constantine XI, 'the Sleeping King'; Charles Howard, 'the Drunken Duke'; Charles II, 'the Mutton-Eating Monarch'; and Richard 'The Lionheart'. One of the more enduring is that of Lorenzo the Magnificent. Lorenzo was a scion of one of the most important families in Europe at the time of the Renaissance. His grandfather Cosimo de' Medici was one of the wealthiest men in Europe, and the first Medici to run the family bank at the same time as running the Republic of Florence. Lorenzo inherited his grandfather's appreciation for culture. A noted patron of the Italian Renaissance, he supported young talented artists such as Leonardo da Vinci, Sandro Botticelli, Michelangelo Buonarroti and the architect Vitruvius. He was also an accomplished diplomat and a powerful political manipulator, becoming the de facto ruler of the Florentine Republic through his network of contacts and the strategic use of his wealth. Lorenzo's court was the epicentre of magnificence – a melee of artists, writers and architects connected to the power, influence and money of the Florentine Republic. Lorenzo was the ultimate network broker in the Renaissance, a schemer, power broker and bully, as well as philanthropist and patron of the arts. But what became his dominant reputation is the epithet given to him by the nobles and storytellers of the time: Lorenzo the Magnificent.

Sadly for Lorenzo, this epithet was not inherited by his son and heir, Piero 'The Unfortunate'. Not only did he squander his father's legacy and wealth, but ultimately he was responsible for the collapse and fall of the Medici dynasty. But Lorenzo the Magnificent's name and epithet live on eternally, testament to the power of a single word to cut through the complexities of history and create an enduringly positive reputation.

8

CONCLUSION

We started this book posing questions about how individuals, companies, institutions, public figures and nation states create, sustain, destroy and rebuild their reputations. We have sought to answer these questions through drawing on peer-reviewed research from leading scholars around the world, supported by insights from people who have played the reputation game in practice, in public and private life. Knowing what we now know, what should we do differently in pursuit of that most precious commodity, a good reputation?

Successful players of the reputation game are better paid, have access to better career opportunities, live happier lives and are able to recover more quickly from setbacks. But believing that you are completely in control of your reputation is a route to disappointment. And you cannot manage what you ultimately do not control. Reputation 'management' is a very dangerous idea. It assumes you can manipulate people's understanding of you on a permanent basis. Successful players of the reputation game understand that they can create a reputation engagement strategy that seeks to influence – rather than control – perceptions about them.

Players of the game should first reflect on the signals that they send through their choice of behaviours. But these behaviours also need to be referenced against others' expectations. Behaving well when you are expected to do so will keep you where you are; but behaving badly will send you crashing down to earth.

Think about the signals you are sending about your competence and your character. This is one of the most useful ways of thinking about reputation. Capability reputations – what you are perceived as being able to do in any given circumstance – take time and skill to earn, and once they are earned they are very sticky. It is hard to destroy them. Character reputations, by contrast, are up for debate and discussion on an almost constant basis. They are flighty, but they are also perhaps the most visible and important factor underpinning your different reputations.

The second major strategy is to think carefully about the networks that surround you. You need to consider the structure of the networks – are they closed or are they open? Closed networks will see trusted information about you move fast. In open networks, however, information moves at a more leisurely pace: you have a chance to engage with lots of different people on a more individual basis, and to be exposed to new perspectives.

We're all part of multiple different networks – family, friends, colleagues, college networks and so on. Being able to connect people from these different networks makes you a valued network broker. As Ron Burt's work shows, network brokers have access to more information more quickly than those who operate only within a closed network, and as such brokers have a better reputation. So, think about the different networks that surround you, and where you can look for opportunities to connect them up. It will be fun and enjoyable, and you will find that people thank you for it later.

Successful players of the reputation game also recognize that networks are not passive. You need to be able to activate people within your network to speak about you at the right time and with the right people. Reputations are contested and we need to make sure that we have our allies marshalled and ready to act when it matters most.

Some of these allies will be more influential than others. Reputation borrowing and lending is a very valuable tactic in the reputation game. Reputation borrowing – associating yourself with high-status and high-reputation others early on – can turbocharge your progress. Later, your ability to lend your reputation to help others becomes greater. This brings benefits – consider the way Tom Jones reinvented his music career – but doing so also exposes you to greater risks as you become associated with the fortunes or failures of others.

Reputations do not live in a vacuum – they are stories we tell one another. Successful players of the game understand that it is not just the sophistication of your narrative that matters, but its authenticity. Inauthentic narratives can backfire, while narratives that manage to be authentic create real and lasting value.

Authenticity rests on two connected things. First, you need to make sure that your narrative actually reflects your core DNA. There may have been a time when it was hard to spot inconsistencies, but in a world of increasing network closure, if there is dissonance there then it will be quickly found and outed.

Your narrative also needs to recognize, and be sympathetic to, context change. This is a difficult balancing act, because being authentic should of course be all about being true to yourself despite the vagaries of the headlines. But if the public context changes and enough people are motivated to speak against you, you can suffer reputational damage and risk being seen as tone deaf. Of course, it is still possible to be out of step with public opinion and win in the reputation game, but it does become much harder. Reputations are constantly being contested, and having the weight of public opinion against you is hard.

We all have multiple reputations for something with someone. Knowing this enables you to invest in the reputations that matter, and ignore others that don't. It's both liberating and practical – we can concentrate on a limited number of valuable aspects of our reputations, and not be thrown off course trying to do everything at once.

We have all experienced times when we wish the ground would open and swallow us up. Canny players of the reputation game can – like Jack Profumo – change their context, open up a new world, and reset the game with new behaviours and narratives, making use of whatever network remains available to them or finding a new one.

Ultimately, we are all playing the reputation game. Most of us, whether we know it or not, are playing to win, and if we play our hand well, our reputations will keep our stock high even after we leave the table.

NOTES

INTRODUCTION

1. Donald J. Trump (@realDonaldTrump) 2 February 2017.
2. Robert G. Eccles, Scott C. Newquist and Roland Schatz, 'Reputation and its Risks', *Harvard Business Review*, February 2007.
3. Global Insurer Aon conducts a biannual boardroom risks survey and the most recent one ranks damage to reputation in position four out of ten – ahead of cashflow/liquidity risk, commodity price risk, and technology /system failure (among others). Boards care deeply about reputational damage.

1 THE RULES OF THE GAME

1. http://www.rollingstone.com/politics/news/the-great-american-bubble-machine-20100405.

2 BEHAVIOURS

1. See John Whitfield, 'The Biology of Reputation', in *The Reputation Society: How Online Opinions are Reshaping the Offline World*, ed. Hassum Masum and Mark Tovey (Cambridge, Mass: MIT Press, 2011), pp. 39–49.
2. Louise Barrett, Robin Dunbar and John Lycett, *Human Evolutionary Psychology* (London and New York: Palgrave, 2002), pp. 260–2.
3. He is Professor in the School of Public Policy and Department of Criminology, University of Maryland.

4. Diego Gambetta and Peter Reuter, *Conspiracy Among the Many*, published in 1995; see: http://www.academia.edu/458525/Conspiracy_Among_the_Many_the_Mafia_In_Legitimate_Industries. A shorter analysis is contained in his article 'Regulating Rackets', in *Regulation*, September/December, 1984, pp. 29–36 and available online at http://object.cato.org/sites/cato.org/files/serials/files/regulation/1984/12/v8n5-5.pdf.

5. In late 2015, Japan's upper house of parliament approved a bill allowing Japan to engage in 'collective self defence', fighting with allies overseas. This overturned Article 9 of the Japanese Constitution that outlawed war as a means of settling international disputes; see http://edition.cnn.com/2015/09/16/asia/japan-military-constitution/.

6. In 'Perverting Trust', her Clare Hall Ashby Lecture, University of Cambridge, 15 May 2009.

7. Rachel Croson and Nancy Buchan, 'Gender and Culture: International Experimental Evidence from Trust Games', *American Economic Review*, 89 (2), May 1999, pp. 386–91 (https://www.aeaweb.org/articles?id=10.1257/aer.89.2.386).

Repeated behaviours build valuable reputations. Four Italian scholars – from the Universities of Breschia and Torino – extended Berg's study in 2008 into a repeated trust game. These four scholars created a new dynamic where both Group A and Group B players had the possibility to rate their opponents' behaviour and also to know their past ratings over repeated interactions. In this way, they hoped to identify the power of character reputational cues based on observed past behaviours. Their results showed that being rated by other players, and letting this rating be known, significantly increased co-operation levels between the groups – in other words, players were more willing to transact in the hope that there will be mutual benefit. And even more intriguingly, they found that reputation is so deeply rooted in human psychological mechanisms that subjects tend to build and maintain a high reputational status even when it is neither rational to do so nor explained by reciprocity motives.

8. David Foster Wallace, 'Roger Federer as Religious Experience', *New York Times*, 20 August 2006.

9. See http://www.bloomberg.com/news/articles/2013-02-20/armstrong-s-cheating-won-record-riches-of-more-than-218-million.

10. Christophe Bassons, from BBC Radio 5, 2012.

11. See http://www.transparency.org/news/feature/global_corruption_report _sport.
12. See http://www.bbc.co.uk/programmes/b06tkl9d.
13. In a speech titled 'Enhancing Financial Stability by Improving Culture in the Financial Services Industry', 20 October 2014.
14. See http://www.ibtimes.co.uk/20-global-banks-have-paid-235bn-fines-since -2008-financial-crisis-1502794.
15. Alain Cohn, Ernst Fehr and Michel André Maréchal, 'Business Culture and Dishonesty in the Banking Industry', *Nature*, 516, 4 December 2014, pp. 86–9.
16. See http://www.goldmansachs.com/who-we-are/business-standards/busi-ness-principles/.
17. See https://profilebooks.com/investing-in-change-ebook.html. In a book chapter for the Association for Financial Markets in Europe, one of the authors argued, together with Professor Alan Morrison of Oxford University and Professor Bill Wilhelm of the University of Virginia, that technology in the financial services industry has in part reduced the power of reputation as a regulatory mechanism.
18. Lord Green's St Michael's Cornhill lecture, 'Belief in the City', 18 March 2015.
19. You can read his open letter here: http://www.starbucks.co.uk/blog/an-open-letter-from-kris-engskov/1249. 'These actions will position us as a company to make a larger contribution in tax and most importantly to the communities we serve while we make the moves necessary to achieve a sustainable level of profitability. We believe that this is the right thing to do. We've listened to our customers and we're taking the actions necessary to pay more corporation tax in the UK, above what we are required to.'
20. See http://www.telegraph.co.uk/technology/google/12151032/Google-boss -International-tax-laws-should-be-rewritten.html.
21. See http://www.mirror.co.uk/money/city-news/costa-coffee-taxing-question-starbucks-1395473.
22. See http://www.telegraph.co.uk/news/2016/09/14/jean-claude-juncker-denies -alcohol-problem-during-interview-in-w/.
23. http://www.economist.com/node/21552243.
24. http://www.telegraph.co.uk/finance/economics/7330761/Michel-Barnier-the-most-dangerous-man-in-Europe.html.
25. http://www.mirror.co.uk/news/uk-news/theresa-may-vicars-daughter-kitten-8399895.

26. http://www.politics.co.uk/comment-analysis/2016/06/27/boris-johnson-the-man-who-broke-britain.

27. http://metro.co.uk/2016/10/24/nicola-sturgeon-and-theresa-may-face-off-in-feisty-brexit-summit-6212835/.

28. See George A. Akerlof, 'The Market for Lemons: Quality Uncertainty and the Market Mechanism', *Quarterly Journal of Economics*, 84 (3), 1970, pp. 488–500.

29. David M. Kreps and Robert Wilson, 'Reputation and Imperfect Information', *Journal of Economic Theory*, 27, 1982, pp. 253–79.

30. This scenario was first explored by R. Selten in 'The Chain Store Paradox', *Theory and Decision*, 9, 1978, pp. 127–59.

31. See http://www.theatlantic.com/magazine/archive/2016/04/the-obama-doctrine/471525/.

32. Alvin Roth was economics professor at the University of Pittsburgh; Francoise Schoumaker, an assistant professor of economics at the University of Illinois. Their paper 'Expectations and Reputations in Bargaining: An Experimental Study' is published in the *American Economic Review*, 73 (3), 1983, pp. 362–72.

33. The computer was programmed to be completely rational in its choices of whether to accept or reject the offers made. Players were divided into three groups, each with different conditions. The first group played against a computer that was programmed to select the outcome that would maximize returns for both sides. This group was called 'the 20–80 group' as per the analysis above. The second group played against a computer that was programmed to select the outcome that split the amount of lottery tickets evenly between the players. This group was called 'the 50–50 group'. The third group was a control group where players always bargained with other real people.

34. 'In order to avoid lengthy and ugly litigation . . . that would hurt the reputation of everyone, I decided to negotiate an assumption of the necessary hedge position of the families who were forcing the sale. They agreed to be responsible for any loss incurred on my part ("hold harmless agreements") and this was key to my taking over the positions. As close as I was to the families in question I felt that, due to the advanced age and poor health of the patriarchs of the families, I asked to have their trust agreements and wills amended to protect my interests in the event of their demise. This was in fact accomplished.

'The sales of the long positions took place, locking in their gains and they [the families] withdrew their moneys to cover their taxes [which were due on these gains]. As some time passed, the market recovered and two things started to happen. The fathers' greed began to get the upper hand and in order to protect their potential commitment to cover my posses on the hedges [that I had assumed] they started to make outside investments.

'I heard that these [outside] investments were not going well and cash withdrawals for outside margin calls were requested. I began worrying that my agreements with them were in jeopardy. I felt that it was necessary to alter my investment mngt [management] business plan and increase my commissions as well . . . to replace the capital I was using to cover the . . . hedge losses that were starting to build.'

35. 'I foolishly convinced myself that I should short the strategy to the clients, losing the spread between the yield on the Treasuries and the expected spread on a successful trade [under the new strategy]. I thought this would only be a short-term trade that could be made up once the market became receptive to actually accomplish a real long trade.'

3 NETWORKS

1. He attributes his success to 'the three As': availability, affability and ability.
2. Nicholas Christakis and James Fowler, *The Amazing Power of Social Networks and How They Shape Our Lives* (London: Harper Press, 2010).
3. Milgram's article 'Small World' appeared in *Psychology Today* in 1967. It showed what happened when a few hundred people in Nebraska were instructed to send a letter to a complete stranger one thousand miles away. On average, it took six letters to get to the right person.
4. Alan Morrison, a professor of finance and law at the University of Oxford's Saïd Business School, has studied behavioural signals within investment banking networks for over twenty-five years. Together with co-author Bill Wilhelm, a professor of finance at the University of Virginia's McIntire School of Commerce, and two others, he created a unique database of share offers and the banks that underwrote them from 1933 to 1969, together with similar data for 1970–2007, to study

long-running trends in investment-bank relationships with their clients, and with one another.

This study found that issuers of securities have placed an increasing emphasis upon the quantity and the quality of their investment bank's connections with other banks over the period. In other words, their place in the network has become critically important to winning new business – it's a reputation-signalling mechanism.

5. See https://www.statista.com/statistics/274911/forecasted-global-diamond-production/.

6. Producing float glass is a fascinating production process. The ingredients for glass are mixed in a vast furnace (called a float bath) of up to two thousand tonnes, creating molten glass at extreme heat – up to 1,500 °C. Once it has reached this temperature and is properly mixed, molten glass pours from the float bath onto a mirror-like surface of molten tin. During this process, it starts to cool down. Then the glass is coated with whatever property the customer requires – it might be reflective glass, or self-cleaning glass that contains a microscopically thin and transparent coating of titanium oxide. The glass continues to cool as it makes its way along the float line – which can be up to a quarter of a mile long – and undergoes further treatment and inspection before finally being cut to order.

7. The City today is a much more open and meritocratic place, but a misstep can mean you are cast into outer reputational darkness. Ian Hannam was a controversial but gifted banker with JP Morgan (Cazenove's ultimate owner today), who was fined by City regulators for disclosing insider information. Hannam told the *Financial Times* over lunch that his former chum Bill Winters, a banker appointed to head Standard Chartered, could no longer remain associated with him. 'He was a friend,' Hannam said ruefully, his eyes moistening, but now that he was in semi-disgrace it was just too difficult for the CEO to keep up the friendship (*Financial Times*, 5 September 2015).

8. A portmanteau of 'ENA', the acronym for these institutions, and the word for monarch.

9. See http://www.dailymail.co.uk/debate/article-2699426/Solid-Gold-Sociopath-Fred-The-Shred-came-personify-greed-banks-But-brilliant-new-book-Daily-Mail-s-City-Editor-shows-toxic-realised.html.

10. See Mark Granovetter, 'The Strength of Weak Ties', *American Journal of Sociology*, 78 (6), May 1973, pp. 1360–80.

11. Mark Granovetter, 'The Strength of Weak Ties: A Network Theory Revisited', *Sociological Theory*, 1, 1983, pp. 201–33.

12. See Ron Burt, 'Brokerage and Closure: An Introduction to Social Capital', University of Chicago Graduate School of Business, Autumn 2005, available at: http://faculty.chicagobooth.edu/ronald.burt/research/files/B&C_Introduction.pdf.

13. Cited in Burt, 'Brokerage and Closure', p. 73.

14. Full disclosure: the other Finsbury founder is Rupert Younger, one of the authors of this book.

15. http://www.guinnessworldrecords.com/news/2015/5/eurovision-recognised-by-guinness-world-records-as-the-longest-running-annual-tv-379520.

16. Dave Troy has documented the social networks of cities as varied as Baltimore, Rio de Janeiro and San Francisco: see www.davetroy.com for more details.

17. See http://www.nytimes.com/2015/08/22/arts/music/dr-dre-apologizes-to-the-women-ive-hurt.html?mwrsm=Email&_r=0.

18. danah boyd, *It's Complicated: The Social Lives of Networked Teens* (New Haven: Yale University Press, 2014), pp. 29–30.

19. Dr danah boyd is a principal researcher at Microsoft Research, and the founder of Data & Society. Her website is www.danah.org.

20. The term was created iteratively by boyd, drawing on research from Joshua Meyrowitz and subsequently used in 2009 by cultural anthropologist Michael Wesch at Kansas State University. See http://www.zephoria.org/thoughts/archives/2013/12/08/coining-context-collapse.html.

21. Alice E. Marwick and danah boyd, 'I Tweet Honestly, I Tweet Passionately: Twitter Users, Context Collapse, and the Imagined Audience', *New Media & Society*, 20 (1), July 2010, pp. 1–20.

22. Tim Pollock looked at this phenomenon together with James Wade from George Washington University, Joe Porac from New York University and Scott Graffin from the University of Georgia. In a 2008 paper published in *Organization Science*, they found clear evidence that celebrity impacted a CEO's earnings potential: 'In analysing how star status affects a CEO's compensation, we found that star CEOs received a compensation premium of nearly 11% immediately after winning a medal. This translates into a pay raise of roughly $265,000 for a medal-winning CEO. The longer-term impact of winning a medal, however, depended to a large

extent on the firm's subsequent performance. If the firm performed well, medal-winning CEOs continued to enjoy higher pay when compared with equivalent performance achieved by their less renowned counterparts. However, when performance was poor, star CEOs received lower compensation than CEOs who had never won a medal and achieved the same level of performance.' See Graffin, Wade, Porac and McNamee, 'The Impact of CEO Status Diffusion on the Economic Outcomes of Other Senior Managers', *Organization Science*, 19 (3), 2008, pp. 457–74.

23. Mike Pfarrer, a professor of management at the University of Georgia's Terry School of Business, picked up this theme in a paper, co-authored with Rindova and Pollock, which tested this hypothesis in the context of stock-market listed companies. The paper, published in 2010 in the *Academy of Management Journal*, found that 'firms that have accumulated high levels of reputation are less likely, and firms that have achieved celebrity more likely, to announce positive surprises than firms without these assets. [And] both high reputation and celebrity firms experience greater market rewards for positive surprises and smaller market penalties for negative surprises than other firms.'

24. See http://proceedings.aom.org/content/2015/1/14966.short.

25. *Financial Times*, 25 August 2014.

26. *MIT Sloan Management Review*, Winter 2014.

27. They took a sample of comments from a five-month period, sorting them randomly into one of three groups – a positive recommendation group, a negative recommendation group and a neutral recommendation group, irrespective of the number of positive, negative or neutral recommendations that the comment had received so far. They then manipulated the initial review as follows: comments in the positive recommendation group were artificially given an added positive review, comments in the negative group were given an added negative review and comments in the neutral group were given an added neutral review. The aim of the experiment was to see the extent to which subsequent reviewers of the comments would be influenced by the positivity, or otherwise, of the initial review.

The results were as follows. Comments in the positive group were thirty-two per cent more likely to receive a positive vote in the future than what had been observed before the experiment. This was also the case with the negative votes, but intriguingly the herding effects were asymmetric. Those comments that were allocated into the negative group did receive – like the positive group – a significantly greater number of negative votes. But there was also, unlike in the positive group, a correction effect – comments in this group were also significantly more likely to be given a positive vote than positive comments were to be given a negative vote. In other words, there was a positivity bias – we want to rate people well if we possibly can.

4 NARRATIVES

1. Keynote speech at MIDEM, the 2015 music industry conference, in Cannes, France.
2. Yuval Noah Harari, *Sapiens: A Brief History of Humankind* (London: Harper, 2015), p. 103.
3. *The Times*, 7 April 2016, p. 24.
4. See https://medium.com/@jaycarney/what-the-new-york-times-didn-t-tell -you-a1128aa78931#.nk0gjzrxs.
5. See http://www.fastcompany.com/3055894/most-innovative-companies/ what-buzzfeeds-dao-nguyen-knows-about-data-intuition-and-the-futur.
6. See https://www.nytimes.com/2017/01/28/opinion/sunday/live-from-the-white-house-its-trump-tv.html?smid=nytcore-ipad-share&smprod=nytcore-ipad&_r=0.
7. See https://www.buzzfeed.com/craigsilverman/viral-fake-election-news-outperformed-real-news-on-facebook?utm_term=.lf6al9nrVd#.toN8wEBVJ0.
8. See https://en.oxforddictionaries.com/word-of-the-year/word-of-the-year -2016.
9. See https://medium.com/@contently/how-i-handled-my-personal-story-going-viral-ad7cae7ec03#.rn7pvxgth.
10. See http://www.samblackman.org/Articles/Suler.pdf.

5 MANAGING CRISIS

1. See http://www.csb.gov/assets/1/19/csbfinalreportbp.pdf.
2. http://www.bp.com/content/dam/bp/pdf/sustainability/issue-reports/ Deepwater_Horizon_Accident_Investigation_Report.pdf.
3. See http://www.bp.com/en/global/corporate/press/press-releases/bp-estimates-all-remaining-material-deepwater-horizon-liabilitie.html.

4. 'Memo to board: we need to talk about BP', *Financial Times*, 1 May 2007.
5. Cited in Mattias Holweg of Saïd Business School's *Oxford Today* article, 18 April 2016. See http://www.oxfordtoday.ox.ac.uk/interviews/what-went-wrong-volkswagen-and-why.
6. 'VW Faces Activist Attack', *Financial Times*, 7 May 2016, p. 13.
7. Catholics are divided on other big questions, Americans and Europeans in favour of marriage for priests and gay people, welcoming to the idea of women priests, while the opposite is true for the developing world. See survey by Univision in February 2014: http://www.washingtonpost.com/wp-srv/special/world/catholic-poll/.
8. See http://www.catholicworldreport.com/Blog/4475/large_decrease_in_visitors_to_papal_events_in_2015_jubilee_numbers_low_so_far.aspx.
9. Writing for the pamphlet OMFIF (n.a.).
10. John L. Allen, 'Pope Francis Faces a Real Dilemma in Vatileaks 2.0', *Crux*, 23 December 2015, available at https://cruxnow.com/church/2015/12/23/pope-francis-faces-a-real-dilemma-in-vatileaks-2-0/.
11. Damian Thompson, 'The Devil in Footnote 351', *The Spectator*, 16 April 2016.
12. Address at the 48th World Day of Communications, 1 June 2014.
13. He had agitated behind the scenes to protect fellow Catholics from the death squads, but he was not a heroic reforming figure like Oscar Romero, the Salvadorian bishop who was assassinated in 1980 while serving Mass.
14. Alec MacGillis, 'Scandal at Clinton Inc.', available online at https://newrepublic.com/article/114790/how-doug-band-drove-wedge-through-clinton-dynasty.
15. Cited in the *Economist* article 'Life After Power: The Loneliness of Tony Blair', 20 December 2014.
16. *Iraq's Weapons of Mass Destruction: The Assessment of the British Government*, published in September 2002.
17. See http://www.woolflse.com/dl/woolf-lse-report.pdf.
18. See https://docs.google.com/document/d/115dQVYUdxoJRvRTsl8uYL9xe9WTp7QUbLBryMRzKqmI/edit?hl=sv#.
19. See www.marketwatch.com for an analysis of this and other types of apologies.
20. Nicole Gillespie and Graham Dietz, 'Trust Repair After an Organization-Level Failure', *Academy of Management Review*, January 2009.

21. https://www.opendemocracy.net/od-russia/mikhail-fridman/fridman-how-i-became-oligarch.
22. See Bill Browder's account of the Hermitage Capital Management affair: *Red Notice: How I Became Putin's No. 1 Enemy* (London: Bantam Press, 2015).
23. Arkady Ostrovsky, 'Russian Oligarchs Dig Up the Dirt to Present a Clean Image to the West', *Financial Times*, 4 October 2003.

6 ADVANCED TECHNIQUES

1. https://www.statista.com/statistics/246501/athletic-apparel-companies-ranked-by-global-market-share-in-footwear-sales/.
2. Peggy M. Lee, Timothy G. Pollock and Kyuho Jin, 'The Contingent Value of Venture Capitalist Reputation', *Strategic Organization*, 9 (1), pp. 33–69.
3. As at April 2017.
4. Most of Silicon Valley's tech titans have been backed by venture capital firms based in Sand Hill Road. It boasts the highest office cost per square foot in the US (US $111 per square foot), more than Manhattan office space (US $102 per square foot). See https://www.bloomberg.com/news/articles/2014-12-04/venture-capital-sand-hill-road-rules-silicon-valley.
5. Scholars have researched the different effects of reputation and status on the performance of firms. In a 2013 paper published in *Strategic Organisation*, four scholars – David Chandler (University of Colorado, Denver), Pam Haunschild (University of Texas at Austin), Mooweon Rhee (Yonsei University, South Korea) and Christine Beckman (University of California, Irvine) – found that status attracts directors to work for an organization, while reputation inspires these people to be more productive. Their study analysed director networks of the three hundred largest US firms over an eight-year time frame from 1985 to 1993, teasing out the relative contribution of status and reputation.
6. C. E. Devers, T. Dewett, Y. Mishina and C. A. Belsito, 'A General Theory of Organizational Stigma', *Organization Science*, 20 (1), January–February 2009, pp. 154–71.
7. See http://www.thisismoney.co.uk/money/cardsloans/article-2597754/Archbishop-Canterbury-Justin-Welby-wages-war-Wonga.html.
8. See https://www.ft.com/content/ac77fe6c-6971-11e4-8f4f-00144feabdc0.

9. Two of the early pioneers in reputation scholarship, Cees van Riel and Charles Fombrun, argue that corporate reputation captures the effects that brands and images have on the overall evaluations which stakeholders make of companies.
10. See http://majkenschultz.com/books/taking-brand-initiative/.

7 LEGACY

1. Mary Beard, *SPQR: A History of Ancient Rome* (London: Profile Books, 2015), pp. 396–7.
2. Chris McKenna is a reader in business history and strategy at the University of Oxford's Saïd Business School and a fellow and tutor at Brasenose College, Oxford.

ACKNOWLEDGEMENTS

1. Titles and affiliations correct as at April 2017.

ACKNOWLEDGEMENTS

The authors would like to thank the numerous interviewees without whose help and guidance this book would have been much the poorer. We are very grateful to the team at our publishers Oneworld, in particular founders Juliet Mabey and Novin Doostdar for their belief in this book, and to our editor Alex Christofi for his thoughtful comments and attention to detail. Bill Hamilton, our agent at AM Heath, provided invaluable guidance and direction. And of course our thanks go to our respective families who now know far more than they ever wanted to know about the ins and outs of reputation engagement.

In addition, the authors would like to thank Stephan Chambers, Emilio Galli-Zugaro, Dr Rowena Olegario, Paolo Scaroni and Nikhil Srinivasan for their comments and thoughts on the draft manuscript; Ian Davis, for supporting the idea for years and giving generously of his time in the early stages of this project; Liz Young, for her energy and enthusiasm and who – together with Noam Gottesman, Simon Lorne and Stefano Lucchini – introduced us to a number of fascinating and insightful interviewees from Jay-Z to Bernie Madoff; Professor Joe Porac and Dr Tim Hannigan for their work in pulling together a group of leading scholars to discuss scandal in Oxford; the research team at the Oxford University Centre for Corporate Reputation; and the assistants of those we interviewed – the unsung heroes of corporate life without whom nothing would ever get done. We thank all those listed below for their help and guidance as we researched this book, and also for those others who have asked to remain anonymous. We are very grateful to you all. All errors of fact and judgement are our own.[1]

Alberto Lopez-Valenzuela, founder and CEO, the Alva Group
André Hoffmann, Vice Chairman, Hoffmann-La Roche
Andrew Walton, Senior Managing Director, FTI Consulting
Andy Marsh, Chief Constable, Avon and Somerset Police
Anna Mann, co-founder, MWM Consulting
Barry Weiss, founder, Records
Ben Rattray, founder, Change.org
Ben Todd, Syco Entertainment
Bernie Madoff, inmate, Butner Federal Correctional Institution, North Carolina
Bill Campbell, former Chairman, Apple
Bill Curbishley, Trinifold Management and Manager, The Who
Biz Stone, co-founder, Twitter
Bjorn Edlund, Principal, Edlund Consulting
Professor Brayden King, Northwestern University
Brian Boylan, Chairman, Wolff Olins
Christoph Walther, founding partner, CNC AG
Craig Carroll, visiting scholar and Adjunct Professor, NYU
danah boyd, social media scholar, author and researcher
David Kelso, JPMorgan Chase
David Taylor, author
Davide Taliente, Partner, Oliver Wyman
Dennis Kozlowski, businessman, former CEO, Tyco
Dominic West, actor
Don Robert, Chairman, Experian
Donald Steel, former Chief Spokesman at the BBC, now a consultant in crisis communications
Doug Morris, Chairman, Sony Music Entertainment
Ed Reilly, CEO, Strategic Communications at FTI Consulting
Professor Ed Zajac, Northwestern University
Emilio Galli-Zugaro, Chairman, Methodos, former Head of Communications, Allianz SE

ACKNOWLEDGEMENTS

Fred Kempe, President, Atlantic Council

Professor Gary Alan Fine, Northwestern University

Glenn Spiro, founder, Glenn Spiro

Greg Burke, Director of the Holy See Press Office

Hannah Burns, Managing Director, Cambridge Global Advisors

Hilary Mantel, author

Sir Howard Davies, Chairman, Royal Bank of Scotland

Howell James, CEO, Quiller, and former Permanent Secretary of
Government Communication

Hugo Dixon, author and entrepreneur, founder of
Breakingviews

Huw Jenkins, former CEO, UBS Investment Bank

Ian Davis, Chairman of Rolls-Royce plc, former Managing
Partner, McKinsey & Co

Ike Sorkin, attorney, Mintz & Gold

Jamie Lowther-Pinkerton, former Private Secretary to TRH Prince
William and Prince Harry

Jamil Baz, Global Head of Client Analytics, PIMCO

Jancis Robinson, wine writer

Jay-Z, musician and businessman

Jeanmarie Mcfadden, Chief Communications Officer, MetLife

Jeff Randall, Non-Executive Director, Babcock International

Jim Ring, author and adviser

John Hinshaw, Hewlett Packard Enterprise

Jonathan Harper, Spencer Stuart

Julia Hobsbawm, Professor of Networking, Cass Business School

Major General Jonathan Shaw, Chairman, Optima

Justin King, Terra Firma

Keith Schilling, Chairman and Senior Partner, Schillings

Les Moonves, Chairman and CEO, CBS Corporation

Liz Young, Director of Communications, Sony Music Entertainment

Lord Chadlington, former CEO and Chairman, The Huntsworth
Group

Lord Green of Hurstpierpoint, former CEO, HSBC plc

Lord Patten, Chancellor, University of Oxford

ACKNOWLEDGEMENTS

Lucas van Praag, Senior Managing Director at Teneo Strategy, and former Global Head of Corporate Communications, Goldman Sachs

Professor Majken Schultz, Copenhagen Business School

Margit Wennmachers, Partner, Andreessen Horowitz

Mark Bolland, former Deputy Private Secretary to HRH Prince of Wales

Mark Ware, Executive Vice President, Vivo Energy, and former Director of Corporate Affairs at BP plc

Sir Martin Sorrell, CEO, WPP

Max Hohenberg, Partner, CNC

Michael Cole-Fontayn, Chairman, EMEA, BNY Mellon, and Chairman, AFME

Michael Diekmann, former CEO, Allianz SE

Michael Fertik, founder, reputation.com

Mike Abbott, Partner, Kleiner Perkins

Mike Barry, Director of Sustainability, Marks and Spencer

Nathalie Gold, Senior Research Fellow, University College, London

Professor Nicholas Emler, former Professor of Social Psychology, Surrey University

Paddy Harverson, Head of Milltown Partners, and former Communications Secretary to TRH the Prince of Wales, Prince William and Prince Harry

Paolo Scaroni, Vice Chairman, Rothschild

Paul Achleitner, Chairman, Deutsche Bank

Peter Henshaw, Group Head of Communications and External Affairs, BP plc

Professor Peter Reuter, University of Maryland

Peter Stanford, author

Peter Stothard, former Editor, *The Times* and *Times Literary Supplement*

Philip Gawith, Senior Managing Director, Teneo Blue Rubicon

Sir Philip Green, owner, Arcadia Group

Philip Thomson, SVP Communications and Government Affairs, GSK plc

ACKNOWLEDGEMENTS

Pierre Goad, Group Head of Communications, HSBC plc

Rachel Botsman, social entrepreneur and writer

Raymond Nasr, sommelier and Lecturer, Stanford University

Reid Hoffman, co-founder, LinkedIn

Richard Hytner, author and founder of beta baboon, and former Deputy Chairman of Saatchi & Saatchi

Robert Douglass, former proprietor, the Admiral Collingwood, Sydney

Professor Robin Dunbar, Professor of Evolutionary Psychology, University of Oxford

Lord Robin Janvrin, Deputy Chairman, HSBC Private Bank

Dr Robin Nuttall, Partner, McKinsey

Sir Roger Carr, Chairman, BAE Systems

Roland Klein, co-founder, CNC

Roland Rudd, co-founder and Chairman, Finsbury

Professor Ron Burt, University of Chicago

Ruth Wilson, actress

Sandra Macleod, founder and CEO, Mindful Reputation

Simon Cowell, founder, Syco Entertainment

Simon Lewis, CEO, Association for Financial Markets in Europe (AFME)

Simon Walker, former Director General, Institute of Directors

Stefano Lucchini, Director of Institutional and Regulatory Affairs, Intesa Sanpaolo

Stephan Chambers, Director, The Marshall Institute, London School of Economics

Steve Easterbrook, CEO, McDonald's

Steve Stoute, founder and CEO, Translation

Dr Theodore (Ted) Malloch, Professor of Strategic Leadership and Governance, Henley Business School

Thomas Schultz-Jagow, Director of Campaigns and Communications, Amnesty International

Tim Allan, founder, Portland Communications, and former Deputy Director of Communications at 10 Downing Street

Tim Cullen, Founder Director, Oxford Programme on Negotiation

ACKNOWLEDGEMENTS

Dr Tim Hannigan, University of Alberta
Tommy Helsby, Chairman, EMEA, Kroll
Tracy Nixon
Baroness Valerie Amos, Director, SOAS
Vernon Jordan, Partner, Lazard
Professor Violina Rindova, University of Texas at Austin
Will Dawkins, Head of UK Board Practice, Spencer Stuart

APPENDIX: SUGGESTED FURTHER READING

Michael L. Barnett and Timothy G. Pollock, *The Oxford Handbook of Corporate Reputation*, 2012

Jamie Bartlett, *The Dark Net*, 2014

Mary Beard, *SPQR: A History of Ancient Rome*, 2015

Tom Bergin, *Spills and Spin: The Inside Story of BP*, 2011

danah boyd, *It's Complicated: The Social Lives of Networked Teens*, 2014

Ronald S. Burt, *Brokerage and Closure: An Introduction to Social Capital*, 2005

Nicholas Christakis and James Fowler, *Connected: The Amazing Power of Social Networks and How they Shape our Lives*, 2011

Robin Dunbar, *Gossip, Grooming and the Evolution of Language*, 2011

Michael Fertik, *The Reputation Economy: How to Optimise Your Digital Footprint in a World Where Reputation is Your Most Valuable Asset*, 2015

Rob Goffee and Gareth Jones, 'What Holds the Modern Company Together', *Harvard Business Review*, Nov–Dec 1996

Yuval Noah Harari, *Sapiens: A Brief History of Humankind*, 2015

Amy Liptrot, *The Outrun*, 2015

Hassun Massum and Mark Tovey (eds), *The Reputation Society: How Online Opinions are Reshaping the Offline World*, 2011

Robin Nuttall and Tommy Stadlen, *Connect: How Companies Succeed by Engaging Radically with Society*, 2015

Partnoy, Younger, Fleischer and Olegario, 'How Reputations are Won and Lost in Modern Information Markets', Oxford University Centre for Corporate Reputation, April 2014

APPENDIX: SUGGESTED FURTHER READING

Daniel H. Pink, *Drive*, 2009

Stephen Pinker, *The Language Instinct*, 1994

Robert D. Putnam, *Bowling Alone: The Collapse and Revival of American Community*, 2000

Steve Stoute, *The Tanning of America*, 2011

Tomorrow's Company, *The City Values Forum – Embedding Integrity & Trust*, 2013

INDEX

INDEX

INDEX

INDEX